ANOTHER DOOR
to
LEARNING

ANOTHER DOOR

to

LEARNING

True Stories of Learning Disabled Children
and Adults, and the Keys to Their Success

Judy Schwarz

with Illustrations and Foreword
by Carol Stockdale

CROSSROAD • NEW YORK

1994
The Crossroad Publishing Company
370 Lexington Avenue, New York, NY 10017

Copyright © 1992 by Judy Schwarz
Foreword and illustrations copyright © 1992 by Carol Stockdale

Printed in the United States of America
Typesetting output: TEXSource, Houston

Library of Congress Cataloging-in-Publication Data
Schwarz, Judy.
    Another door to learning : true stories of learning disabled
  children and adults, and the keys to their success / Judy Schwarz ;
  with illustrations by Carol Stockdale.
        p.   cm.
    Includes bibliographical references.
    ISBN 0-8245-1191-3 (cloth); 0-8245-1385-1 (pbk.)
    1. Learning disabled children—Washington (State)—Case studies.
    2. Learning disabled — Washington (State) — Case studies. I. Title.
    LC4705.5.W2S39   1992
  371.9—dc20   91-22731
                                                             CIP

This book is meant for educators
and for all those who cherish education.
For that reason I dedicate it to my finest teachers:

to my mother,
who taught me to believe, even in the face of doubt;

to my father,
who taught me to persevere,
even in the presence of overwhelming pain;

to my husband,
who taught me to embrace the day with joy and hope;

to my sons,
who taught me to wonder, as only a child can,
why clouds flip over and stars linger long into winter's morning;

and to my illustrator friend,
who taught me to practice my faith by honing the gifts that I have been given
and giving them back to the community so that others can use them.

Contents

ACKNOWLEDGMENTS

——————

Many years of work preceded the actual writing of this book. Although two of us produced it, one with words and the other with pictures, the book would not have been possible without the contribution of many individuals. Carol and I want to thank them.

We are indebted to the eleven clients who wanted their stories told, even if the telling meant reliving pain. By sharing their stories, they hoped that a student like themselves might be helped or that a parent or a teacher might understand. "Boy," Frank recalled one day during his clinic lesson, "teachers sure didn't know how to do this here stuff when I was a kid! If they did, "betcha' I coulda' gone to college . . . maybe . . . but then," Frank added, forgiving those who unwittingly wounded his self-esteem because of their own ignorance, "maybe they just didn't know how to teach me." We are grateful to Frank and to the all the others who not only shared their pain but who had the courage to move beyond it.

We are thankful to all the teachers and administrators within education who see beyond the confines of what is and who work for what can be. We are particularly thankful to one elementary school teacher who talked to her husband of the need for this book, to him for publishing it, and to a college teacher who listened, applauded, and advised in just the right spots.

We are deeply grateful to our own clinic staff, all of them women, though gender is not what makes them special. What is uncommon about every one of these women is their willingness to be vulnerable to one another and to those we serve as well as their willingness to attempt what at times seems impossible. Yet they do, over and over again, sometimes scaling mountains they never knew existed. We are particularly grateful to the staff member who pays the bills and takes on the burden of financial worry so that the rest of us at the clinic can direct our energies to teaching and dreaming.

We want to thank a gentle man we lost along the way, a school

administrator who brought the two of us together. We also want to thank
an Irish pediatrician who believed in us long before it was fashionable to
do so and two orthopedic surgeons who enlarged our horizons as well
as our space.

We are indebted to our six initial board members who not only believed in our dream but also helped us give it to the community by
becoming a nonprofit agency. We thank all the other board members
who have since followed. All of them, in their own way, have given us
the very gifts that we have needed to flourish. We thank the community that supports us through their time and their dollars. Because of the
financial support of individuals, foundations, and service clubs within
our community, we can serve individuals of all economic levels.

Finally, we want to thank our husbands, whose love has sustained
us, and our sons, whose lives have inspired us.

Foreword

TO KNOW THEY ARE THERE

Peering into the darkness requires courage when eyes in the shadows return our gaze. This book tells the stories of people who once lived in gloom. Their eyes peered back from the shadows for years before they stepped into the sunshine. The characters who follow, Clark and Frank, Lucille and Ethan and Albert, emerged to tell us much about the countless others who remain hidden. Most of the eyes staring back are veiled with discouragement, but some are angry slits raging at anyone who ventures into their gloom. These shadows border each community, each school, each classroom.

Sometimes alone, often brought by another, the folks who tell their story in these pages each ventured from safe obscurity to enter Another Door to Learning; hesitant or aggressive, shy or belligerent, hundreds and hundreds have come to the learning clinic. The youngest was five; the oldest thus far was sixty-three. For twelve years they have been coming.

How the clinic started is significant. About a dozen years ago in the evergreen state of Washington, teachers and administrators worried, as educators everywhere still do, about the children who fail. Two women teachers who saw their own lives enriched by sons who learned differently became friends. They probed the research emanating from expanding study into brain functions, taught, and watched their sons grow. With the mediating push from a school administrator, they began the clinic. First they tried out their theories by teaching a graduate class for educational specialists. They also talked long hours together and with their businessmen husbands. Teachers are often strangers to money and business skills. They became convinced that the clinic should at least begin as a "for profit" business, because the actual costs of testing and teaching these students needed to be acknowledged and built into the clinic plan. Change is not free.

After the first years, the baseline costs of service were established, and the time came to give the clinic to the community. Six community leaders representing public and private education, business, parents, and the minority community guided the transition to nonprofit status. The cost of delivering the services is carefully monitored, and fees reflect those costs. But now grants from foundations and donations by individuals fund scholarships. The clinic, begun in a medical center for ease in collaborating with referring physicians, moved after five years to a second medical building. Two years ago the board of directors purchased a large house. To the delight of the staff each room now has a window. People from many states climb the front steps. Children come with fear-generated tummy aches lest they be asked to read. Others read well but cannot spell or perhaps are unable to write. Math is the crucible for quite a few. Many are adults. Some are professional people sharing a carefully hidden restriction. All are intelligent. Some are gifted. They all walk in the shadow of their pain. First we talk to find out if this is the time to make changes and if Another Door is the place to rehearse them. If so we start probing. The function of clinic tests is to describe how learners learn and, based on this information, how they can be taught. Former students attend twenty-three different colleges and trade schools. They are teachers, firefighters, electricians, dentists, salespeople, accountants, janitors, attorneys, nurses, and farmers. Some are now bringing their children. Several who passed briefly through the doors are now in jail.

Students who come to the clinic are expected to learn because learning is natural. We do not make them learn. Our task as teachers is to define the open routes and shape instruction to fit those pathways. It is also our job to remove artificial obstacles and get out of the way. The instruction is responsive to the individual learner and thus is never "canned." Instead, each lesson is developed and shaped for its one-time use.

We who are the staff teach and are taught by the students who come to us. Looking into these eyes is painful for a reason. We see our own reflection, our own eyes mirrored back. We are not better or brighter, or more talented, or in any way more wonderful. The singular difference is that we are in the economic and social mainstream, and they are not. We have access to light while they are in the shadows. Until we penetrate the darkness, we will not even know they are there. That is the unique job description of the clinic teachers, to cherish learning disabled students, including their differences and to teach them skills for stepping into the sunshine. After all, everyone can learn. That is the guiding philosophy of the nonprofit clinic.

Neither learning differences nor learning disability puts these people into the shadow. Usually definition does it. Children's learning differences may well mean that they cannot succeed through traditional instruction. Moving into the lowest reading group does not change the nature of that instruction. Drill and practice do not cure the misspelled words. Inevitably, the children are defined as at fault. Either they are labeled as unmotivated or, sadly, simply as not capable. Sometimes both.

Very soon these children participate in the most confining step of all. They agree with the definition that they are lazy, that they are dumb. The walls build silently a brick at a time. Neither the children nor their families hear the builders. A few escape to become "late bloomers." Special skill at making friends or throwing a football or singing provides a window for light. So, too, does dogged belief by a parent or a teacher, friend or spouse that nicks the boundaries of definition. Most individuals stay in the shadows, deterred by inadequate academic skills and limited educations from functioning successfully in this society.

Both before and beyond these limits is a shadow of the damaged spirit. Intangible emotional wounds provoke the greatest pain. Obstacles to learning cast a shadow not only on the skills of living, such as reading and writing, but on the human spirit. Frank, one of the characters in the book, expressed gratitude for his disabled body because retraining channeled him to a new definition of self. Reading was indeed useful, but appreciating himself was joy.

Joy is the natural lubricant smoothing each system. Learning does indeed take place in integrated systems in which concept and emotion are wrapped by memory, even while they reconstruct new memory. Each of us arrives in the classroom with a basket of tools, including language, imagery, and memory, which tangle into an intricate personal web as we learn. This book deals with two segments of that web, the system of language and the system for understanding space, although it does not pretend to portray all the principles within those patterns. To underscore these interdependent systems of thought, each story is illustrated. Illustration is the visual image while story is the linguistic image. That is what we do at the clinic — blend these two pools of intellect. As a result, failing students succeed.

Learning differences are glitches or variations common to everyone. However, if the glitch blocks academic progress, the result is a learning disability. When traditional methods in the classroom or on the job do not work — but no other options are available — a learning difference becomes a learning disability. Each year students reach university level without realizing they have been navigating around a learning disability. As the demands of learning change, the glitch may become a chasm, unbridgeable without assistance.

Like the clinic, this book is built upon the philosophy that each of us can keep only what we are willing to give away. Our lives touch at those points where we exercise our gifts. However, the wonder of gifts is only found as they are given. These stories are an effort to pass on to others some of the gifts given to us by the remarkable people who come to the clinic. Most clinics fade with the passing of their founders. This book is part of the effort to have the clinic live on beyond its founders. The intent of these stories is to teach and thereby to take readers beyond what they now know.

The people who reach out from these pages, thank God, are different one from the other. Individuals remain unique even without obvious exterior markers. They learn differently. The clinic and the book celebrate this infinite variety within the unifying patterns that guide instruction. Nature coats surface differences over our unique cores. A distinctive spirit moves each of us. These stories expose that extraordinary spirit for a fleeting glimpse. Divergence undoubtedly helps sustain the human race by generating both a broad range of enterprises as well as the explorers to undertake them. Nourishing differences, then, becomes part of the job description for parents and teachers.

Frank, Steve, Lucille, and all the others disclose their pathways in the journey out of the shadow. The stories are true although individuals are disguised to protect their privacy, some so well that they might not recognize themselves. The function of the telling is to sharpen the vision of all who wish to see, to amend the sameness of instruction, to take away homogenized technique, and to redefine the paths to learning. The need for courage to take the step and look still remains. Who has failed? Whom have we failed? Concealed in the shadows, eyes are looking back.

CAROL STOCKDALE

Part 1

THE LANGUAGE SYSTEM

Elevators inspire an etiquette that its riders understand; however, when two strangers are stuck in one, the unwritten rule of silence quickly disappears. In fact, whenever two or more strangers share a perilous journey, they turn as though instinctively to their language for survival, for nourishment, and for understanding. Learning is that: a wonderful yet perilous journey full of pitfalls and dark winding alleys that lead us to places we least suspect. Language is one of the systems that helps us weave our way to meaning.

We use language to impose order upon information, to understand it, and to store it in memory. We use language to control and embellish our mental images — the sometimes fleeting but ever-present glimpses of another kind of knowing. Not only do we link our language to our imagery, we also use it to orient ourselves to events, to times, and to tasks. Who hasn't overheard the considerate husband stopping at the grocery store on his way home from work trying to remember the items that he promised his wife he would bring home. "Let's see . . . what did Blanche tell me to buy? Five things, I remember that, five of them . . . now, what are they?"

Most of us talk to ourselves internally, particularly about emotionally charged events, like a disagreement with our spouse or an ultimatum we're about to impose upon the kids. We use our language to talk our way through tasks, verbally rehearsing them, questioning them, or in some way examining them with our own language. In fact, we use our language as a filter, pouring our experience as well as our learning through it. We attach language to the concepts that we learn. Once we can explain an idea in our own words, we feel that we really "know" it, we truly understand it, so much so that many of us feel compelled to teach it or, perhaps, preach it to others. Finally, we use language to reduce, to emphasize, and to assimilate details, events, or ideas into some type of schema or stereotype, all for the sake of efficiency. In summary, language is an intermediary between thought and action, between ideation and endeavor.

The classroom is a language-dependent environment. Most households are that too, of course, though some are surely more than others. To operate efficiently, both families and classrooms need some amount of language. In the classroom, for example, teachers explain a skill through language, model and rehearse it with language, and test their students' understanding of it by measures that are language-based. As students advance through school, the amount of language required of them increases in quantity as well as complexity; moreover, the amount of modeling provided for him diminishes in direct proportion to that increase. Stated another way, as the grades advance, teachers tell more and more and show less and less. In the first grade, for example, a student listens to short blips of teacher talk seasoned heavily with modeling, reads language that is fairly straightforward and unadorned of fancy phrases, and produces a limited amount of written language. In fourth grade, however, the explanations get longer, the modeling shorter, the printed language more convoluted, and the written expectations greater. The vocabulary increases as well. By eighth grade the language demands increase again. More than one foreign language is introduced here; languages like "earth science," "pre-algebra," and "metal shop" are common to most eighth-graders. Modeling is reduced even further by the limits of a fifty-minute period.

The language requirements, then, both receptive and expressive, continue to increase as the grades advance. As they move up the grades, students are not only expected to assimilate more language, they are also expected to produce more language. Small wonder, then, that students with language difficulties perform poorly in school. Small wonder too that students who performed well in the earlier grades earn poor marks in junior or senior high school. Their grades are an indication of their ability to keep up with the increasing linguistic demands.

Some language is learned through the deliberate instruction that happens at school. A lot of it, however, is "caught" through casual and accidental exposure at home and other places. Fortunately for those of us who teach it deliberately, language is a system with a set of governing rules that help us understand its operation. The system is dynamic. Hence, we do not know all the rules of the system nor should we be so arrogant as to try. Learning changes our intellect, not only making it different from before but also positioning it outside the boundaries of a finite set of operating rules. Like the expanding cosmos out there, the universe of our own intellect unfolds as learning happens. Hence, we need not demean what we know about language or about learning by reducing it to an irrefutable set of truths or a hierarchy of skills through which all students must pass. As educators, the best that we can hope for is to help learning happen and amend our own understanding of the process as we go along. If we do it right, learning changes the cognitive soup of the teacher as well as the student.

The learners in the chapters that follow teach us something of those principles within the system of language. The first four stories illustrate the relationship between language, reading, and writing and some underlying principles about print. Print is that: language put down on paper. Reading is a matter of bringing meaning to the printed language, gathering meaning from it, and interpreting meaning of it. Reading is exchanging meaning with absent authors who left their language lying on a page. Reading is not a matter of saying all the sounds nor even all the words. It is always an exercise in meaning. Meaning and understanding are inseparable. Hence, reading does not happen in the absence of comprehension. The first four folks — Ethan, Frank, Tyler, and Bert — all had difficulty with reading and writing. They could not make meaning of print or express meaning through it. Since imaging, questioning, and controlling the form of print are at the heart of this meaning process, it is in those arenas that each of them made a cognitive leap. Bert, for example, learned to catch the vivid images that filled his thinking and translate them into printed language. Ethan learned to link the name of a printed word to its image so that he could later recognize its face. Tyler learned to anticipate and control the form of printed language, and Frank learned to make his own language rhyme with it. Each discovery produced a gentle "aha" that resounded throughout their intellect.

The other two folks, Lucille and Clark, had difficulties that extended far beyond the printed word. They had difficulty with the broader and more basic language activity we call communication — that is, making our meaning known and understanding the meaning of others. Lucille had such profound expressive language difficulties that she could barely be understood. Even though she abstracted the meaning of what others told her, Lucille could not convey her own message in such a manner that others understood with ease and accuracy. Because of her instruction, Lucille made a cognitive leap that resounded in a chorus of hallelujahs rather than a string of hushed ahas.

Clark had extensive language delays as well, both receptive and expressive delays, the ingoing and outgoing features of the language system. Clark had tremendous difficulty deciphering what he heard, not because he had a problem with hearing but rather because he could not abstract the essence of language meaning. When a system holds little meaning, an individual does not use it, and that was true for Clark. He did not use language for any of the functions described at the beginning of this section. He did not use it to program or guide his behavior or to orient himself to task or event. Instead, when events happened, Clark acted, spontaneously, "without thinking," his classroom teachers said. Often, he bit. Clark made a leap too, a quantum one, though the reason for it is not exactly clear. We can only surmise. Perhaps he changed because once the complexities of the environment were reduced, the instruction previously provided could take hold. Perhaps the change was a matter of time, inevitability. Perhaps it was God's gesture of kindness. That's the wondrous quality of learning. It happens when we least expect it and for reasons that lie just a reach beyond our grasp. Perhaps these folks can teach you to wonder, at least about some principles of language.

- 1 -

THE GIANT WITH A BOY TUCKED
INSIDE HIS POCKET

None of the tutors wanted to teach Ethan Groat, for he was as cross as his name. Jean Loomis was elected. She was the oldest and wisest teacher at the clinic. Centered in the joy of more than forty years of marriage, enriched by the wonder of raising five children, and humbled from the wisdom of losing one to an early death, Jean understood those truths that cannot be learned from a teacher's manual. Turned outward, rage bloodies the world. Turned inward, rage kills the spirit.

Jean understood the reason for Ethan's rage. He was not only several years older than his sixth-grade classmates, he was also many inches taller, taller even than his teachers. Ethan was thirteen, nearly fourteen, frozen in time as well as in sixth grade, retained three times in the earlier grades because he could not read any "new" material.

"*God!*" he screamed at Jean one morning during his lesson at the clinic. "Don't *tell* me I can read. Don't *tell* me that! I can't read any new stuff!... only old stuff... *old*, just like you!" Jean did not wilt from the criticism. She recognized the symptoms of despair turned hateful against the world. What Ethan meant by "old stuff" was print that he had heard before or print that he had dictated himself. Ethan could not read unless he first heard the story read aloud to him, and even then he could not manage stories beyond the primary level. Ethan was tired of listening to taped stories and equally tired of dictating them so that he could later read them back. In fact, asking him to dictate a story was the question that triggered the day's explosion.

"God! Don't *ask* me to tell you any more stories," he warned Jean. "I'm thirteen, for God's sake. . . . Teach me to read. . . . I'm goin' to seventh grade next year, for God's sake. . . . I gotta' read library books and social studies books, and science and health books. . . . Don't you know that? . . . For God's sake . . . I gotta' be able to read! That's why I'm here! Remember?" he baited his tutor. Jean remained calm, silent.

"God," he said, now folding his arms around his middle as if to shut himself off from the world. Ethan lowered his eyes to avoid witnessing the cruelty of his last blow. "God," he said, "you don't know *anything!*" Jean did not flinch from the insult nor reprimand him for his continual use of the word "God." Ethan used it like seasoning, sprinkling his talk with the almighty as a power mark to give himself courage. Jean waited for the storm to pass. She knew that his anger would abate if she listened without so much as a hint of argument or judgment. Acceptance always reduced Ethan's rage, and so Jean did not attempt to disprove his statements and said nothing as his anger continued. "God! This is stupid! This is dumb! *Dumb! Dumb! Dumb!*" he screamed, each word falling in beat with his fist.

Ethan's intimidation tactics produced the desired effects at school. With the exception of his special education resource teacher, Alice Quenton, Ethan's classroom teachers did not instruct him, at least not in the printed word. They believed that as a learning specialist, Alice Quenton must have a corner on the truth, at least in those matters relating to Ethan's reading instruction. His classroom teachers also believed that since Ethan could not read, all they could expect of him was to be quiet and cooperative, which he was, unless they asked him to read. Then Ethan exploded. Because he qualified for the resource room for reading and language arts only, Ethan spent many hours in the regular classroom completing math drill sheets, watching the paint peel off the wall as well as helping it along, and threatening to disrupt the order.

Although she knew she must pretend otherwise, Alice did not feel much like an expert. Of all the children she had ever taught, and during the past twenty-five she had taught many, Ethan was her most difficult as well as her most trying student. She had been Ethan's resource teacher as well as his ally for the past six years, sometimes defending him even when she shouldn't. During the six years she taught him, Alice endured, with the equanimity of Jean, many of Ethan's verbal tirades. She found it best to instruct him individually, a privilege afforded few students, even those in special education.

Alice tried first one reading program and then another. She consulted other specialists in the district. Desperate, she even asked one of them to teach him for a trial period, an unheard of request. Nothing seemed to work. Ethan's greatest difficulty was recognizing words. He could, of course, read a few primary stories, but only if he heard them read to him first. He could also read the language that he dictated. However, he could not read words when they appeared all by themselves. In fact, with the exception of his name and a few billboard words, Ethan could not recognize words at all. He recognized "Coca-Cola," "Pepsi," "STOP," "McDonald's," and a handful of others, but he could not consistently read even these unless environmental cues accompanied them. He recognized "McDonald's," for example, only if a golden arch was adjacent, the word "STOP" only if it appeared on an octagon, and "Coca-Cola" only if it was printed in bold white letters on a red background. Even then, Ethan often misread "Coca-Cola" as "Coke." Because of his difficulty with word recognition, Ethan could not read "new" material. He hated himself for that, and he vented his rage on Jean that morning.

"God . . . this whole idea of my teacher sending me here is dumb!" Ethan went on, Jean still silent. "This work isn't helping me . . . you're not helping me . . . not even one little bit . . . I can't even read these dumb words!" he said, now edging toward tears. "God . . . Miss Quenton is gonna ask me to read these words today when I get back to school . . . and I can't even read them . . . and God . . . you're not even helping me!"

Alice Quenton tried numerous ways to teach Ethan word recognition, even methods she considered a bit questionable. She began, of course, with phonics. For five years Alice taught Ethan all about the sounds that symbols make. After years of struggle, he learned to match the sounds that went with symbols. He learned how to blend the sounds together. He even memorized some phonetic rules: "When two vowels go walking, the first one does the talking." However, after all that time, Ethan could not consistently apply those skills to words. Alice resorted to other means — tracing around the shape of words, writing them in sand, drawing them in the air. When those methods failed too, she tried the more unorthodox procedure of having Ethan draw words in shaving cream. After two weeks, Alice concluded that shaving cream produced nothing more than an incredible mess! Frustrated, Alice resorted to the standard procedure of drill and practice. She gave Ethan a packet of sight words. She met with him several times a day, reviewed the words with him, insisted that he write them down as she said them, and chided him to remember. She praised him too when he actually read one of the words in the packet, but Ethan's ability to read them again later was hit and miss at best. That's why she referred him to the clinic.

The referral required substantial courage on Alice's part. Not only was she supposed to know what to do, Alice was responsible for Ethan's instruction in reading and language arts. Wary of the criticism that might befall her, Alice reasoned that she had to maintain control of Ethan's clinic reading instruction. Without Jean's knowing it, Alice Quenton evaluated the correctness of her referral by the number of words Ethan knew after each instructional hour at the clinic. Words were the hidden agenda. Alice Quenton tested Ethan on them each time he returned from the clinic.

"*God!*" Ethan screamed. "She's gonna ask me, and you're not even helping me! I can't even *read* these dumb words," Ethan wailed, slamming this week's stack of word cards on the table. The stack that Alice Quenton had given him just the day before burst into confusion — corners here, corners there, words right side up, upside down, and overturned.

"Oh, God," Ethan signed. "Now I'll never get 'em right. I'll never get 'em right, Jean," Ethan said, appealing to her for forgiveness. "I had 'em in just the right order. Now I'll never know 'em for my test." Unable to remember the look of the word, Ethan relied upon irrelevant information on each card — a smudge, a frayed corner, a splotch of ink. He tried to recall the words by remembering the sequence of the extraneous detail. Tears welled, and Ethan swallowed hard to prevent their fall. "God," he said softly, "now I'll never get 'em right. Oh, God," Ethan called lowering his head to his hands, his rage turned inward to despair.

Jean did what she does best — remain present to her student and to his sorrow. She asked for his forgiveness saying she did not understand. "I didn't know you were being tested on these words, Ethan," Jean apologized. "Give me another chance," Jean asked. "Give me one more chance," she asked again. Ethan looked up bewildered by his tutor's request. No teacher had ever asked for his forgiveness. He was the one who always had to apologize. "Let me try to teach you some words the next time you come," Jean asked. He allowed her to wipe the tears of discouragement that streaked his face. "Well, God . . . sure . . . one more time . . . just once though . . . for God's sake."

Jean called Alice Quenton later in the day. She wanted to tell her of that morning's explosion and sort out what Alice expected from Ethan's clinic work. Jean spoke of Ethan's rage. Alice wondered if some event at home hadn't triggered it. "I know this sounds awful," Alice whispered into the phone, "but Ethan is just like his father. They have the exact same temperament. Mr. Groat can be an absolute dictator with us at school. He blusters in, unannounced, and demands that we do this, demands that we do that, and threatens to sue us if we don't."

Jean didn't know anything about that. "I wouldn't be surprised if an argument happened at home this morning," Alice went on. Recognizing the relationship between anger and despair, Jean offered a different interpretation. Perhaps, she said, that Mr. Groat saw himself in his son and felt tremendous guilt for having passed the learning problem on to Ethan.[1] "Maybe Mr. Groat can't read either," Jean suggested. Alice paused. She didn't know anything about that. "Well," Alice said, tempering the criticism that stemmed from her own feelings of failure, "Mr. Groat can be a very gentle man. I have seen that. He wants the best for Ethan." Jean concurred.

Alice and Jean agreed that Ethan's clinic work would center on teaching him to recognize words. "I'm not quite sure how to do that just yet," Jean admitted. "You aren't?" Alice asked incredulously. I thought *you* folks were the experts!" Jean said she really didn't know much about being an expert, especially where learning was concerned. Like other members of the clinic staff, Jean believed that teaching required as much learning on the instructor's part as it did on the learner's, and that if she wasn't learning while she was teaching, she probably wasn't teaching at all. Instead, she was telling. For a moment, Alice wished she could teach at a place where the state of uncertainty was not treated as a social disease.

Alice agreed to send Ethan's packet of sight words with him for his next clinic appointment. Before abdicating her control over word recognition, however, Alice Quenton offered a piece of advice. "I've found," she said, "that Ethan's writing the words immediately after I say them is terribly important . . . well, I think that's important," she added humbly. "Tell me," Alice added, "if you don't know how you're going to teach Ethan, how are you going to figure it out?" Jean explained that she would ask her colleagues for their ideas and solicit their opinion. She would also ask her mentor, the teacher she met with every week to discuss her cases. "Mentor?" Alice questioned. "You have a mentor?" Jean laughed. "You don't think I'd have the courage to teach this kid all by myself, do you?"[2]

At the next staff meeting, the tutors concluded that we learn to recognize words like the "faces of friends."[3] Some words are plainer than others, prettier than others, longer or smaller or fatter than others, but each of them has a personality of its own. Like faces, words are visually distinctive.[4] We do not learn to read words by sequentially identifying their parts any more than we learn to identify a friend by examining, piece by piece, every feature of his face. We do not read a word by saying its sounds or decoding its pieces. Instead, we learn to "read" a word by recognizing it as a familiar face and linking that face to the unique features of its meaning.[5] Learning always depends upon meaning.[6]

"That's easy for *you* to say!" Jean said to the staff, laughing to cover her own uncertainty. "You don't have to teach this kid! How am I gonna' teach him? Just tell me that," Jean prodded, urging them for more input. They weren't sure, but they knew she would have to try some method that linked meaning to configuration. Jean spent the next two nights tossing and turning, rehearsing ways to teach the boy who would give her just one more chance.

Ethan arrived the following morning, his hair uncombed and his face unwashed as though someone had dragged him from bed. Jean recalled Alice's whispered observations. She greeted him, but Ethan did not respond. Instead, he threw himself down on the chair and slammed his word cards on the table. "There," he growled, "she *told* me to bring 'em." Jean wondered how, or even if, Alice and Ethan's teachers had the patience to endure his tantrums day after day. Jean greeted him again. "Good morning, I said!" Ethan folded his arms and looked away, his only means of protection except, of course, his appeal to the almighty. "God this is dumb," Ethan announced. "This is so dumb...God...." Jean remembered the relationship between anger and despair.

She ignored the rebuke, thanked Ethan for coming, and reached for his cards. Jean smiled. Alice Quenton selected words that had similar counterparts — words like "nothing" and "neighbor" and "giant" and "giraffe" — twenty word cards in all. "You're going to learn these words today," Jean said as though to convince herself. Ethan lifted his head a few degrees.

"Bet you're gonna have me sound 'em," Ethan scoffed, trying to anticipate as well as demean Jean's method of teaching. "No," Jean answered. "Then you're gonna have me write 'em," Ethan continued and seeing Jean shake her head added, "stupid, dumb writing...in the air...for God's sake." Again Jean said no. "Then you're gonna have me draw around 'em." Jean continued to indicate the negative. "Good," Ethan replied, "that dumb trick doesn't work either...for God's sake."

Jean sure hoped that God was listening. "Ethan," she asked, reaching for the card that read "neighbor" and showing it to him, "what do you think of when I say the word 'neighbor.'" Without hesitation, Ethan jeered, "a fat lady...God is that old neighbor lady fat!" He looked up ready to dump his anger. "She's disgusting she's so fat," Ethan smiled, confident in his assessment

Jean pressed further, not commenting on his discrimination. "But what does 'neighbor' mean, Ethan?" He could not believe the simplicity of her question. "It means someone who lives next door...for God's sake...and my next door neighbor is a real tubbo," Ethan laughed as he threw his head back.

Jean handed him a blank index card and asked him to draw a picture note to capture his own personal meaning of the word "neighbor." She drew a note as well. Jean hated drawing. Ethan did too. "I know," she said. "It's the pits, but do it anyway. I have to." Ethan smiled. He kind of liked Jean. The two of them doodled quietly. Their artistic expression complete, Jean and Ethan explained their drawing to one another. Jean had drawn a series of houses, each with a neighbor standing outside it. Less stereotypic but just as accurate as Jean in his definition, Ethan drew a picture of a woman with a very large stomach. "Tubbo!" Ethan chortled, holding his card in the air. "Hey, this is kind of fun. Let's do another."

They did, several more of them. If Ethan did not quite understand the meaning of the word, Jean and Ethan tossed ideas back and forth. They discussed the word and put it in context to resolve any lexical misunderstanding. If Ethan clearly understood the word, which was frequently the case, he simply drew his picture note to capture the word's meaning. Artistic considerations were not important. It did not matter if Ethan drew with a controlled, clean line. It did not matter if he drew his image with sensitivity or accuracy. It did not matter if his drawing actually looked like what he said it was. What mattered was his ability to identify the word from his picture note alone later in the hour. The single criterion of a good drawing, then, was if Ethan could call it by its correct name — see the tubbo lady, for example, and say "neighbor." Only then could he take the next step — sort through the stack of printed words, find the one that said "neighbor," and read it.

Occasionally Jean needed to shape the specificity of Ethan's image before he sifted it through his language system. That was the case with the word "giant." When Jean asked him what he imaged when he heard the word "giant," for example, Ethan readily replied. "God, that's easy," he said and sketched a picture of a very large man. As with the previous words, Jean asked him to explain and thereby attach language to his image.[7]

"Oh, come on, Jean," Ethan begged. "This guy's a giant! I mean he's a big dude for God's sake." Later in the hour, however, Ethan could not call his drawing by its correct name.

"God, what is that?" he asked himself, looking at his stereotypic rendition of "giantness." "What is that?" he asked again, but he simply could not recall. Even pounding his fists against his head did not dislodge the name. "God . . . what is that word?" Ethan demanded of himself. He simply did not know.

Jean told him the word. She also asked him to personalize his drawing, to add more significant and relevant features to capture his image of giant. Ethan thought again, scanned his mental image for the meaning of giant, and began to draw. He added what appeared to be meaningless squiggles. Yet they were not meaningless at all. When Jean asked him to explain the addition, Ethan replied with a grin, "My giant has a boy tucked inside his shirt pocket." He could then match it to its correct word card in the stack.

From that day on, whenever Ethan saw the word "giant," he called it by its correct name without the picture present. A typed "giant," a cursive "giant," a "giant" with other words around it or a singular "giant" appearing all by itself, Ethan always read the word correctly. He called it by its correct name. Always. In fact, whenever he imaged to the meaning of the word and then described the image in his language, he was able to read the printed word from then on.

"God!" he yelled at the end of the emotionally charged hour. "God . . . I don't believe it!" Ethan yelled again in surprise. "I know 'em all . . . every one! It's a miracle!" he marveled.

Ethan read his word cards several times more to certify the reality of the day's "miracle." "God," he said, finally satisfied. "Miss Quenton won't believe this day," he predicted. "She'll be soooooo happy with me," he teased, "that she'll start dancin'." Ethan stopped talking momentarily, long enough to model the motion. "Waitl' she sees me 'cook' on these words," Ethan grinned as he scooped up the cards in a rush. Suddenly he stopped, the cards clutched in his hand. He raised them high and yelled "God" again as though he finally realized a window to the future.

In one continuous move, Ethan repeated his dance, blanketed Jean with a hug, and burst toward the exit, ready for his day. For the first time, for the very first time in all his years of school, Ethan read words in isolation — twenty of them, every time, with no pictures present, in any order they happened to appear. Relishing his achievement, Ethan reminded himself on his way out the door, "God, this is awesome . . . just awesome . . . God."

Jean chuckled as she tidied up behind him. Realizing that she would see him soon enough, Jean did not call Ethan back to remove his morning clutter. Besides, she did not want to interrupt his joy. To flourish, a child needs joy, another truth Jean understood. She hoped that Ethan's would last, at least all day.

- 2 -

THE MEANING OF RHYME

Frank fell from the roof of a construction project and nearly killed himself. He stepped on a hammer that another workman had inadvertently dropped near the edge of the open steel structure. Frank stumbled over the tool, lost his footing, and fell to the pavement three stories below. He landed on his back, and six of his vertebrae crumbled on impact. In that instant, Frank's future, the future of his wife, Delores, and their young sons, Paul, Thomas, and Matthew, tumbled into poverty. No insurance except workman's compensation. Less than a thousand dollars in savings. A mortgage, car payments, monthly bills. A second mortgage, money that Frank and Delores had borrowed to remodel the attached single-car garage into a large bedroom for two of the boys. Now this.

A team of orthopedic surgeons used steel and bone to stabilize Frank's damaged spine — bone to patch it together, steel to strengthen it and ensure its straightness. Days later the chief surgeon, Alex Milanich, gave Frank a simple yet brutal explanation of the physical limitations that a fusion imposes upon a man, even a strong twenty-nine-year-old one like Frank. Like most surgeons, Dr. Milanich left nothing to chance. No carrying sleepy children off to bed, he told Frank. No racing for the football in the backyard with the kids. No jogging, riding dirt bikes, or playing racquetball. "Remember, Frank," the surgeon warned, "you've got two steel rods in you, one on either side of your spine. They add strength, keep you straight, and prevent your spine from breaking. Better face it, Frank... you can't pretend you're superman anymore."

"Yeah," Frank replied, fighting the overpowering presence of pain and the haze of medication administered to mask it. "I sure ain't feelin' like no superman." Doc must a been talkin' to Delores, Frank thought. Superman Frank. Delores always teased Frank about his superhuman strength. She affectionately called him her "big bear," the only grizzly she'd ever known that had the temperament of an affectionate pup.

Frank relied upon physical prowess to solve life's problems, like the problem of a growing family that lived in too small a house. Frank solved the dilemma by taking a second mortgage on the house and working longer and harder. Every night after an exhausting day at a construction site, Frank pushed his body to labor four or five additional hours, sawing and hammering, plastering and painting, until he transformed the garage into a third bedroom complete with built-ins and bunk beds he designed and made himself. The boys were delighted with the end product, particularly Paul. A strong boy built like his father, seven-year-old Paul climbed to the highest bunk in one swift stretch. "Daddy!" Paul squealed. "This is like bein' on a mountain. Watch, Daddy, watch! I'm gonna' jump off it!" and he leapt from the oak precipice into his father's arms.

As he lay in his hospital bed, Frank realized that he could no longer catch his son in mid-air nor rescue Paul from the daring, often reckless play, which reminded him of himself. Perhaps, Frank thought, he would not be able to provide for his family or afford the dreams that he had promised, like the remodeled kitchen he had promised Delores. Dr. Milanich was thorough. No remodeling jobs. No climbing up on ladders to paint the house, inside or out. No lugging groceries in from the car. In fact, no lifting any item that weighed more than five pounds. The words hit Frank like harsh, silent blows. No lengthy standing. No pushing. No pulling. No job, no job of any kind, that required hard physical labor.

"You can learn to do other work, Frank," Dr. Milanich said casually, while examining his despondent patient during morning rounds. "As a matter of fact, Frank, you can go back to school at government expense!" An accomplished academician himself, Dr. Milanich assumed that Frank would relish the chance of attending school and suggested that this juncture could actually be an opportunity! "Just think, Frank, you can use your mind, and the government will pay you for it!"

Frank did not show the slightest hint of emotion. Instead, he pretended that sleep was about to overtake him. Quietly, believably, Frank sighed, "I'm tired, Doc, real tired . . . more tired than I been before." Frank closed his eyes.

Whenever he felt assailed, Frank barricaded himself off from the world. The suggestion that he attend school exposed Frank's most vulnerable spot. He couldn't attend school. He couldn't even read! A guy like him couldn't attend school. They'd find out, and then what would they do? What would Doc do if he found out, a fine smart man like the doc and all, a fine smart man like him. The doc wouldn't talk to him, that's what, a dumb man like Frank.

Confined to a bed and restricted to a cast, Frank freed himself from the shame of the moment by pretending it did not exist. He had no other means of escape except to close his eyes. Frank pretended that he was asleep until Dr. Milanich left the room, until the nurse tidied up and closed the door to a crack, until he was absolutely certain that he was alone and his secret was safe. Only then did Frank weep.

Not even Delores knew of Frank's illiteracy. She realized that Frank hated reading and that he found numerous ways to avoid it, but she never realized that Frank couldn't read, except for a few words scattered here and there. Had she known, Delores never would have insisted that Frank buy the weekly groceries. "With three little kids pulling at me, Frankie, I just can't go to the store. I need your help, Honey Bear."

Frank had trouble resisting Delores's requests when she called him "Honey Bear," the appeal she used most frequently to convince him to go to the store. Before he left the house, however, Frank made certain that he had enough cash on him to cover the cost of the groceries. "No, I ain't writin' no checks, simple as that." He also made certain that Delores read the items on the list out loud. At times, he found ways to have her read them more than once. "What's that you said, honey?" Frank asked. "I never heard what you said. Ya' know how bad my ear is."

As he drove to the store, Frank rehearsed all the items that he could remember. When the number of items on the list did not match the number in his basket, Frank walked up and down the aisles scrutinizing the products on the shelves. He matched the words that Delores wrote to the ones that appeared on cans or boxes. At times, finding the items on the list took Frank as long as three or four hours. He always had an excuse for taking so long or for omitting an item. "Pickles? No, honey, I didn't forget no pickles. They was out a them kind we like best, so I just didn't get none."

Although she did not suspect he was illiterate, Delores wondered why Frank refused to read to the boys even though they asked him repeatedly and why he refused to write any of the checks for the monthly bills. Frank shrugged off these and other unmanageable reading tasks as "women's work." "I ain't doin' no women's work," Frank announced. Delores could not understand her husband's attitude. He was genuinely helpful in other ways, in fact, in many other ways, but occasionally, for reasons Delores did not understand, Frank was just plain unreasonable. She did not realize that Frank dug in his heels when he felt his secret, or his manhood, threatened.

"I ain't no cripple!" Frank shouted at the nurses the first day they got him out of bed and tried to help him walk. "I can do this by myself . . . on my own! I ain't no cripple, ladies!" Frank complained, unwilling to call any woman by an unsavory name. "I don't need no walker neither," he announced as he pushed the chrome contraption away with his large hand. The physical effort of getting up so drained this bear of a man that Frank's push merely made the walker teeter, then topple reluctantly to the floor. It lay a few inches in front of his feet.

"Get that damn thing outa' my way," Frank demanded. "Outa' my way!" he repeated. "Now, you ladies ... you're next," Frank insisted as he motioned the nurses away with his free hand. Frank held onto the overbed table so tightly that his knuckles whitened. As he took his first steps, Frank huffed and puffed out the pain caused from muscles and nerves screaming insults at the two steel intruders attached to his spine. The pain would lessen, he told himself, once his body got used to moving again, so he forced himself up and led with his chest, heaving with each step. Frank insisted on walking without assistance. His stubbornness helped him mend so that he could walk again, but it did not help him heal. Mending requires only time to pass, but healing requires transformation.

Frank spent the next several weeks recuperating, first in the hospital and then at home. His days became an endless string of game shows, broken only by Delores muting the television and encouraging Frank to alter his activity. "Come on, Frankie," she said, "Let's walk up to the stop sign and back. The doctor said you need to walk. You can walk that far, Bear." Frank declined, needing instead to distance himself from the world. "Nah," Frank shrugged, "not today ... too tired, honey ... too tired." Frank closed his eyes and brooded about the future. What would he do? How could he feed his family if he couldn't work, and how could he be retrained to do different work if he couldn't read? What if she found out, if Delores found out that he couldn't read? He'd lose everything. Delores and the boys would leave him if they found out about a guy like him, what he was really like, not being able to read and all.[1] God, what would he do? How could he make good on his promises, the ones he made to Delores when they married. He promised to support her and the children that they wished to have. How could he do that now? He'd just have to find a way, that's all. He always had before. He'd just have to do it again. Maybe he could become a licensed electrician, like he planned on being years ago, like his old friend Henry told him he could be. Henry always told Frank that he was the best damned electrician he'd ever trained. A natural, Henry said.

Henry Sullivan was an electrician by trade, an independent contractor, in fact. He was also a close friend of Frank's father, who had died years earlier of a lengthy illness. Henry made good on his promise to care for his friend's headstrong son. When Henry learned that Frank dropped out of high school, he came to the house and asked for an explanation.

"I ain't learnin' nothin'," Frank offered. "For years I ain't learned nothin', just plain nothin,' and I'm in tenth grade. Imagine that, Henry, tenth grade and I can't even read!" Henry was the only other person besides his father who understood. "Besides, Henry, I just can't stand to go back no more. I just can't stand it."

Right then and there Henry offered Frank a job. He asked Frank to work for him, hoping that in the process he could prepare this young man for what school had not: employability.[2] For the next four years Henry orchestrated Frank's learning with the skill of a master teacher. He used pictures rather than written words, modeled rather than told, encouraged rather than advised. "Now that's the finest job I ever did see!" Henry often proclaimed. "You're a 'lectricity man, that's for sure Frank, best damned 'lectricity man I ever seen."

Frank felt safe with Henry. When he didn't understand, Frank said so, and Henry gave his student additional opportunity to observe and practice the skill without judgment. Henry believed unconditionally in his student and told him so, repeatedly. "You're pretty damn good with this here wirin' stuff, Frankie. I do believe you're gettin' better than me. Yes, sir, better than the old master."

Frank listened intently as the two of them worked. "Bet if you learned to read, Frankie, you could pass that old 'lectrician's test quick as anything. Yep, bet you could. In my day," Henry went on, "we didn't have to take no tests to be a 'lectrician. Just learned how to do the work, that's all. Then them damned politicians and union bosses got together, and whadya' know!" Henry disliked anyone who relied upon false authority. "Damned crooks," Henry muttered. "Just a damned good thing I got grandfathered, Frankie . . . damned good thing."

"I wouldn'ta listened to them crooks anyhow," Henry went on. "I wouldn'ta taken their damned tests." Frank smiled at this brave little man. "But you don't have no choice, Frankie," Henry continued. "Course, maybe you don't wanna be no 'lectrician and take over my business like we talked about, so I can retire. Maybe you don't wanna . . . but damn, you're good at this wirin' stuff, Frankie. Yes sir, better than me. If you can learn how to do this here wirin' stuff, Frank, you sure can learn how to read. Never met a young man as smart as you is, no never did."

Frank savored Henry's words of praise, even the way Henry sounded. Frank talked just like Henry, which explained why he could repeat Henry's exact words in his head. Frank said them over and over to himself until he began to believe them. "If you can learn how to do this here wirin' stuff, Frank, you sure can learn how to read. Never met a young man as smart as you is. . . ."

Then, at the end of a very difficult wiring job, Frank announced his news. He was going to learn to read. He had seen a reading program on a television advertisement, which guaranteed success. Frank asked his mom to send for it. "Yep," Frank promised, he was gonna learn to read, and then he'd take the test and become a licensed electrician, just like Henry. With his own license hanging in the office, Frank could do some wiring jobs by himself so that Henry could go fishing or spend the afternoon at the bowling alley if he wanted. Henry beamed with pride. The two of them drank a beer on the promise.

Frank received his individualized reading program in the mail. The following week, Henry dropped dead of a heart attack while playing a few games at the bowling alley after work. When he heard the news, Frank couldn't believe it. Damn, how could he have died, just like that? Didn't Henry know he needed him? He was like his father, his hope for the future. How could Henry have died, just like that? Initially, Frank mourned the loss of Henry's promise as much as he grieved the passing of this beloved little man. Frank could no longer do the work at which he was so skilled until he first passed a test to prove his competence.

For a concentrated month, Frank labored on the home study program, but he simply could not make sense of it. Like all the other ones used with him before, this program tried to teach Frank to read from a phonetic base — parts to whole, this sound then that sound, then blend the sounds together. For years teachers drilled Frank in the sounds that symbols make and taught reading as a decoding activity, but even the best instruction did not work — the years and years of special instruction at school, the literacy program through his church, even the tutoring he received after school. Frank simply could not learn phonics.

The harder Frank tried to sound out words, the more confused he became until he finally boxed up the books and sent them back to the address on the front. As he did so, Frank felt simultaneous anger and guilt. It woulda' been better, he thought, if Henry hadn't ever taught him to be an electrician so's he wouldn'ta known what he was gonna' miss. Silently, Frank asked Henry to forgive him for breaking his promise. He wondered if Henry would understand.

Shortly after Henry's death, Frank found work in the construction industry. He met Delores, and they married soon after. Frank and Delores had been married eight years when the accident happened. In fact, a few weeks after his return home from the hospital, they celebrated their eighth anniversary. Having neither the money nor the stamina to take his wife out to dinner, Frank planned a special celebration, reminiscent of their courtship days. Frank and Delores went on a picnic, this time at home. Frank spread a blanket out on the living room floor, unpacked the basket filled with food, and presented his wife a bouquet of artificial flowers that the kids had found in the closet.

"These have been good years, Bear," Delores said reassuringly, but she too worried about the future, especially in light of her man's stubbornness and his distrust for authority. How could he be so wonderfully kind yet at times so damned unreasonable?

"I know you don't want to see a vocational counselor, honey," Delores said. "I know you don't, Bear, but you don't have a choice if you want to get paid by Labor and Industries. You know the rules, honey. You've got to go, Frank. You've just got to go."

Delores did not need to say any more. Frank realized they needed the money, and he knew what he had to do to get it. Frank drove himself to the office of the vocational counselor who was assigned by the state. No, he didn't want Delores to go with him. Absolutely not! He would do this himself. The counselor soon learned that Frank could neither read nor write. Almost as soon as he sat down in front of her desk, Frank told her. Wouldn't do no good to hide it, Frank figured. Couldn't fill out the damn forms anyway. That didn't matter, the counselor reassured him; she could fill them out for him if he just told her the information. Frank felt her kindness.

As part of the vocational plan, the counselor suggested that Frank learn how to read. She knew of a clinic in town that helped people like Frank learn to read and write. Frank pulled back like an animal smelling danger. "Hell, no," he said. "You think I'm gonna' make myself feel dumb all over again. I ain't goin' to no damn clinic. Hell, no!"

The counselor paused, took a deep breath, and tried to explain the futility of Frank's situation. Like many other adults in this nation, Frank could neither read nor write, and unfortunately he was now physically disabled. He could not receive disability benefits unless he participated in a job retraining program. However, his inability to read or write would prevent him from participating successfully in any retraining program.

"You're talkin' 'bout a rock and a hard place," Frank summarized. The counselor nodded. She explained that the Department of Labor and Industries would not recognize that Frank's reading and writing problems were part of his disabling condition. What made Frank disabled was a fused back. Illiteracy didn't count. That was the rule.

"That don't make no sense! That's the dumbest damn rule I ever heard!" Frank replied. The counselor agreed that the ruling was stupid. Many of the rules written by government agencies were stupid. She felt Frank soften, just a little. The counselor promised to try to buy Frank time on benefits, if he agreed to attend the clinic. Frank realized that he was at the mercy of a system and maybe a cagey counselor. Reluctantly, he agreed to try again. "But don't you tell no one!" Frank insisted. "If my wife, Delores, calls you, if she asks you 'bout my program, don't you tell her nothin'." Frank's request surprised the counselor, but she agreed to his demand.

Frank knew that he'd have to find a way to explain this clinic stuff to Delores so she wouldn't guess the real reason he was going. "Sure," he said aloud on the way back home. "She'd believe that. I'll tell her 'bout this place where there's little kids that don't learn good, and my job is helpin' to figure out how to teach 'em. That's how I'm bein' retrained. Sure," he repeated, "that would work. Delores would like my doin' that." Delores did.

Frank liked his clinic teacher almost immediately. Maggie was little yet sturdy, just like Henry, demanding yet kind. She believed in Frank, and she demonstrated her belief by her expectations. She gave him lots of homework. "I ain't gonna be able to do all this, Maggie!" he complained. " What do you think I am, a college student or something?" Frank asked. However much her student complained, Maggie sensed that Frank liked homework and the accomplishment he felt from completing it. "Now listen here," Maggie teased, "you have enough time at home to do all this work and more. You get frisky with me, fella'," Maggie went on, "and I'll give you some more!"

Maggie was not aware that Frank rose at 3:00 o'clock in the morning to complete his homework so that Delores would not find him out. She did not realize that Frank hid his books and school supplies in the closet that hung on the inside wall of his tool shed. Every morning at 3:00 A.M., however cold or wet the weather, Frank walked outside, unlocked the shed, and pulled out his secret. He returned to the house, made coffee, and sat at the kitchen table to complete his day's homework.

Frank promised Maggie that he would always do his homework, no matter what. He'd work as hard as he could and as long as had to so that he could learn to read and pass the electrician's test. Frank planned on taking it the next time it was offered. "Now, let's just hold on here," Maggie said. "One step at a time, Frank, one step at a time."

Within the next few months Frank took many steps. Within two months, for example, he could read the sentences and paragraphs that he dictated to Maggie. He could read a compendium of individual words that he made visual notes for as well as simple predictable stories.[3] At the end of four more months, Frank could read certain articles from hunting and fishing magazines, portions of a first aid handbook, and large chunks of his electrician's codebook.[4]

Frank could read some third-, some fourth-, even some fifth-grade-level print, but surprisingly, he could not read all print written at that level, only some of it. He could read an article from *Field and Stream* or *Mechanix Illustrated*, for example, but he could not necessarily read a story from a child's reader. When Maggie asked why, Frank explained, "It don't rhyme, that's why!" Maggie asked Frank to explain. "Well, little lady," he said, "what else can I tell ya'? It just don't sound good. Ya' know . . . like it don't rhyme good!" For the same reason, Frank could not read dialogue unless, of course, he dictated it himself. "It don't rhyme neither," Frank complained of the author's talk. "It just don't rhyme."

What Frank meant when he said, "It don't rhyme" was that the syntax of the author's language did not match the syntax of his own. Frank didn't talk the way that the characters in children's readers talked, and as a result, he couldn't read the dialogue. He didn't speak the same way that many of the stories or articles were written, and, for the same reason, he couldn't read them. Teaching Frank to understand and use complex language was the key to his instruction, but he was resistive to change. He tried to leap ahead, like a leashed puppy chasing after a cat that raced across the road in front of him. Frank didn't want to be constricted. He didn't want to be confined to a certain type of language nor practice making and questioning complicated language. "I talk good enough," Frank reasoned. "How come you're wantin' me to say things other ways and write 'em other ways?" he asked. "One way is all I need." Maggie tried to explain the reason for the language work, but Frank dismissed its importance.

Maggie recognized that Frank could not understand print that organized and arranged language differently from his own. She recognized that Frank could not get meaning from print until his understanding and command of syntax matched the author's use of syntax. Frank had to be able to produce the same kind of language that he met in print in order to understand it. In other words, he had to be able to say and to write, in his own language, sentences that incorporated subordinate clauses and other complicated structures in order to be able to read other print that used the same kind of language.[5]

In spite of his need to produce more complicated structures, Frank resisted doing so. "I know I'm learning how to say stuff other ways," Frank acknowledged one day, "and I know I'm talkin' better because Delores said I'm startin' to talk like her. . . . But Maggie," Frank went on, "I gotta' get goin'. I gotta get ready for that electrician's test in two weeks!"

Maggie urged him not to take it. She knew that Frank understood the concepts in the electrician's test, but she also recognized that he wasn't ready to take it. She told him so. The language was too complex. For the same reason, he wasn't ready to take the test orally. Complex language quickly overwhelmed Frank.[6] Let's rehearse this language awhile longer, Maggie urged, trying to prevent another disappointment. "Besides, Frank, why do you want to be an electrician anyway? Scooting around on your belly like that and crawling around in the rafters . . . wouldn't that kill your back?" Frank denied the potential pain with a shrug. "Nah," he said, "wouldn't be so bad."

Two weeks later Frank took the electrician's test and failed it, by how many points he wasn't sure, but he failed it all the same. As soon as he received his grade in the mail, Frank stopped by the clinic to tell Maggie. He reassured her that his failing was not her fault. Yeah, he knew he was stubborn. Sure, he could take the test again — six months from now, he thought — but he didn't want to take it right now anyway. No, he didn't think he wanted to come for any more classes right now either, but he'd let her know when he was ready. Yeah, he'd call her. Yeah, he would.

That night at dinner Frank felt as glum as Paul looked. "What's wrong, Paul?" Frank asked. Paul shrugged just like his daddy. "What did you say, Pauliwog?" Frank asked again. "Tell your daddy what's wrong. Remember? I'm you're best friend." Paul pretended not to hear, but the hurt inside him would not be still. His disappointment tumbled out. "I'm still in the turtle group," he cried. "I'm the only kid in the turtle reading group! Teacher says I might have to stay back if I can't learn to read better than a turtle." Tears streamed down his face and onto his plate. Through his tears, Paul asked, "How come you help other kids to learn, Daddy, but you won't help me? If you can help other kids, why don't you help me?"

The question stunned Frank into action. Right then and there, Frank slid his son onto his lap, wrapped him tightly in his arms, and began his confession. Frank explained his weakness in detail as Delores and the boys sat spellbound. Paul listened to his daddy tell the story, what he really had been doing all these months at the clinic, not teaching other kids how to read but learning to read himself. Frank told his boys how he got up in the middle of the night so that Mommy wouldn't know. He told them why he spent so long at the grocery store looking for items on Mommy's list, how he walked up and down the aisles trying to match the words on the list to the words on the cans and boxes. Frank told them how sad he felt when his boys asked him to read and he wouldn't, too scared to have them know he couldn't. He told them how he failed the test 'cause he couldn't read good enough yet but was too plain stubborn to admit it. Maggie tried to tell him. She tried to explain that he needed more work, but he just wouldn't listen. Frank ended his confession with a promise. "Now you listen to me, Pauliwog. If I can learn to read, you can too, and your daddy's going to help you."

Frank put the boys to bed that night. He helped them brush, tucked them in, and led them in their prayers. As he switched off the light, Paul called his name. "Daddy," he called from the top bunk, "would you tell me the story again? Would you, Daddy?" Frank remembered how desperately he needed to hear Henry's words over and over again. He walked across the room to embrace the child who called him. "Daddy," Paul whispered, "tell me again, 'specially the part about the grocery store and how scared you got if anybody knew. Tell me that part too, Daddy." Leaning his elbows on the top rung, Frank retold the story in detail, being careful not to omit any parts.

The following day Frank called Maggie at the clinic. "You got any more room for a stubborn guy like me in your schedule, little lady?" he asked. "I want to learn more about this rhyme stuff and introduce ya to my boy, Paul."

Frank attended the clinic a few more months and Paul less than that. Paul learned to read better than a turtle and, at the end of the year, advanced to the next grade. Frank required several months of language work so he could read the language he met in books. To read any piece of print, Frank had to be able to produce and question the type of language that appeared in it. "I gotta' make it rhyme," he said.

Frank combined sentences into one according to the rules that Maggie set down.[7] "Put these two sentences together," Maggie instructed, "without using the word 'and.' " When he was unable to comply, Maggie modeled an alternative. Frank looked at the resulting sentence, shook his head, and said in disbelief, "Well, whadya' know!"

Sometimes Maggie represented the sentence in three-dimensional shapes with each shape signifying its appropriate part of speech.[8] "Hmmm," Frank said. "So that's what it looks like!" Once Frank could produce a sentence that followed a specific pattern, he personalized it by giving it a name. He called compound sentences "tape sentences," for example, reasoning that the "and" or the "but" in the sentence acted like a piece of tape that joined the two ideas together. Frank wrote each type of sentence he learned to produce. He named them and questioned them and looked for them in books. "Look at that, Maggie!" Frank exclaimed while scanning through a reader. "These little tape guys are all over the place!"

Frank became so adept at reading that he decided to take his electrician's test again. This time he passed it. However, even before he learned of his final grade, Frank decided that he no longer wanted to be an electrician. "I gotta' face reality," he explained to Delores. "I can't scoot on my belly any more or crawl around in the rafters. I'd get stuck, sure as hell, and my back would kill me for days!" Delores chuckled at her husband's honesty.

One night in the quiet of their bedroom, Frank shared his plan for the future. "Ya' know, honey," he said, as they climbed into bed, "I'd be a lot better school janitor than I would be an electrician. Maggie said I'd be the best janitor a school could have. A natural she said. I could learn to run the boiler easy. I could fix all the broken equipment for the teachers. Maggie told me teachers never know how to fix anything, not even a simple little tape recorder. Can you imagine that? Ya' know what else?" Frank asked, waiting for an affirmation from a wife who was nearly asleep. "I bet I could help some of those kids . . . ya' know the scared little kids who don't think they're good enough to be there . . . Maggie says I could . . . I bet I could."

Delores thought Frank would be a wonderful janitor. "Umm hmm," she said sleepily, "I think you'd be a wonderful school janitor, Bear." As Frank drifted off, he bet that Henry would think so too.

– 3 –

THE FISHERMAN

Why did he ever tell the principal that he'd do it, Tyler asked himself, the bed covers still over his head. Boy, that was the dumbest thing he'd ever done, that's for sure. Well, Tyler thought, he couldn't back out now, not today, unless of course he died right there in his bed. Tyler wondered if kids his age ever died from fright. He waited several moments under the darkness of his blankets to see if death might save him. No such luck, Tyler thought. Might as well face it. He threw the covers off, slipped quietly from bed, and tiptoed across the hall to shut his sister's bedroom door. The last thing Tyler wanted to do now was to wake her. Amanda would really make a fuss if he woke her on a morning that wasn't a school day. Amanda complained about darned near anything, Tyler thought. He breathed a sigh as he heard the latch of her door slip quietly into its pocket. Now to prepare for the battle that faced him, he thought. Wise warriors always prepared for their battles.

Wanting to be certain that every piece of himself was cleaned and armored for the day's challenge, Tyler showered, shampooed, and dried. He brushed his teeth and counted to ten before moving the brush to the next section of his mouth. He pulled the comb through his hair, tugging at the thick brown curls that defied a part. Tyler wished that once, just this once, his hair would cooperate. It didn't. Doesn't matter, Tyler muttered to himself. His cap would hide his recalcitrant curls.

Tyler remembered the word that his father, a defense attorney, used to describe a teenager whose crimes had been detailed on the news several weeks before. Words stuck with Tyler like dog hair to polyester. Once heard, he remembered them. "Recalcitrant." Tyler liked the way the word echoed in his mouth. He savored words and the ways he could use them. "Recalssssssitrant," Tyler hissed, accentuating the "s" sound so as to fight back the fear that nibbled at his insides. Tyler reached for his Cub Scout uniform. He admired the clean crisp creases in his trousers and the badges that adorned his shirt. He liked his newest award, the bear badge, best of all. Tyler traced around the edges of the bear with his finger, hoping that somehow this ferocious giant might send him strength and protect him, as it protected other brave scouts in times of danger.

Later that day, Tyler and several other scouts from the community would participate in the city's Veterans Day celebration. Tyler had been selected to play the leading part. At the end of the traditional parade, he would walk to the front of the reviewing stand, lined with dignitaries and scouts from throughout the community, and address the onlookers. Heady stuff for a third-grader. Tyler told his principal that, yes, he was pleased to represent his school . . . no, no, he wouldn't be scared . . . well, maybe a little . . . but scouts are supposed to serve, he argued, and he wanted to serve, even if he were scared . . . yes, of course, he would do it!

For the past several days, Tyler questioned his decision. In fact, he thought of nothing else. He worried that his monstrous problem would return. He feared that the words on the page might all run together again the way they used to, and he would not be able to decipher them. The more Tyler tried to sound them out, the more confused he became until the print made no sense at all. Just recently, only three weeks before, Tyler learned to read. Previous to that momentous breakthrough, he "talked" the print. That is, he added huge hunks of language to whatever he read, said an entire string of words when only a few of them appeared, added words and phrases as well as entire ideas that did not appear on the page. What he read always made sense, of course, but the words never matched the number and seldom matched the actual language on the page. Just three weeks earlier, in the fall of his third-grade year, Tyler abandoned his embellishments and read the print that appeared, read it like any other student. He wondered if he could do that again today.

"Don't worry, Tyler," the den mother exhorted. Unaware of her prized cub's reading difficulty, she nominated Tyler above all other scouts to participate in the ceremonies. "If you forget what to say, just read your speech that's written on the card!" That was the trouble. Tyler wasn't sure he could do that! Maybe, when he got up there on the stand, his terrible affliction would return and he wouldn't be able to read. Of course, he could paraphrase the lines that he was expected to say, for he had a keen memory, but today of all days he couldn't, no he wouldn't paraphrase. This was a military operation, after all, and the language had to be perfect. Exact. As precise as his uniform.

Tyler imaged himself in front of the crowd — his mom and his dad . . . his sister Amanda . . . his grandparents who at this very moment were driving all the way over from the other side of the state to watch the event . . . his classmates . . . his third-grade teacher, Miss Nelson, as well as a special former teacher, Mrs. Wilson . . . his fellow cubs and the older scouts . . . and then the governor, gosh, the governor. . . . What would he say to the governor? His parents knew the governor. Tyler's whole insides fluttered. What if he couldn't remember how to read? Tyler shuddered as he slipped into his uniform.

Two years earlier at an end-of-the year conference, Tyler's first-grade teacher, Edna Wilson, described Tyler's reading to his concerned parents. "Tyler reads funny," she said. "In fact, in all my years of teaching," Edna reported, "I have never had a student read like Tyler. He reads like a fisherman. He throws his language out onto the print, like a net flung out onto the water, hoping to gather up meaning that might be there. Sometimes he's right, but often he's not. Seldom does he read the language that is actually on the page!"

Edna could not explain why Tyler struggled so with reading, but she could describe with absolute clarity how he read. "He reads like a fisherman," she said simply. Throughout that year, Edna did what all astute first-grade teachers do. She linked the print on the page to language, thereby unlocking its mystery. In many different ways, Edna helped her students discover that print was language put down on paper.[1] She read to them and asked them to retell the story. She wrote down their retellings as well as their own personal stories, and she helped her young authors read their stories back to her. She labeled items in the room, like the chalkboard and the windows and the garbage can with their appropriate names. She taught them the names of other printed words, reviewed the names of any letters that were a little shaky to the children, and instructed them in how to make the letters. She taught the sounds that letters make and how to blend them into words. And she did one thing more. Edna waited, expectantly.

Edna expected that her students would bloom in January, certainly no later than February. Blooming, as Edna affectionately called it, was that time of the year when her youngsters could suddenly read "new" print — words they had never seen before, stories they had never heard before. Blooming was the time that her first-graders could take a book off the shelf or from under their bed and plunge into the print without ever being instructed in it. Tyler never bloomed. Well, he read in a fashion, Edna acknowledged, but never the way other students did. He never read what actually appeared.

Edna often wondered why Tyler couldn't read the words on the page. "How can he make a meaning match," she asked herself repeatedly, "yet not make a language match?" Throughout the winter and early spring of that first-grade year, Edna conferred regularly with Tyler's parents.

She reassured them that Tyler would learn to read, sometime soon, but exactly when she was no longer certain. She really had expected him to be reading by now, but certainly he would learn. Certainly. Edna made suggestions that the parents carefully followed. Tyler's mother practiced reading with him every night he asked, for example, and on those nights he didn't ask to read to her, she asked if she could read to him. She praised him for his attempts and coaxed him to "say the words that are on the page." Even with these gentle reminders and Mrs. Wilson's daily instruction, Tyler could not match the words on the page. In fact, whenever he tried, his reading deteriorated into nonsense.[2]

Before the end of the school year, Edna reported with great sadness what the parents already knew: Tyler was not reading, at least not reading like all the other students. Instead, he read like a fisherman, with meaningful yet abundant additions. Tyler was not ready to meet the reading demands of second grade.[3] "What do we do?" the parents implored. Edna wanted to say that she would keep him for another year. To Edna Wilson, Tyler was a treasure she had not had time to finish. She recognized the selfishness and the inappropriateness of such a solution. Tyler was the intellectual and social leader of the class. His peers sought him out. They knew he could always answer their questions or solve their problems. He simply couldn't read, that's all. Most certainly he would learn in second. Edna had already talked with the principal and with the strongest second-grade teacher in the building, Martha Oldenkamp. Miss Oldenkamp had a little sterner style than hers, that's true, and she insisted upon structure and order, but perhaps Tyler would benefit from that, Edna reasoned. To retain him in first would only penalize him.

The next fall on the first day of school, Miss Oldenkamp greeted Tyler at the door of her second-grade classroom. "Halooo," she said, her voice high and scratchy like metal scraping against slate. "You're the boy I'm going to teach to read!" Tyler flinched. He realized he couldn't read, and all of his classmates knew he couldn't, but Tyler did not want to be reminded of it so publicly. Still, he was not about to be disrespectful of a woman who held out such promise. "Yep, I'm the one," he smiled and rushed, as quickly as he could, past the well-intentioned spinster with iron gray hair.

Miss Oldenkamp believed in her instructional powers as well as the absolute need for all of her students to be thoroughly schooled in phonics.[4] That's why Edna recommended Miss Oldenkamp for Tyler. Edna wondered if she hadn't unwittingly omitted some secret ingredient of phonetic instruction in first grade. She urged Tyler to try his hardest on all the reading lessons Miss Oldenkamp taught him in second. Tyler pledged that he would. He drew letters in the air, even though he felt a little silly doing so. He repeated the names and sounds of letters as well as the directions on how to make them as Miss Oldenkamp spat them out... "bee... bu... down and around to my writing hand ... dee... du... down and around to my holding hand... kay... ku... down and angle in and angle out." Over and over he rehearsed as Miss Oldenkamp directed the action.

Tyler listened to the strings of sounds that Miss Oldenkamp called out and blended them into words, often incorrectly. "P-I-N," Miss Oldenkamp said, enunciating each sound with clarity. "Pen," Tyler responded. "Listen again, Tyler. Listen again," Miss Oldenkamp demanded. Tyler sat up straighter. "P-I-N," she repeated. "Pen," Tyler responded quickly. *"Tyler,"* Miss Oldenkamp raised her voice in frustration. "Carefully, Tyler, you must listen *carefully!* I spelled the word 'pin' not 'pen'!" Tyler blinked away his teacher's rebuke and summoned the courage to ask her a question. He truly wanted to understand. "But what did I do wrong?" Tyler asked, not realizing he had erred again. "You didn't listen carefully," Miss Oldenkamp responded.

Care had nothing to do with Tyler's errors. Neither did his hearing or his ability to listen. He listened intently, and he had normal hearing. However, he had difficulty with the phonological or sound aspect of the language. Tyler simply could not recognize the subtle differences in the sounds that words make. He often said "death" when he meant "deaf," for example, or "pen" when he meant "pin." He never caught his error nor was he able to recognize that he had made one when corrected, sometimes insensitively, by Miss Oldenkamp. Tyler also could not recall the direction of letters, particularly certain letters, or remember their position within a sequence of other symbols. Even though he and Miss Oldenkamp had written letters in the air all year, Tyler almost always confused them when he saw them. He almost always said "b" when he saw "d," for instance and "d" when he saw "b." He often reversed the position of letters within a word even when the word remained in view. Tyler was dyslexic.[5]

As the year progressed and Tyler's reading performance didn't, Miss Oldenkamp increased the frequency, duration, and intensity of her drill. "All right, all right, all right!" she announced from the reading table located in the back of the room. "All right," she called again, none of the students daring to turn around in their seats. "It's you, Tyler. Your turn! Come, come, come," and she clapped three times to emphasize the urgency of her command. Tyler dreaded his daily notoriety, but he wrote and spat and wrote and spat as Miss Oldenkamp directed him through his drills... "bee... bu... down and around to my writing hand... dee... du... down and around to my holding hand."

Unfortunately, the daily drill did not make a difference.[6] Neither did the additional instruction Tyler received from the building reading specialist. At the end of second grade, he read no better than before. He still tried to make meaning rather than to make sound. Tyler still read like a fisherman.

At another year-end conference, this one more ominous than the last, Tyler's parents met with a larger group of school professionals. They asked again, "What do we do?" The building psychologist recommended that Tyler be included in the building's special education resource program. Tyler qualified not only as a learning disabled student but also, and interestingly, as a gifted one. Unusual, the psychologist remarked, very unusual that Tyler is both gifted and learning disabled. "Special education?" Tyler's father reacted. "Tyler would hate that. Nothing against the resource program, you understand, but from Tyler's point of view, that's not a safe place. He told us what happened to his best friend, David, who went into the resource room this year. David went into the resource room smart, Tyler observed, and he came out dumb. Tyler would absolutely hate being placed there. My wife and I want our son to feel good about himself, and I can't think of anything that would make him feel worse!"

Miss Oldenkamp recommended that Tyler repeat second grade. She believed that Tyler needed more instruction in phonics, and he would not receive a sufficient dose of it in third grade. "Tyler cannot sound out words," Miss Oldenkamp reminded them, "and until he can do so, he will not be able to read." Tyler's father, a pragmatist by trade, wondered aloud how another year of the same thing would improve his son's reading. Edna Wilson, who attended the conference at the request of the parents, suggested that the school tape the books that Tyler needed for the following year and that his parents find their son a tutor. She recommended the clinic.

That July Tyler arrived at the clinic, scrubbed, pressed, and shiny, his parents wavering a few steps behind. "Come on," Tyler urged them. "Come on, hurry up, we don't want to be late!" Tyler did not suffer any of the distrust that gripped his parents, wary now of educators' recommendations. "Mrs. Wilson said that they can even teach adults to learn to read. I've got to be easier than an adult," he reasoned. "I bet they can teach me," he predicted as he reached for the door.

Bonnie Morrison, one of the teachers at the clinic, thought that she could. "Well, I can't guarantee that I can teach you to read, Tyler, but I do promise to try my hardest to find a reading method that works for you." That was good enough for Tyler. "Let's get started," he urged. During the remainder of the summer and into the fall of his third-grade year, Tyler and Bonnie worked together twice a week to unlock print.

Bonnie recognized that motivation was not the problem. Nor was intellect or opportunity. Tyler's reading difficulty did not stem from either of these but instead from his talking the print. Tyler equated talk with print. He treated them as equals, even though their forms are very different indeed.[7] Nouns, pronouns, verbs, articles, and other grammatical categories are distributed differently in print than they are in talk. That's why print sounds so different from talk, and that's why Tyler sounded like a fisherman when he read, scooping up meaning that might be there. Even though he was more intelligent than most of his peers, Tyler did not recognize what most other first-graders discover sometime in January or in February, after which they "bloom." Tyler did not recognize that print is the same as language but *not* the same as talk.[8] Unlike most readers who make that discovery on their own, Tyler had to be taught the difference for no amount of telling him would help. He had to be instructed, and that was Bonnie's job.

"Would you try reading one of these for me, Tyler?" Bonnie asked as she handed Tyler a selection of books. "Mrs. Wilson tells me that you can read . . . sometimes," she added.

The name of Tyler's favorite teacher made him beam. "You mean you talked to her? Did you?" he asked. Bonnie nodded. "Wow, Mrs. Wilson is just the best teacher a guy could ever hope to have. What'd she say about me?" Tyler asked eagerly.

"Well," Bonnie paused, not wanting to embarrass him. "I bet I know," Tyler grinned. "Mrs. Wilson used to say that I read like a fisherman . . . you know," he explained, "that I say a whole bunch of stuff that isn't there. But you know what?" Tyler added. "That's the only way I can read." He selected a first-grade book from the stack to demonstrate. Bonnie agreed. Tyler did read like a fisherman.

Not only did she concur with Mrs. Wilson on how Tyler read, Bonnie also recognized what he did not do. Tyler did not cue himself. In other words, as he read, Tyler did not ask himself questions that were sensitive to the actual language on the page. He asked general questions, of course, like "what's this story about" or "what does the picture tell me about the story." In first grade Mrs. Wilson taught him to do that, but the questions he asked were neither specific nor sensitive to the exact language on the page. Tyler did not control its form but instead approached the print as talk and, as a result, read "a whole bunch of stuff" that wasn't there.

To be able to cue, Tyler had to learn the basic ingredients of a good question. What makes a question a good one? A cue is effective if it sorts out the important from the unimportant, the relevant from the irrelevant, and if it examines alternatives. Tyler came to understand these essentials by learning to ask certain types of questions of information that was highly similar. Bonnie showed Tyler five similar pictures and had him ask questions that followed certain rules.

"Gee," Tyler pondered, "these pictures are a lot alike." Bonnie agreed that they were. "And you want me to ask a question of each picture, huh?" he asked as he chose one from the group. Bonnie nodded, and whatever question Tyler asked she would write down on a card.

"You want me to ask a question that doesn't have a 'yes' or a 'no' answer," Tyler told himself, "and a question that only this picture can answer," he said as he held it up to look at it more closely. "You know," Tyler said after several moments of examination, "you have some tough rules here, real tough. How can I ask a question of this picture when it is so much like the other ones?" he wondered. That was the point, of course. To ask questions of pictures that were visually similar, Tyler had first to identify the distinctive characteristics within each picture. Bonnie was about to tell him to notice how the picture was different, even slightly different from all the others in the group, but Tyler stopped her. "No, wait, wait!" he urged. Tyler wanted to solve the puzzle himself.

"Hmmmm," he said, "all these pictures show a little girl in a ruffled dress. Boy does she ever look like my sister," Tyler observed. "Amanda really likes ruffles. Hmmm," he continued, "so what's different between these pictures?" he asked himself. "What's different about this one picture?" he asked again. By asking himself "what's different," Tyler narrowed his attention, focused it on the distinctive characteristics of the picture so that he could then ask a "good" question of it.

"Hey! That's it! That's it!" he exclaimed. Tyler always said "that's it" whenever he made an important discovery. "What is the little girl holding under her arm?" he asked. Bonnie applauded and wrote Tyler's question down on a card; on a separate card, she wrote down his answer. "The little girl in the ruffled dress is holding a brown teddy under her arm," Tyler replied to his question. For the other pictures, Tyler and Bonnie did the same. Later, Tyler easily matched question to answer and answer to question and read each pair flawlessly.

"Hey," he said, "this is neat. I know exactly what this card says!" For the next few lessons Tyler and Bonnie wrote several more question-and-answer cards, and he took them home to practice. Late at night his parents found him, sitting in the middle of his bed, sheets tossed over his head and flashlight in hand so that he could match and read his stack of question-and-answer cards.

"Okay," he said when he returned to the clinic one day for additional instruction. "I know how to do this now. Teach me something harder," he told Bonnie. She taught him to ask questions of more extensive language. Tyler dictated, and Bonnie wrote. He dictated sentences, for example, and Bonnie wrote them down. His job was to ask syntactically sensitive questions of each sentence so that Bonnie could read them. For example, if the sentence read, "The athlete ran onto the field," Tyler would ask, "Where did the athlete run?" Tyler dictated directions, small stories, and remembered events, and Bonnie wrote those as well. Again, his job was to cue Bonnie so that she could read his language that appeared on the page.

Not surprisingly, once he could ask syntactically sensitive questions of his dictated language, Tyler could ask those same questions of an author's language. He made one reading leap after another. Without additions or embellishments, he read his dictated language in the form that it appeared. He read other language as well — stories in basal readers, small paperback readers, riddles and rhymes and poems — in the form that they appeared.

He could not yet read the *Hardy Boys,* one of his greatest longings. He could not yet read the sports page or the newspaper nor even a third-grade reader. Those leaps required different reading instruction, atypical reading instruction. He could not yet write so that others could decipher his meaning even though he himself could read what he wrote. Learning to record correctly spelled language would happen later and would also require a different type of instruction. What was important for now was that Tyler could read first- and second-grade level print whether that print was new or old. He could read birthday invitations from his friends, comments from his teachers, portions of his grandma's letters, which arrived with monthly regularity, even the text that he had prepared for today's celebration. But Tyler wasn't certain. Could he do it today? In front of all those people, his parents and his grandparents and even the governor . . . gosh, the governor. Could he really read, even in front of all of them? Tyler wasn't certain. His insides were so full of butterflies that morning that he picked at his breakfast.

"What's the trouble, pal?" his father asked at breakfast. "You look mighty impressive in that fine soldier uniform of yours. Doesn't he look impressive, Mom?" Tyler's father added, soliciting additional family support. "What's the matter, bud?" his dad continued. "Is your oatmeal a little mushy this morning?" Tyler looked down at the cereal bowl and ummmmed. "What's that?" his dad asked, unable to distance himself from his son's worries. "Is it the oatmeal or the whim whams that's got you?" Tyler ummmmed again as he poked the spoon up and down in the oatmeal.

"Hey, Ty, what can your dad do for you this morning besides hassle you with questions?" his father pressed further. "Questions, questions, questions," Dad repeated. Tyler paused. He dropped his spoon and broke into a wide grin. "That's it!" Tyler hollered. "That's it!" he proclaimed again as he rushed from the table, leaving his family wondering what "it" might be this time. Tyler returned several minutes later, his text for the day in hand. Written across it were all the questions he needed to ask himself so that he could read the print that appeared on the page.

Later that morning, Tyler walked across the stage to the podium as several hundred onlookers prepared to witness an act of courage. A cool autumn breeze blew the bill of his cap that covered his brown curls. Tyler unrolled his text, now moist from the anxious moments of waiting his turn. He ironed the paper flat with his hands so that it would not flap in the breeze. Decorated in pins and badges reserved for the bravest of bears, Tyler began. He read the text slowly, carefully, pausing occasionally to refer to the questions that he had written in the margins. Not once did he embellish the text or say language that did not appear. Tyler no longer read like a fisherman. He missed a few words, of course, but all his substitutions were appropriate.

At the end of his speech, the crowd burst into applause and hoorays and whistles. Family and friends gathered around him. Tyler noticed that his mother had been crying. So had his grandma. Even Edna Wilson appeared a little teary. The next day in school she sent him a card with a note written inside. Tyler was not certain he understood its meaning, so he took it home for his parents to clarify. The note read simply: "Congratulations, my dear friend. You have bloomed!"

– 4 –

TAMING A BULLY

Albert Lincoln's third-grade teacher reminded him that his imaginary friends belonged in the hallway, outside the classroom door. They wouldn't all fit in the hallway, Albert argued. He had too many of them! Line them up sideways against the wall, Miss Robinson urged. Then they would fit. But how could he explain to his companions that they were not welcome in the classroom, Albert asked. Don't explain, Miss Robinson insisted, just instruct them to leave. They were distracting Albert and the rest of his third-grade classmates from their story writing.

Albert paused for a moment to weigh his teachers request. He uncurled his legs, which were tucked underneath him, placed his feet on the floor, and stretched his long frame up. Like a music man directing a raggedy band, Albert led his friends out of the room. His classmates smiled but did not laugh or even chuckle as Albert marched back to his desk, the pretend baton still in his hand. He returned to the task that Miss Robinson had assigned to the entire class that morning. Casually, she walked toward Albert's desk to check his progress on the creative writing assignment. "Why, Albert," Miss Robinson exclaimed. "You've forgotten to write the story! You've drawn a picture instead, a wonderful picture I might add, of a dog and a boy. I think that boy is you, Albert!" Miss Robinson exclaimed, "but where is your story?"

Albert Lincoln explained that he always drew a picture first, always, always drew a picture first, that's the way he did it, and then, if he had the time, he wrote the story. "Well, the story is what you're going to read to the class after recess, Albert!" Miss Robinson warned. "Better hurry," she urged him gently. "Don't worry!" Albert grinned. "I'll be ready," and he returned to his imaginings, adding more color to the German shepherd and to the trees in the background.

As predicted after recess, Miss Robinson called her students individually to the front of the room and asked them to read their stories to the class. Believing that Albert needed additional time to finish his, Miss Robinson called him up last. Like youngsters cuddling into warm laps, the third-graders settled into their chairs as though anticipating the enchantment that was about to unfold. Albert always told such good stories.

This one was about a boy named Albertino and a German shepherd named Aroma. The dog, a very unusual canine, the storyteller added, lived in the wooded area at the edge of Albertino's home. Many years ago, centuries in fact, a wizard bestowed two gifts upon the dog: the ability to speak and the ability to sniff out magical treasures like pots of gold at the end of a rainbow. Hence the name Aroma. The wizard foretold that one day a young boy, an extraordinary child, would arrive with a knife in his hand at Aroma's den to set him free. The wizard chained Aroma to a pole to wait for the boy who appeared centuries later. His name was Albertino. The whisper of the trees called Albertino into the deep and dark woods one late afternoon. He took his knife for safety. Albertino came upon the dog's den, crawled in, and set Aroma free. The two became fast friends and planned how they would find treasure to disperse to poor people in the community. At the end of rainstorms, frequent in the Northwest, Albertino and Aroma ran to the end of the rainbow to uncover magnificent riches, which they circulated to the needy, just like Robin Hood and Tuck.

"Wow!" Billy Morgan exclaimed with wonder in his voice, "that was a terrific story, Albert. That was the best one you ever wrote!" The other third-grade students agreed. Albert was the best storyteller in the class, probably in the whole school! Miss Robinson smiled. "That was a wonderful story," she said. "Bring it here so that I can save it. I'll hang it in a special place in our room." Eagerly, Albert complied. When he placed his paper on her desk, however, Miss Robinson gasped in surprise. "Albert," she whispered so as not to embarrass him, "you forgot the words! You didn't write anything down at all." Albert smiled. "I know," he said. "I read my stories better when I don't write them down."

Miss Robinson paused to measure her reply. She did not want to curtail Albert's creativity, but she wanted him, somehow, to recognize his reading difficulty. After all, how could Albert overcome the difficulty if he didn't realize he had one? For the first full month of third grade Miss Robinson worked with Albert — individually, daily, and intensely. Like all his teachers in the past, Miss Robinson was intent on teaching Albert to unlock the printed word, but her efforts, just as the efforts of previous teachers, simply did not work. Albert could not read. More troubling, he denied the problem existed. Albert was a puzzle, a mixture of conundrums — large but graceful, creative but illiterate, intense but unconcerned, at least about inconsequential matters and everyday tasks such as reading and writing. "Hmm," Miss Robinson finally responded. "You may not be ready to write the words down just yet, Albert, but at least put your name on the story. Artists sign their name, you know. First and last, please," Miss Robinson requested as she pointed to the bottom of the picture.

Albert stopped and thought for a moment. He put the tip of his pencil between his teeth and bit down lightly on the lead. He cocked his head to one side, removed the pencil from his mouth, and scrunched his eyebrows up. "Albert," Miss Robinson called, "I'm waiting for you to write your name, just your name, dear," she said coaxing him to risk a response. "I'm thinking," Albert replied. "Thinking?" Miss Robinson questioned. "Yeah," Albert responded, "thinking about how I want to be remembered!" Miss Robinson waited for the artist to decide. "Well, let's see here," he said to himself, his pencil now in its writing position. Albert signed "Albret Licon" on the bottom of the page, stepped back, looked at his signature, and promptly erased it. "Hmm," he said, "I don't like that one." He tried again. "Aldert Licoln" he wrote and erased again. "No, that won't work either." Albert tried two more signatures, omissions or reversals apparent in each one. Finally he settled on the following: "Al L." From that day forward, Albert called himself "Al."

Melanie Robinson could not wait until November, the normal time for parent conferences, to communicate with Mr. and Mrs. Lincoln. She invited them in at the end of September to talk about their son's learning difficulties. Both parents appeared. Tom and Helene Lincoln were keenly aware of their son's reading problem and of his reluctance to admit it. "He absolutely refuses to admit defeat or to lose an argument," Tom observed. "I call him pig-headed," Tom went on. "His mother has another name for it, of course, but Albert . . . excuse me, I mean Al . . . has his own view of the world, doesn't he, Helene?" His wife agreed. Al was definitely stubborn, Helene said, but he was also warm and sensitive, characteristics that both parents cherished. That's part of the reason that he's so well liked, Helene surmised. Al could not read print, but he certainly could read feelings, and he did so skillfully, his mother observed. Al felt as comfortable with people as he did with a soccer ball, and on that score he was also skilled. Al swooped down the soccer field, his appendages flying with the grace of an eagle. Al had many talents.

Tom concurred and identified another one of Al's abilities. "You know that little guy can make just about anything!" Tom said. "For Father's Day he made me a papier-mâché pig to put in my office, the most handsome little pig," Tom went on, estimating the size of the gift with his hands, "about this big. As expected, he chose a pig for a reason — to illustrate to his father what a pig's head actually looked like!" Tom and Helene laughed in unison. "Yep," Tom said, "he's quite a guy." Helene nodded.

Melanie Robinson recognized all these gifts — Al's sensitivity and wit, his intellect, his remarkable creativity, his physical grace and grandeur — but what concerned her was his reading. "You realize, of course, that he isn't."[1] The Lincolns nodded. They described the steps that they had already taken: selecting one of the best private schools in the area to ensure small class size and thoughtful instruction, the kind that Melanie Robinson provided; having Al repeat the first grade; employing one reading specialist after another to tutor him for three full years; and taking him to the largest university in the state to have him tested. Dyslexic, the psychologist concluded, severely so.[2] The psychologist explained that Albert demonstrated a form of "word blindness" that was so severe that he might not ever be able to read.[3] They conferenced with the psychologist just a few months ago. They had not tried additional tutoring since.

"He complained so," Helene explained, "For years he complained! Albert ... I mean Al ... said he could not learn the way his tutors taught him. Still, we insisted that he continue. After each tutoring session, Al whined when he couldn't do their homework. Sometimes he cried. He was so desperately unhappy that Tom and I simply gave up. Al hasn't been tutored since the end of June," Helene Lincoln confessed. It was now the end of September.

Melanie Robinson agreed that Al needed his summers free, but she encouraged the Lincolns to resume tutoring now that school had begun. She also encouraged them to find a different approach. "What's been tried to this point simply hasn't worked," Miss Robinson reasoned. "Find something else for Albert ... I mean Al. Find a different route for him." The Lincolns thought they had exhausted all sources. Miss Robinson encouraged them to try the learning clinic. Tom and Helene debated, worrying about the consequences of another disappointment. Another failure might break his spirit.

"Al desperately wants to read," Tom explained, "but he's worried that he can't." "He appears unconcerned," Helene observed, "but he really isn't." "Al's indifference is his way of protecting himself." "He worries a lot, about things kids shouldn't have to worry about," Tom added. Miss Robinson asked them to explain. "At dinner last night," they began in unison, then stopped, each deferring to the other. Helene continued, "Last night at dinner Al said he wanted to be a doctor, probably a surgeon, if things turned out all right. When we asked him to explain, Al said that 'turning out all right' meant learning to read. See," she said, her hands gesturing to emphasize her vision, "Al worries about that, about the future and being okay. We tell him in lots of ways, 'Al you're okay,' but when schoolwork is involved, he doesn't feel he is. The thought of not being able to read absolutely terrorizes Albert... I mean Al. That's why he denies he can't. The thought of not being able to read is simply too horrible."

Beneath the veneer of Al's nonchalance, worry swelled. He worried about the ride to school in the car pool, especially when Molly Wilkens was present. Molly had red hair and freckles and a space in her front teeth, which she always stuck her tongue between when she wasn't talking. Todd and Austin, two other students who were some of the best readers in third grade, rode in the car pool too, but Molly was the most annoying, always looking for ways to read, especially when it wasn't necessary. On the way to and from school, for instance, Molly convinced her classmates to look for the funniest billboards along the roadside and read them aloud. Al never read any. When Molly asked him why, Al explained that he couldn't find any billboards that he liked sufficiently well to read, but, unwilling to risk his secret, he joined them in their laughter. Al used Todd as his cue. Al watched him intently, laughing only when Todd did. Melanie Robinson assured the Lincolns that the students in her class never teased Al for not being able to read. "That makes sense," Tom said. "None of his classmates knows... except, of course, for his best friend, Billy Morgan."

Al would not be able to hide his shame much longer, however. Miss Robinson urged the Lincolns to try again. She asked them to make an appointment at the clinic. "I'll reassure Albert... I mean Al... that his secret is safe with me, but he needs to find a different way to learn to read."

Al and his parents appeared at the clinic a few months later. A clinic assessment explained Al's "word blindness." He recognized so few letters and words on sight that he appeared to be blind to them. Al was not sightless, of course, but his memory for symbols was so vague that he could not recognize words and even many letters on sight. He could not remember what sounds to attach to them or recall how to make them. Al was a "broad-ranged" dyslexic. In other words, his visual, auditory, and motor memories for letters and words were vague and inexact. Al would have to learn about symbols and about reading in a way different from than his peers. Unlike them, Al could not rely upon the three sensory channels that teachers traditionally use to instruct their students in reading. Al could not learn to recognize words, for example, by writing them over and over again. His motor memories were unreliable. So were his auditory memories. As a result, Al could not remember what sounds to attach to the symbols on the page. He could not remember what name to call them because his visual memories were also inaccurate. Hence, a traditional sight approach would not work either. Al needed atypical instruction.

For most of his third-grade year, Al attended the clinic, until a red-headed classmate with a space between her teeth wounded him. Two mornings a week Al came to the clinic and met with his tutor for an hour before school began. Those were the mornings that Helene brought Al to school. Al liked that. On those days, he only had to endure Molly for the ride home. During those months, Al learned the reading skills that most children acquire easily and automatically in the first grade. Al had to learn each of the skills in a way different from his peers. He learned to recognize bothersome letters, for example, by storying them — that is, by devising a story that linked the shape of the letter to a high strength cue that incorporated the label of the letter, not its sound.[4] He recognized the letter "e" once he saw how its shape resembled a snake, which he named "eel." He recognized the letter "m" once he saw it on a piece of candy and associated that with its name, "m and m." Al learned more about letters — how to identify them by their tactual features, how to recognize them by their visual features, and how to write them.[5] Al learned to recognize words by the same unusual route he learned letters, from a base of imagery. To learn to recognize individual words, for example, Al drew a picture that captured the word's meaning as well as its name.[6]

Understandably, reading words in context was significantly easier for Al than recognizing isolated words. When words appear all by themselves, recognition depends heavily upon symbols. When words appear in sentences, however, meaning surrounds them. Al needed meaning in order to read. He dictated sentences and stories and later read them back with cuing from the teacher.

"I don't believe this," Al grinned when he read his first story at the clinic. "I didn't think I'd ever learn to read!" he said to his tutor the day that he read back his dictated language. Al learned to read simple stories written at the primer, first-grade, and even second-grade level, but like other broad-ranged dyslexics, Al needed instruction to do so.[7] He could not read language "cold" — that is, he could not read without preparing himself by scanning the story and predicting to himself what it might be about.

Al's learning affirmed him — so much so, in fact, that he began to take his clinic notebook to school so that he could share it with Miss Robinson. She encouraged Al to work on his clinic homework assignments in class. Al thought that was a great idea. One day on the way home from school, however, Molly retrieved Al's notebook from the floor of the car. Recognizing that print was inside, Molly looked in, believing she had a responsibility to uncover its mystery. "What's this, Albert?" she asked. Molly knew his name was Al. "Huh, why do you have this notebook? Look!" she cried holding the notebook in the air to expose its pages. "It's got little stories inside! Oh, Albert, these are cute," Molly squealed and then fell silent. "Gosh," she said thumbing slowly through the pages, "these are baby stories, Albert. How come you read stories like these, Albert?" Molly asked questions the same way she talked — in an endless string of one after the other. Al shrugged. "Huh? How come?" Molly asked. "Oh, these are really cute, Albert!" Without a word, Al grabbed the notebook away from her, closed it firmly, and stared out the window all the way home unable to look at the pain inside.

Whether it appears for a moment or a lifetime, pain fills the entirety of whatever universe it occupies, becoming an insult or a blessing, a burden or a gift.[8] The pain of exposure humiliated Al that day. "I'm *not* going back to the clinic!" he announced at dinner that evening. "I hate being different," Al screamed as he stomped away from the table and returned moments later to add, "and I'm not gonna be . . . either!"

No amount of encouragement or explanation from Miss Robinson would change Al's mind. "I've already learned to read, Miss Robinson," Al reasoned. "I've accomplished what you asked," he went on. "I learned how!" Miss Robinson knew that, in a way, Al now could read. She also knew that he did not read sufficiently well to meet the demands of fourth grade, and she recognized that unlike most other readers, Al would not continue to become a better one without additional and specialized instruction.[9]

"But Al," she explained, "fourth grade is a lot harder than third. You'll be expected to do so much more. . . . " Al would not budge. He would not even consider returning to the clinic, not because he disliked it, but because he absolutely refused to be singled out. His parents did not argue with him. Long ago, Tom and Helene Lincoln realized that their youngest son could not be coerced into a decision. He had to arrive at it himself, through his own experience. Besides, Al's fourth-, fifth-, and sixth-grade teachers reinforced his point of view. Al needed to be in school, they said, and treated just like anyone else in the class.

For the next three years, Al blamed his teachers for agreeing with him. "Mr. Olson can't teach me anything!" Al complained soon after fifth grade began. "He might be able to teach some people some things," Al acknowledged, "but he sure can't teach *me* anything!" Al spent most of his fifth-grade year building papier-mâché replicas of Northwest buildings, each one grander than the last. "Albert!" his father complained, "Sorry, sorry, I know it's Al . . . Al," his father cautioned, "consider the size of our house! The Narrows Bridge won't fit in the living room, let alone the car." Sixth grade was the year that water colors captured Al's attention. He liked the way they wept together and how he could make them move. Al painted whenever he had free time in class. "May as well paint!" Al complained to his parents. "Then I learn something. I can't learn a *thing* by listening to Mrs. Hardy. She doesn't make any sense to me, any sense at all!" Al protested. "First she explains things one way, then another way. I wish she'd make up her mind!"

Tom and Helene Lincoln worried about Al's readiness to handle the demands of seventh grade. "He can't read well enough, can he?" Helene asked Tom. Tom wasn't sure. He only knew that Al's writing was undecipherable, not because of the way he formed the letters but because of the way he put them together. Al threw letters down on the page in a scramble, and the result did not even vaguely resemble the actual spelling of the word. Al's spelling was so off the mark, in fact, that no one could read his writing, not even Al himself. Al had succeeded in the lower grades, ego intact, for several reasons: his mother's reading necessary material to him in the evening, his intellect, and his great set of ears. Al could understand and remember anything he heard if, of course, the teacher explained it to him the right way.

His seventh-grade teacher, Arlette Burns, explained ideas thoroughly, sometimes too thoroughly, but Al did not mind her explanations. What he minded was Mrs. Burns's written expectations as well as her civilized brutality, which she defined as "honest criticism." Al wondered if dishonest criticism hurt as much as the honest variety. Before he would graduate from *her* seventh-grade classroom, Al Lincoln must compose his ideas in written form, record those ideas in his own hand, and read them to his classmates! Billy Morgan couldn't help. Nor could his mother.

"I've got your number," Mrs. Burns told Al, loud enough for the class to hear. "You stretch back," she said, mocking his long-legged repose," and dictate your ideas to someone else without even trying to write them down yourself," she said, criticizing him with her waving finger. "Don't you realize writing is hard work?" Mrs. Burns asked as though Al did not know. "You can't ever expect to get better if you have someone else to do your work for you! This paper you've given me is someone else's work, not yours," Mrs. Burns said as she hung Al's paper between her fingers for all onlookers to see. "It is not in your hand!" Without a word Al retrieved it and returned to his seat, intent on proving her wrong.

For weeks Al worked on his spring writing project every day after school. One afternoon Helene came home early from work to find Al lying face down on the living room floor amid a pile of rumpled up papers. What's wrong, his mother asked. "It's the bully," he said. "The bully beat me . . . he beat me again." Helene did not understand. In fact, she was amazed, assuming that "the bully" referred to one of Al's classmates. With that one exception in third grade, Al's classmates never taunted him about his reading problem.

"The bully?" Helene asked incredulously. "Tell me about him, Al." The bully lived in his head, Al explained, on one side of a lake. "He throws the letters and words across to me," Al wailed, "but most of them land in the water, and I can't get them. I know them, but I just can't get them," he cried. Helene tried to soothe him, but Al continued to cry. "What do you think, dear," she asked, "is it time to go back to the clinic?" Al nodded. It was time.

He arrived a few days later, the unfinished writing project protruding disrespectfully from his school notebook. Al met with the clinic teacher who first taught him to read in the third grade. Her name was Ellyn Landry, a bird dog of a teacher. Al was embarrassed for having to return. He knew Mrs. Landry would poke around until she found out the truth. No, Al said, he didn't want help on his writing project. Actually, he'd like to forget it, but he couldn't if he ever wanted to get out of seventh grade. He'd finish it somehow, but he didn't want to do it today, that's for sure. What he wanted . . . no, what he needed, was to become a better reader. Yeah, he'd try some reading today, no writing though. Al hated writing. His ideas never came out the way he wanted — in bits and pieces and disconnected blurts that were neither sensible nor decipherable.

Still worried over the burden of the assignment, Mrs. Landry asked Al how he planned to finish the spring project. "If I have to," Al replied, "I'm gonna copy straight from the book, but I'm gonna get it done," he said, unwilling to submit or even acknowledge his difference. "How will you be able to read it?" she asked. "Remember," Al grinned, "I'm good at remembering what I hear, and I'm even better at making things up."

Like Tom and Helene Lincoln, Mrs. Landry recognized that Al could not be coerced. Instead, she granted his request. In an attempt to find his reading level, Mrs. Landry chose different selections of print, which ranged from fourth grade all the way down to beginning first. After struggling with the harder pieces, Al chose the easiest selection. Without questions to warm him up or cues to guide him, Al stumbled over the words, his index finger tracking each one until finally he reached the end of the page. Al stopped, unable to continue. After all this time, Al read more poorly as a seventh-grader than he did when he was in the third grade. Wounded and weary from the insults of the day, Al lowered his head to hide his tears from Mrs. Landry. Al did not want her to witness his defeat. The bully had beaten him, again.

The two of them sat in several moments of silence. Al spoke first. Quietly he promised, as though to himself, that he would learn to wrestle the bully another day, but not just then. The pain was too great, and surely he would lose his spirit if he tried.

The following year Al honored his promise. He attended the clinic throughout eighth grade and learned strategies for deciphering the printed word. He learned an image-based strategy, for example, to recognize words on sight. For Al, every word was a matter of sight recognition. He had to learn them "like the faces of friends."[10] Whenever he came across a word he absolutely needed to know — one in his science or math book or any other word he needed to recognize in isolation — Al drew a picture note, which captured the word's meaning as well as its label. He rehearsed matching the picture note to the printed card, thereby linking meaning to configuration.

Al never took on methods directly but instead slid up to them, with his shoulder first, as though needing that amount of distance to ease the awful pain that print inflicted. With reluctant deliberation, for example, Al brought his background to the print, telling himself all he knew before he began. "Do I have to read this?" he seemed to say, whenever Mrs. Landry asked him to read. "Do I really have to?" Al knew the answer. He could not ever take the bully to the mat unless he learned how to wrestle him. His opponent was a mean contender, devious at times, and so Al always approached him cautiously. He approached print as language and made predictions about its content before beginning to read.[11] Like someone fearful of the dark, Al asked himself questions of the print aloud, as though quizzing the bully before engaging him in combat.

Al learned another device that gave him even greater control. He asked questions of the language as the print unfolded.[12] Al became so skilled at cuing that when he tired of asking questions of the print, he cued his clinic teacher so that she could read. He asked questions of Mrs. Landry, for example, so that she could read the actual language on the page. When she asked him to model the complex moves of printed language by writing difficult written structures himself, however, Al withdrew from the battle. "Enough," he said at the end of his eighth-grade year. "I've had enough," Al said as though to guard his spirit. "I have to save something for ninth grade!" Al reasoned. "I'll learn to write then."

When high school began, however, Al did not have the heart to quarrel with the bully and at the same time to contend with all the changes — new subjects, different teachers, greater expectations, even a rotating schedule. Al struggled to keep up with them all. He could not battle the bully too. Besides, he believed that he had found a way to live with him. "Don't worry about teaching me more reading," he reassured Mrs. Landry in the fall of his ninth-grade year. "What I need is help getting through the ninth grade!" Al always knew what he wanted and what he needed. The two of them negotiated, the teacher and the artist. Al began to look like one — his long hair pulled back in a pony tail, his open sandals, which he wore year round, his blue jeans, which were tattered just the right amount and in just the right places. Mrs. Landry agreed that she would teach Al how to use taped textbooks and questioning strategies to control his ninth-grade classes if he would learn to type. "*Type?*" Al cried. He preferred to communicate with a brush, but reluctantly he agreed, recognizing, at some level, that he needed the skill to prepare himself for the next encounter. Al expressed ideas and emotions with a strong, cool line, but he could not remember how to reproduce words, in part because of his inaccurate motor memories. In order to write, he would have to learn to type.[13]

Al insisted that he try tenth grade on his own. No help from the clinic. No help from home. Al could manage on his own. He had, after all, learned to live with the bully, if he slid up to him quietly, unobtrusively. Al could now read his textbooks, although maintaining the task was very difficult indeed. When the assignment was too long or the frustration too near, Al listened to his taped textbooks. He knew how to study for tests. He knew how to ask for oral ones when he felt he needed them. He even knew how to have others write his thoughts down on paper for him. He talked, they wrote. Yes, Al could manage tenth grade on his own. He knew how to live with the bully.

But could he live with him into the future? That was the question that flashed before him, often in the middle of the night or when he was alone in his room completing his homework. Then the future terrified Al even more than the bully. Would he turn out all right? Al wondered. "All right" no longer meant being a surgeon. He changed his mind in tenth grade once he took a class in pottery and felt the power of clay. Molding a wet lump of clay into a definable form appealed to Al far more than slicing and suturing flesh. After he graduated from high school, Al intended to enroll in college and earn a fine arts degree. Like other adolescents, Al needed to verify his gifts. College meant that he must face the tormentor that prevented him from writing decipherable, sensible language. Al still preferred to read his writing from his imagination, not from his paper.

Al returned to the clinic during the fall of his junior year and announced his readiness to face the brute that taunted him. "I've changed my name to Bert," Al said. "What do you think of that?" As predicted, Mrs. Landry asked him why. "Well, when I was little," Al explained as he crouched down like a child and smiled impishly, "I thought that changing my name from Albert to Al would solve my problem of wiggly letters. Creative, don't ya' think?" he asked. "Well, it might have been creative," Bert grinned, "but it sure didn't work. Do you know . . . I still reverse my letters! Besides," Bert added, "I hate the name Albert. I even hate the name Al, but the worst part is that my parents still can't remember which one to use. Who wants to be called 'Albert, I mean Al' all the time?" he asked. "Not me!" Bert concluded. "From now on," he announced, "my name is Bert" even though he occasionally spelled his name "Bret."

For the entirety of his junior year, Bert wrestled with the tyrant, reading him and writing him. He wrote daily and learned atypical methods of control. Bert learned to write from a base of imagery, not from a traditional outline.[14] He identified his images first, captured them in visual form, reduced them to a simple three-word sentence, and defined the actions that best expressed each image.[15] He evaluated the effectiveness of his images, how they worked together, and created a visual design before he ever put fingers to typewriter. When he wrote argumentative papers, rather than narrative ones, Bert concerned himself with ideas rather than words, meaning rather than spelling, proof rather than punctuation.[16] In fact, he was never graded on the icing of writing, only on its content, on idea or image and the clarity of each. To express them clearly, Bert and his teacher constructed his own personalized list of rules to follow and added to them with each paper.[17] Bert could not write from a list of someone else's rules any more than he could read from a base of phonics or learn a skill from a compendium of pieces. Bert had to learn from the top down and from the inside out.

"I don't learn that way," he complained when Mrs. Landry asked him to predict the rules for an argumentative paper so she could list them. "I don't learn the way that teachers do ... the way you do ... and other kids do!" he added. "If I try, the bully always wins. I have to see it ... hold it in my head, like a piece of sculpture," Bert said, acknowledging his gifts. "Tell me what the paper should do," he directed, "so I can make a map of what it looks like." Bert sketched out his argumentative paper in doodles to capture the function of each paragraph. He wrestled the bully to the ground that day, and with each match that followed, his writing improved.

One day after a particularly grueling meet, Bert shared his plans for the future, casually as always. He planned to apply to college, he said, to study for a fine arts degree. What did she think? Bert's teacher always asked more questions than she answered. Mrs. Landry returned his question with another.

"Clay and sculpture," Bert answered when she asked what type of art he liked to produce the most. "I don't like drawing as much," Bert mused, "or printmaking either," he added, asserting as always his autonomy. "I dunno, though," he shrugged when asked to examine the future, "I worry a lot about it ... I mean if I can really compete and all. . . . My folks tell me that I've already turned out all right, but I'm not so sure about the future ... I'm not so sure."

Soon now he will begin his formal training at the university level. Bert's worry is understandable as well as necessary, especially for an artist. He has already lived the life of one, enduring all the pain that can be borne without breaking. Artists can do no less, especially in their childhood years, for anguish leads them to recognize their gifts and teaches them to accept the ownership of them. The bully lurks silently behind every corner, on every signpost of this print-dependent society, lying in wait to wound Bert's spirit. He meets him daily.

– 5 –

LUCILLE, HOW DO YOU DO?

Lucille loves her Lord. She clings to the joy that he promises her future. Without a trace of doubt, Lucille believes that, like the brothers and sisters before her, she too will escape to a better life, if only she endures this one. And so she does. Lucille trudges through life obediently. She ignores the constant intrusions of physical pain and the daily reminders of her grinding poverty. Instead, Lucille devotes her life to others. She volunteers her days as a cook in the soup kitchen of her neighborhood community center, which is affiliated with her church.

"Needin' no baby, the lettin' goin' hunry," Lucille said adamantly. "Hurtin', real true, a baby. If so bad, so bad, wantin' quit," she said shaking her head. "Ma littleprettybaby," she said all in one word, "any hunry *all* a time! Cowin' on!" she said explaining further. "Ma kitchen I'm in cookin' in foo real good wi a baby.... Lotta' foo.... Evry day wi a wee... on lunch," she added. "Lordie, Lordie," Lucille went on, softly now in reverent tones, "My Lord be the speak at Lucille... little speak.... little little.... Lucille be the cookin' ma baby," she said. "So Lucille do!"

What Lucille meant was that she saw no reason to allow people, especially children, to go hungry. Hunger hurts the stomach and insults the spirit, particularly the delicate spirit of a child. The intensity of children's hunger is directly related to the dependability of their next meal. When youngsters cannot count on that next meal, hunger hurts their very souls. Lucille's mission, given to her by her Lord, was to reduce the hurt and cook a "real good" dinner for her babies, Monday through Friday at the community center. On an average weekday at the center, Lucille fed between two and three hundred citizens, most of them children.

Actually, Lucille directed more than she cooked. Many years of arthritis confined her to sitting. From her solid oak stool, given to her years earlier by the staff of the community center, Lucille directed all action. She helped plan the day's menu, organized kitchen volunteers, exhorted them to use every scrap, and insisted upon the taste test for each item. "To here a Lucille," she directed. "For here with a green good . . . seein,'" she repeated.

Many times, the volunteers misconstrued what Lucille said or politely ignored her because of their confusion. When that happened, Lucille rose from her stool. Slowly, painfully, deliberately, she pushed her round frame up, intent on demonstrating what she meant.

"Honey, the be you watch to Lucille," she chided the woman who was cooking the day's greens. With gestures and nods and utterances of approval, Lucille modeled what her spoken language could not accurately convey.

Deciphering Lucille's language was difficult for any listener. Even her children had occasional trouble understanding her. In fact, without the immediacy of her presence, Lucille was often misunderstood. For Lucille and the listener at the end of the line, a telephone conversation was nearly impossible. As a result, Lucille used the phone only in case of an emergency, as she did when her mother fell to the floor moaning of chest pains.

"*An Mamma, an Mamma,*" Lucille yelled at the operator. "'tackn for the floor, "*'Tackn,* real bad, real bad 'tackn! Mamma hapin comin' a hel . . . *merchee, merchee* . . . now!" Lucille yelled.

"Excuse me?" the operator asked. "Tell me what's wrong!"

Phone in one hand, gesturing frantically with the other, Lucille pointed to her mother now doubled in pain on the kitchen floor. "*Mamma,*" she repeated. "'tackn bad, for real bad 'tackn. Not be die to here comin' now. To here, an mamma," she repeated for emphasis.

Still confused yet hearing the urgency in Lucille's voice, the operator asked, "Are you hurt? Tell me your name! Tell me your problem!"

"*Lucille!*" she screamed into the phone. "*Lucille! An a Mamma 'tackn for a floor.* Please, merchee, hapin a hel, to the dyin,'" Lucille wailed. "*Please an mamma.*"

At that moment, Lucille's oldest son, Curtis, walked through the back door. He often stopped by on his way home from work. Curtis worked the night shift as a stocker at a large supermarket. Several mornings a week, Curtis dropped by to see his mother and grandmother. They always fixed him breakfast and fussed over him a little, just as they used to when he was unmarried and still living at home. This morning Curtis found his grandmother gasping at life and his mother, desperate to communicate their plight, screaming into the phone. He grabbed it from her.

"We have an emergency," Curtis translated. "My grandmother. She has heart trouble. I think she's having a heart attack. She needs help right away," Curtis implored. He gave the operator the address as Lucille cradled her mother in her lap.

"Lordie, Lordie," Lucille prayed. "Be to the mamma, to the mamma," she repeated.

In minutes the rescue unit arrived. While Lucille continued to pray, the paramedics worked their earthly knowledge upon the old woman who lay deathly blue, motionless, and ready to exit this life. Jolts of electricity, drips of solution, and a mask of oxygen revived her. The ambulance raced grandma to the hospital, where she spent the next two and a half weeks.

Lucille went to see her daily, sometimes twice a day. Curtis offered to drive her, but Lucille declined, recognizing that her son had to sleep during the day if he were to work all night. "Curtis boy, no, no" she said, "workin' time for nigh . . . all a nigh . . . ma Curtis boy to be sleepin' . . . for workin' be drivin' all a nigh . . . jus' a busin' me to."

The time Lucille spent waiting and riding and transferring busses consumed most of her day. For the two and a half weeks her mother was in the hospital, Lucille did not have the time to volunteer at the community center, but she carried each and every one of the children in her thoughts. "My babies, my babies," she worried aloud as the bus traveled across town to the hospital. "Charl, and Toma, and Pamla," she said again shaking her head, "any hunry all a time!"

Lucille worried about the children. She worried about their parents. She worried about the other volunteers at the center. Would they fix good meals? Would the meals be sufficient for the crowd that always increased as winter lengthened? She worried about Curtis. Who would feed him breakfast? Curtis's wife left for work before he arrived home. Would he take the time to eat? Curtis didn't have "no sense . . . ma Curtis hard for workin'. Too hard for workin'."

Lucille also worried about her mother. Would she get well? What if she didn't? What would Lucille do? Lucille relied upon her mother for more than love and companionship. She relied upon her for formal communication. When an appointment had to be made with the doctor, Lucille's mother made it. When she had to appear at the welfare office, Lucille's mother accompanied her. When a bill or a notice appeared in the mail, Lucille's mother read it.

Lucille's children recognized that her words often needed interpretation, but neither Curtis, Vanessa, nor Louis knew that their mother was unable to read. Lucille was too ashamed to tell them, as though somehow she was to blame for not learning, as though she had committed some awful, unspeakable wrong. Lucille worried that if her children knew she could not read, they too would be unable to learn. If they knew of it, her sin would befall her children. Lucille would not allow that to happen.

Throughout their early years in school, Lucille listened to her children read nightly, in fact, insisted that they do so. She held them close and heaped them with praise as they read so beautifully, like song birds, Lucille thought. "Uh, huh, uh huh," Lucille chanted as her children performed the wondrous feat that she wished she could have accomplished. Lucille could not read. Not the directions on her own blood pressure medication nor that of her mother's. Not the names of her children or the names of her grandchildren. In fact, she could not read many of the letters by name, not even the letter "Q" even though she had lived on Q Street for most of her forty years. Lucille was illiterate, totally illiterate, and she was not likely to be otherwise.

Lucille could not read because her language was highly unpredictable. She did not talk like books talk. In fact, she did not talk like anyone else at all! Not the members of her family. Not the volunteers at the community center or the members of her church. Lucille did not arrange her language according to the agreed upon rules of grammar.[1] Instead, she strung words together randomly, it seemed. Verbs here, nouns there, strewn but not located. Misplaced, incorrect, or unnecessary articles. Conjunctions in the place of prepositions. Language that turned and spun and swirled in confusion. Gesture rather than syntax was the glue that held Lucille's language together. When gesture was not present nor observable to the listener, as in phone communication, Lucille could not be understood, even by her children.

Lucille's disordered language was not a matter of experience or of environment. Her mother spoke syntactically predictable English, language that followed the agreed upon rules of order. So did all her children. Lucille had heard English all her life, but hearing it had not helped her learn how to put it together. Her disordered language was not a matter of her race. Black English, like Puerto Rican, Chicano, and Asian English, has a predictable syntax — different from standard middle-class white American English, to be sure — but predictable all the same.[2] Lucille's English, however, was not syntactically predictable. Often she mispronounced words, used them incorrectly, or omitted the sounds that comprised them. She also did not use plurals with consistency nor express events in the past or future tense. Her word selection contributed to the swirl of confusion. The words Lucille chose often conflicted with her intended meaning. In summary, Lucille was difficult to understand because her knowledge of the sounds, meanings, and ordering conventions of the English language was insufficient and often incorrect. Because of her scrambled language, Lucille could not read . . . at all . . . and the only person she dared ask to read for her was her mother.[3]

Now that her mother was in the hospital, Lucille did not want to trouble her with daily reading demands, the mail for instance. "No frettin', no frettin'," Lucille urged when her mother asked. "Mamma to be well...eatin' and restin' and better and better," she urged. "Be readin' hard by restin'," Lucille insisted. No, she would *not* bring the mail to the hospital for her mother to read. Lucille would not even ask her mother to decipher an important-looking notice that was hung one day on the front doorknob while she was away at the hospital. Lucille wanted her mamma to use all of her energies recuperating. Returning home that night, Lucille looked at the orange notice quizzically, hoping its color did not convey importance. Unbeknown to Lucille, the orange notice announced that this Friday, between the hours of 9:00 A.M. and 2:00 P.M., the water would be shut off so that the mains could be repaired.

Friday morning Lucille pulled the faucet up, then down to draw her bath. Again she pulled it. No water came out. "Hmm, be broke," Lucille concluded. "Fixin' Curtis, by eggs." Lucille would ask Curtis to repair the trouble when he stopped by for breakfast the following morning. Already late, Lucille dismissed the problem and promptly forgot to unplug the bathtub or turn the faucet to its off position. She dressed hurriedly and spent the day as she had spent the previous ones, commuting on the bus and comforting her mother. Weary and cold, Lucille returned late that evening to a houseful of water, the tub down the hall still overflowing its banks.

For the next several hours Lucille mopped and wrung while she cried softly. Unlike all the other tears she had shed before, Lucille did not shed these for her babies. She did not cry for her own children or even for her mother. Instead, she cried for herself. Lucille recognized that she would be left alone, victimized by a world dependent upon print and no one within it to decipher it for her. "Bein' for doctor too, scitions...and if to the warfare lady to me seein'.... What I be, what I be to doin'?" Lucille asked herself throughout the night. Hours later, the water now mopped from the floor, Lucille fell into bed exhausted after she had said her prayers. Lucille gave thanks and asked for guidance.

On the way to the hospital several days later, Lucille knew what she must do. "Ma Lord be the speak to Lucille...Pator Robin'...Pator Robin'...yes, yes," Lucille announced. She would talk to Pastor Robbins, that's what she would do. Pastor Robbins would forgive her for not learning to read. He would know what to do. Lucille's faith and Pastor Robbins's recommendation brought her to the clinic. He learned of the agency through one of the clinic's board members, a leader of the minority community himself. "Don't worry, Lucille," the pastor explained. "This is a good place I'm sending you to. I know your mamma's sick and needs care, but members from the church will take care of her while you're at school. You go learn how to read. Soon as you can, now. You go learn how to read."

Such faith Pastor Robbins expected from his parishioners! Lucille had to endure endless hours of urban captivity as well as face the fear of the unknown. Every time she came to the clinic for an hour's lesson, Lucille spent at least three hours riding one bus to freedom, and then another, finally repeating the cycle of enforced patience again for the ride home. Waiting in the rain. Waiting in the cold. Riding and waiting. Waiting and riding. Far more frightening than the bus, however, was the white, upper-middle-class world that faced her: a clinic located in a complex of medical buildings full of authority figures dressed in suits or stylish dresses. The first day of her instruction, Lucille would not remove her coat, a purple one, its arm seams ripped slightly, uncovering the white batting bulging from its interior. For her second instructional hour, however, Lucille felt sufficiently safe to remove her purple armor.

Annie O'Loughlin, Lucille's teacher, made it a point to make her student comfortable. She was little lady with gray hair and delicate hands. "You want a cup of coffee, dear?" Annie asked. Lucille liked coffee. She liked to be called "dear." And to think that someone would pour coffee for her, put cream and sugar in it, even bring it to her on a tray with a napkin! "My, my," Lucille told her mamma that night. "Coffee a Lucille . . . and it be me, and a namkin, orange, by a teacher! *My* teacher! My, my." Lucille was impressed.

Annie wondered how to teach Lucille to read, or if she even could. Lucille did not lack the intellect to learn, her teacher reasoned, for she could accomplish what Annie and many others could not: plan and orchestrate nearly three hundred meals for members of her community, most of them wiggly, demanding children. Though she did not lack the intellect, Lucille lacked the expressive language skills necessary to communicate and be understood as well as the language skills necessary to read. Her language difficulties involved all features of the expressive system: articulation, semantics, and syntax.[4] Lucille could not articulate many of the sounds of speech. That's why she cut off parts of words, their beginning or their end, or omitted portions within them. She said "scition" rather than "prescription," "tackn" for "attack," or "merchee" for "emergency." Lucille also had difficulty retrieving the correct name for objects, actions, or events. As a result, she might say "eggs" when what she really meant to say was "breakfast." Right category, wrong label.

Lucille's greatest difficulty with language, however, was neither articulation nor word retrieval. It was putting it together. For some reason, she had not learned how to put language together in the way that others do. She had not learned the internalized, unconscious set of rules that most children learn, not by formal instruction or by drill and practice, but by mere exposure to and rehearsal with the language.[5] More importantly, Lucille had passed the critical period for learning it.[6] Linguists report that the crucial period for acquiring grammar is a window during the childhood years. When it is passed, future language development is severely restricted if not prevented. At the age of forty, Lucille was well beyond that critical period. Lucille knew nothing of linguists, however, and although she surely lived through many critical periods, Lucille did not equate them with language. All Lucille knew was that her Lord directed her to Pastor Robbins, and he, in turn, sent her to Annie. Lucille knew that Annie could teach her.

"Ummm ummm," Lucille would say on those days Annie greeted her at the clinic. "And how are you today?" Annie asked. "Fine, fine, bein' fine to me, darlin', an' workin' hard, real hard for me! Lucille workin' hard and hard!" she would say.

For weeks Annie floundered with her student, trying this, discarding that, Lucille always trusting the wisdom of her teacher. Annie knew that the focus of Lucille's instruction had to be language. How could Lucille ever learn to read, let alone be understood, unless her language changed, unless it began to approximate the language of others?[7] And how could Lucille acquire a sense of language structure now that she had passed the critical age for learning it? How, Annie asked herself, how? Or is it how? Is the question "how," Annie wondered after all. Doesn't Lucille already have a sense of language structure, at least a passive sense of it?[8]

"Hmmm," she wondered, continuing to badger herself, and others, with questions until she arrived at an understanding. Annie was a plucky little woman who debated with defeat even when it seemed to stare her directly in the face. She questioned defeat to death. A "passive sense" of grammar, Annie continued, Lucille must have that or she would not understand what others said to her, and clearly Lucille understood.

"How are you today, Lucille?" Annie asked. "Bein' fine, honey, fine to me an' workin' hard, real hard a Lucille," Lucille responded. "Can I offer you some coffee?" Annie asked. Lucille smiled, "Oh yes, darlin'." Lucille liked her coffee. "I don't recall, Lucille, what do you put in yours?" Annie asked, deliberately not reducing the complexity of her own language. "Little sweet," Lucille answered, "little tiny sweet, an' a whee," she added referring to the powdered white cream she liked so much. "Than you, honey," Lucille always said, "coffee a Lucille . . . for me . . . an' with a namkin my teacher! My, my, so ni a Lucille, so ni," she said, relishing the thought that someone as important as a teacher might pour her a cup of coffee.

Yes, Annie reasoned, Lucille understood. She simply did not know how to put language together according to the agreed upon rules that most children learn by the age of five. How could Lucille learn those rules now, at the age of forty? Annie wondered. If Lucille hadn't learned the rules by hearing the language, how would more hearing make a difference? Obviously, it wouldn't; the language must be accompanied with a visual referent, Annie concluded. In other words, Lucille needed to rehearse a language that was *seen* as well as heard.

What would such a language look like, Annie questioned herself as she walked through the halls of the clinic, into one room and then another, up to the office and back to her own, as though the walk might help dislodge some wisdom. What form would the language take? How would this visual communication system capture the dynamic and creative quality of spoken language? How could it move like spoken language moves?[9]

Questions, questions, questions. For weeks Annie carried a bushel of questions around in her head, until at an unexpected moment, a bolt of "aha" struck. Annie understood. She realized that she needed to invent a system of shapes to accompany the spoken word, thick colored shapes, ones that Lucille could pick up, feel, and move about. Annie cut shapes out of heavy cardboard: red triangles for action verbs; black triangles for helping ones; blue rectangles for nouns; clear rectangles for adjectives and clear triangles for adverbs; fat orange arrows for prepositions; gray circles with a nose pointing out on the edge for articles; question marks for question words like "how" and "who" and "when," and on and on.[10]

The reason for the shapes was to make language sit still so that Lucille could examine it and the relationships it captured. With the shapes, sentences did not vanish as spoken ones do. Instead, they remained frozen, horizontally on the table. The goal of representing spoken sentences in visual patterns, then, was *not* to teach Lucille to label parts of speech. Instead, the goal was to teach Lucille about the rules and relationships of language; to teach her about completeness; about what words do, how they act with one another, what jobs they perform, how to arrange them, and how their arrangement changes their form. The goal, then, was to teach Lucille more about the form of language and the relationships it captures. Lucille never once doubted her teacher's wisdom.

"Hi, darlin'," Lucille greeted Annie at the clinic one day. "Thank you, honey, me to," Lucille said acknowledging Annie's dose of tenderness as she poured the coffee. "So good, an so good," Lucille said, sipping its warmth.

Lucille took off her coat and reached into her cloth bag for the yellow tablet that Annie had given her just a few days before. Lucille was eager to show her teacher the homework she had assigned herself. Lucille liked to copy letters and words, the one academic skill she could perform with ease. Although she knew how to write them before she ever came to the clinic, Lucille did not know how to read letters — that is, she did not know how to call them by their correct name until Annie and she worked out a series of stories.[11] Lucille practiced writing her letters and reading them back. She also practiced copying words. Pages and pages of them she copied, even though she could not read them.

"To me be workin' hard, real hard Lucille," she said, proud of her accomplishment. "Yes, this is wonderful," Annie said as she examined Lucille's writing.

"I have something new for us today, Lucille," Annie began, and she spread the shapes on the desk. "Oh, pretty, so pretty!" Lucille said approvingly. "For a Lucille?" she asked, delighted that her teacher would actually make her something special. Annie nodded. "Yes, Lucille, I made these for you. Today we're going to learn how to use them."

With a picture in hand, Annie said a sentence and represented it in shapes as Lucille listened intently. "The wind is blowing through the trees," Annie said. Lucille looked at the colored tokens strung across the desk. "Hmm," she said. "Say it with me, Lucille," Annie urged. "The win' is blowin' through the tree," Lucille said, repeating the sentence spontaneously as she touched the colored tokens.

Lucille immediately recognized the one-to-one correspondence between words and shapes, and with minimal rehearsal, her sentences took on a quality of completeness not observed before. "Tha is a looong senence," Lucille remarked while looking at the string of shapes before her, " . . . real long." Lucille listened to Annie say a sentence and repeated it several times until she could reproduce the sentence in shapes herself with minimal guidance from her teacher. Soon Lucille could build and say her own sentences, each of them complete. "I be tellin' you one," Lucille announced. "Listen to me!" Lucille not only realized that each word had a predictable form but that the word's form was determined by its function. "A doin' word," she said matter-of-factly while building a sentence. "Tha be a doin' word, huh?" she concluded, and held up a red triangle for affirmation.[12] Annie nodded, believing that her student's trust might be justified.

For the next several weeks Lucille built sentences to accompany pictures. After she built them out of shapes, Lucille wrote the words that corresponded to them. Lucille looked back at the shapes to guide her response, and Annie helped her with the spelling. By now, Lucille could spell a number of words — function words, several nouns and verbs that she had made visual notes for, and a handful of other words as well.[13] Spelling was not an issue, however. Annie encouraged Lucille to write a word the way she thought it might be spelled. She did not require nor even encourage exact spelling, for she knew that spelling would develop much later. Annie wanted Lucille to focus on the structure of language.

One day Lucille came to the clinic eager to share her latest accomplishment: several pages of sentences she had first built with shapes and then written in words. "Look what I be to doin'!" she told her teacher proudly. "I be writin' and writin'," Lucille said. "My mama be hollerin' at me, 'Lucille, you workin' too hard, too hard, Lucille,' but I workin' and workin'... wantin' to read!"

Annie asked Lucille to read back the language that she had so carefully written, and although Lucille tried, she could not. She looked at Annie and asked, "I can't be readin'?" Annie looked at Lucille and asked her to repeat the question, "What did you say, Lucille? Tell me again." Lucille repeated her question, "Darlin', I can't be readin'?" she asked sadly.

Something was wrong with the question, Annie thought. Its form was incorrect. "I'm not sure, Lucille, but ask me some more questions. Let me hear some more of them. Ask me a question about the color of this cup," Annie directed as she held up Lucille's coffee cup. "A queshion?" Lucille repeated. "What color this cup is?" Lucille asked. "Ask me another question, a question about coffee," Annie directed. "A queshion, a queshion," Lucille repeated, "Annie be liken some queshions. Hmmm," she thought, "I can have some coffee?" Lucille asked. "Ask me another question!" Annie directed as she went to pour her another cup. "Think of a question about me, a how question about me, while I get you some more," Annie said. "Hmm, 'bout you," Lucille thought. "Hmm, a how queshion 'bout Annie. Oh, I got a queshion 'bout you," Lucille said as Annie returned, "How you are, Annie?"

"Well, I'm just fine, my dear," Annie replied as she gave Lucille her cup of coffee on a tray with a napkin. "Ummm, ummm," Lucille said, "little darlin' Annie is so good to me!"

Annie realized that Lucille asked questions the way that small children do — by positioning the verb after the subject, not before it. Lucille would ask "I can have some coffee?" rather than "Can I have some coffee?" Even with "ising" and "areing" questions, Lucille could not transpose the verb. Like small children who ask a question by raising the inflection of their voice at the end of a statement, Lucille would do the same. "What color the cup is?" rather than "What color is the cup?" or "How you are, Annie?" rather than "How are you, Annie?"

Lucille could ask questions, of course, but she could not ask ones that were syntactically correct.[14] Annie realized that Lucille needed to be able to do so. A question is an internal scanning device that nourishes the intellect, makes it grow and flourish. By asking a question, the individual examines the status of her knowing, like Annie examined hers, and proceeds to the next level of understanding, as Annie moved when she discovered how to teach Lucille about language structure. A syntactically correct question is a more strategic and effective probe than asking one that is arranged incorrectly. A question that asks, "What color the cup is?" is ambiguous. One that asks, "What color is the cup?" is not. The information requested is clear. Learning to ask a syntactically correct question was important, then, because questioning not only guided

Lucille's thinking, it aimed it, allowing her to formulate relevant probes of ideas and specific questions of content.

Lucille learned to ask these questions by building simple statements out of the shapes and changing the statements into questions. She thought of a sentence, for example, and built it with the shapes. She read the sentence aloud, transposed it into a question, and said it again before returning it to statement form. Then, with minimal guidance from Annie, Lucille wrote the sentence. As self-imposed homework, Lucille wrote pages of statements, questions, and answers and brought them back so that she could read them to Annie. "The banana is yellow," Lucille read. "Is the banana yellow? Yes, the banana is yellow." Lucille constructed, wrote, and read trilogy after trilogy.

Initially, Lucille had great difficulty transposing the verb to its proper position at the head of the line. "Is the boy is riding down the street?" she wanted to say, but the shapes prevented her from doing so. Lucille realized that she had added another word and that she could only write a word if she had a shape for it. She learned to ask different forms of a question as well as to answer them.

One day Lucille came to the clinic with a surprise for her teacher. On her own, Lucille discovered something wonderful. If she put a person's name in front of the question, she constructed a message that sounded "just like talkin'." Lucille pulled her prized writing tablet from her bag and peaked Annie's curiosity before reading the discovery. "I have a big surprise for you...yes darlin', a *big* surprise!" Lucille added. Annie's eyes twinkled, a sure sign of her pleasure. "Well, I'm waiting!" she smiled.

Lucille never needed coaxing to read her sentences aloud. "Louis," she began, "you are going to work. Are you going to work, Louis? Yes, Louis, you are going to work!" Lucille looked up from her paper to remind Annie that Louis was her middle child. Quickly she returned to her reading. "Curtis, the dirt is on your trousers. Curtis, is the dirt on your trousers? Yes, the dirt is on your trousers!" Again she looked up. "That boy still gets hisself filthy," she explained. Ever since he was little, Curtis found a whole bunch a ways to get hisself dirty. He just do like the dirt." Annie laughed out loud and acknowledged the attraction for dirt in one of her own children.

Again, Lucille returned to her reading. "Vanessa, you are crying. Why are you crying, Vanessa?" Annie greeted Lucille's newest form of question with applause. "A 'why' question, Lucille," Annie said, "my you are getting fancy!" Lucille and Annie had worked on the meaning of why's and their resulting subordinate answer. Lucille beamed. "You are crying because you are sad. Vanessa, are you crying because you are sad? Yes, you are crying because you are sad."

Unable to wait for her teacher's praise any longer, Lucille asked Annie if she too had noticed the discovery. "Did you look what I just did?" Lucille asked, unaware of the structural complexity of the question she just posed. "I just be puttin' in names!" Lucille answered. "See," she went on, "this writin' is just like talkin'!" With joyous words of approval, Annie assured Lucille that, yes indeed, she had noticed.

Saving the best for last, Lucille read her favorite group of sentences. "These are my *favorites*," she announced, a smile stretched broadly across her face. "Lucille," she read, "how do you do? You are doin' fine, Lucille. Are you doin' fine? *Yes, Lucille*, you *are* doin' fine," she read, loud enough for her Lord to hear. Lucille looked up and asked her teacher, "You know why I'm feelin' so fine, honey?" Without waiting for a guess, Lucille whispered to Annie, "I be readin', darlin'. This be just like talkin', and I be readin', that's why." Annie nodded softly, showing that, yes, she understood. Lucille had made the link between talk and print.

As she learned how different structures worked and the relationships they expressed, Lucille's expressive language skills increased, particularly her vocabulary. One day as part of her lesson, for example, Lucille selected a picture from a stack and dictated the following sentence to her teacher: "The stout old man is standin' by the pretty flowers in the park." Annie nearly dropped her coffee cup in surprise. "Stout!" Annie exclaimed. "Stout!" she said again. "When did you learn *that* word, Lucille?" Delighted with herself, Lucille replied assuredly, "Eaaaasy, honey. That is real easy for me! Now I can think of a lot a words I'm 'ginning to remember!" Annie understood the meaning of Lucille's puzzling explanation. What Lucille meant was that she could recall words, even ones she'd heard long ago, now that she had a schema or a framework for them. The framework of a language is its grammar. Without a sturdy internal scaffold to attach them to, words cannot be learned. Nor can they be retained or retrieved from memory. Once the schema is in place, however, once the rules are internalized, the learner can "think of a lot a words" that they can now remember.

Lucille's scaffold strengthened as she represented and manipulated language with shapes and wrote that language down on paper. Her expressive skills increased as well. Lucille now converses on the phone even though she dislikes using the "contraption." Her language has an order to it that others share. Equally important, Lucille can read and write, though the level is not yet where she wants it to be. It hovers between the second- and third-grade level, but the fact that she has learned, despite the odds, delights the staff as well as Lucille. She now reads to her "grandbabies" and to herself for pleasure. "I be readin' and readin' to them every night," Lucille says. "I tell them to work real hard in school, just like their grandma. And they do! My grandbabies listen to me!" So do other members of her community. For the past year, Lucille has participated in community efforts to keep all of her babies free from drugs and crime. "They need to be studyin'," Lucille concludes, "and workin' hard like Lucille! I tell 'em, and they listen to me."

Faithfully, Lucille continues to attend the clinic, except, of course, when she is down with an occasional illness or enjoying a well-deserved gift as she did last spring. Family and community friends sent both Lucille and her mother back home to Georgia to visit the relatives. Lucille came to the clinic to tell the staff members of the good news as well as to make an appeal for her safety. Ever since she came to the clinic, Lucille included the clinic staff in her daily prayers, each of them separately and by name. When Lucille arrived at the clinic with her Georgia surprise, she said to the staff gathered round her, "Oh, darlins'," she said, "I need you to pray for me! I have never been in no airplane afore . . . never, never," she said shaking her head. "You be prayin' for me to keep that airplane up in that sky!" All of us assured her that we would.

- 6 -

I BIT HIM 'CAUSE I BIT HIM

Like a mean gale in winter, Clark Honeycutt, a sixth-grade student at Pacific Elementary, blew through the main door and settled on the trouble bench just outside Mr. Redding's office. Clark rocked back and forth, waiting for the principal to open the door. Waiting was part of the punishment. Students were sentenced to Mr. Redding's trouble bench for behavioral outbursts of the worst kind. The teachers and staff at Pacific Elementary handled other student misconduct themselves. Marvin Redding refused to police the skirmishes that happened on the playground or the misbehavior that occasionally occurred in the classroom. Instead, he empowered his staff to settle disputes themselves; he believed that misconduct could be resolved by talking to students in a reasonable fashion. When that did not work or when the misconduct flagrantly violated school rules, Mr. Redding saw the student in his office. However, he insisted that offenders first sit on the long oak pew to the left of his office door to examine the error of their ways. The length of time that the offender waited on the oak bench reflected the seriousness of the transgression.

Clark had been waiting a long time now — since morning recess, in fact, when the playground duty sent him to the trouble bench for biting Jesse Taylor, one of his sixth-grade classmates. Jesse's accusation triggered Clark's attack. "You were actin' like a dodo bird in reading this morning!" Jesse taunted. "Bet you don't even know what a dodo bird is!" Jesse continued as he flapped his arms to mock the bird and demean his peer. In a flash of anger, Clark grabbed Jesse by the arm and bit him.

Jesse screamed loud, piercing wails while Clark dug his teeth deep into his classmate's flesh.

As soon as she heard the screams, the playground duty knew that Clark was involved. Clark was always involved. Halfway across the playground, the duty yelled, "You're hurting him, Clark! Stop it, you're hurting him!" Clark released his jaws, fell limp, and began to cry, silently, as he always did. His breath quickened, and his shoulders heaved. Tears fell, but he did not sob with sounds or words. After each outburst of anger, Clark cried this way, in despair, without a noise. "To the bench!" the duty commanded breathlessly as she approached. "You belong on Mr. Redding's bench...now!"

Clark complied without one word of protest. Clark seldom complained. Occasionally at home he complained, of course, about inconsequential matters like the dinner menu, but he seldom complained about anything else. Nor did he try to dismiss his behavior with excuses, to explain his biting, for example, as an understandable consequence of Jesse's merciless teasing. Clark did not know why he did what he did even though he regretted his actions, especially hurtful ones like biting Jesse. Clark only knew that he was in trouble, *big* trouble. In the eyes of Mr. Redding, Jesse's teasing would not justify Clark's behavior. The way Jesse threw words at Clark, the way he always pounded him with language, the way Jesse danced around him like a pesky fly, none of that would matter either. Biting was not acceptable. Simply not acceptable. Clark knew that, but knowing the rules did not deter his actions. He bit him anyway.

While the duty and several hovering sixth-grade girls comforted Jesse, Clark left the playground as instructed. At times like these, Clark always did what he was told. Silently, his head lowered, he swooshed into the building, through the hall, and to the office, where he plopped himself down on the trouble bench, a label given it by the student body of Pacific Elementary. Clark remained on the bench throughout that Wednesday morning as the office staff and student helpers busied themselves, like ants, with the tedium of the school day. Hurry scurry, they rushed around him. Busy, busy, they bustled by him as though he did not exist, and in a way, he didn't...really. For the most part, Clark occupied space on Mr. Redding's trouble bench. During his many years at Pacific, Clark spent so much time on the trouble bench that he had worn a slight dip into the oak seat. Clark scooted his rump back and forth across the bench while he waited for Mr. Redding to appear. As the wait lengthened, Clark's scooting increased.

"You here again, Clark?" Mrs. Patterson asked as she returned to her desk from a morning of sorting, tallying, and distributing. Elsie Patterson was the head secretary of Pacific Elementary. Her desk was the closest to Mr. Redding's office, which meant that all serious offenders waited next to her. She instructed them during the wait. That was another part of the punishment. "I swear, Clark Honeycutt, you are going to wear a hole right through that bench. Now stop your scooting back and forth," Elsie Patterson demanded. Clark stopped. His black hair looked as disheveled as his shirt, which hung loose from his jeans. He'd lost several buttons in the morning combat.

"You got into another fight I see," Elsie surmised. Clark did not answer. "What's the reason for the fight this time?" she asked. Clark still did not answer. "Who else might I be talking to except you, Clark Honeycutt?" she asked.

"Dunno," Clark responded.

"You do too know! Who else is sitting on the bench except you?" Clark wished Mrs. Patterson would stop. She had a way of saying things that made him so confused. "Who else might be sitting on that bench except you, Clark Honeycutt?" Elsie asked again in reverse.

"Dunno," Clark replied.

Selecting another way to release his anxiety, Clark moved his knees. Up and down he moved them like pistons in high gear. "Stop it, I said. Quiet!" Elsie Patterson commanded. Clark tapped his fingers instead. He cupped them around the edge of the pew and droned out a monotonous rhythm. Again Elsie looked up, lowered her glasses, and released a sigh of irritation. "Clark Honeycutt," she said peering over the rims, "why do you make such a racket? Why is that, Clark?" Elsie asked, staring directly at the boy who refused to return her gaze. She bore her eyes deep into her charge and asked again. "Now you know I'm talking to you, Clark Honeycutt! Why do you always make such a racket? Just answer me that, Clark Honeycutt!"

"Racket?" Clark blurted out at the sound of his name. His long, slender frame jerked in surprise.

"Well, I knew someone was home!" Elsie smiled, reassured by the connection she had established. She continued her morning instruction. "You know what I mean by that, don't you?" she asked. In spite of the frustration he caused her, Elsie Patterson liked this strange child, one of the few adults at the school who did. She recognized an unexplainable emptiness in him, which she tried to fill with her casual form of instruction. "Racket means noise, honey. You're always doing so many noisy things, noisy this and noisy that, just like my youngest grandson . . . except you're skinnier," Elsie added.

Elsie Patterson's observation was not entirely accurate. Clark made numerous sounds with his body, like the clicking of his teeth or the rumbling of his fingers, but he actually said very little. Clark used language only under certain conditions: when he was asked a direct question, when he recognized the need to be polite, or when he and another member of his family, usually his mother, were together. Clark was the most communicative with his mother, but even she could not press for language directly.

"Why do you like to be so noisy, Clark?" Elsie asked.

"Dunno," Clark shrugged, and he slumped his head into his shoulders, trying to escape further dialogue.

"Oh, you do too know," Elsie Patterson went on, unwilling to allow him to retreat into himself. "You know very well why you make so much racket. You just don't want to tell me, that's all," she said with a grin. "You just like to tease and pretend you don't know, when of course you do know all the while. I know you know why, I just know you know why!" Clark wished Mrs. Patterson would stop. He felt so confused. "Look at me when I talk to you, Clark Honeycutt!" Elsie commanded. "I like to see your beautiful black eyes."

Clark looked up, but he could not bear to meet Mrs. Patterson's gaze. He looked at the desk instead and smiled his half smile. "For heaven's sake," Elsie directed, "get your head out of your shoulders, sit up straight, and stop that silly smile!" Clark complied except for the smile. He sat motionless, hoping that Mrs. Patterson would relent.

"That's better," she concluded, satisfied now with the thoroughness of her instruction. "You don't have to tell me why you make such a racket. You just spend your time thinking about what you did and why you did what you did. That's what you need to do!" Elsie Patterson said as she returned her attention to the paper work on her desk.

Clark sighed, wrapped in the safety of silence. As he waited for Mr. Redding's door to open, however, anxiety returned. Clark struggled to keep himself calm. He knew that big trouble lay ahead and that the amount of trouble he was in with Mr. Redding was somehow related to the amount of time he waited on the bench. The longer the wait, the deeper the danger. Clark didn't understand the relationship, of course why that was so. He simply knew that time on the bench and danger were a fact. Restricted by the presence of Mrs. Patterson, Clark found an acceptable way to release his anxiety. He picked at his fingers until they bled. He pulled all the cuticles off his fingers and smeared the blood into his hands.

Several hours later, a few moments before lunch, in fact, Mr. Redding opened his office door. "What did you do to your hands, Clark?" he asked. "Is all this blood from your fight this morning? Is it?" Clark shrugged his shoulders. "You've had long enough to think about what you did to Jesse," Marvin Redding continued. "Let's come into my office and talk about what happened," he said. "Your mother is on her way. I've called her to join us."

Clark wished Mr. Redding hadn't called his mother. She'd be real sad again. She'd be real soft with him, like she always was, and she'd try to understand, but she wouldn't and neither would old man trouble bench, especially when he couldn't explain why, especially when he couldn't say why he bit him, and then she'd cry again, and old man trouble bench would shake his head again and stroke his beard again and send him home again to spend the next few days in his room again, and then he'd have to listen to his sister, Colleen, his high-school-hot-shot-sister Colleen, who'd tell him to quit being so dumb again, and then he'd have to go through it all over again at the end of the week again when his dad got home from his business trip, and "crap . . . shit." The words fell from Clark's mouth unguarded. "That kind of language will get you into deeper trouble, Clark. Clean it up before your mother arrives!" the principal directed.

Katie Honeycutt arrived with her name tag still emblazoned across the lapel of her wool suit. Katie always wore a suit whenever she volunteered at community functions, as a representative of Junior League. Katie Honeycutt, the name tag read, Junior League Volunteer. Of all the members of the women's organization, Katie best mirrored its goals: socially responsible, gracious, and lean. Katie moved like a dancer, and she had the discipline of one. She believed in doing things the right way, whatever the cost exacted of her. Katie was willing to bear costs. If the school needed someone to organize a cake sale, Katie would do it and buy any of the leftover items for distribution at the local nursing home. If no one was willing to run for the presidency of the Pacific Elementary PTA, Katie volunteered for another year. If the classroom needed a party, Katie threw it. She always threw parties just right, both at school and at home.

Katie believed that raising children was really a matter of her doing things the right way, of providing the right nourishment, both spiritual and intellectual, of providing the right support, of modeling the right expectations, and of being there for her children. Katie was always there. She arrived at school breathless, only minutes after Marvin Redding called her at a Junior League luncheon to inform her of Clark's incident on the playground. She apologized to Marvin for having to track her down that way. She sat next to Clark and touched him on the hand. He did not respond. Clark never responded to physical contact, not even to his mother's hugs. When she embraced him, Clark hung limp, nonresponsive. Still she tried. Katie touched him anyway. She spotted the blood.

Marvin Redding explained the morning's incident in detail. "You add anything I might forget to tell your mother," he suggested. Clark shrunk into himself. Marvin described Clark's biting with such detail that Katie winced and reached for a tissue from her leather bag. "Oh, Clark," she said. He bit so hard, Mr. Redding continued, that the duty thought he would never let go. "Somehow in the fight," Mr. Redding concluded, "Clark scraped his hands. How did they get so bloody?" he asked. Clark could not admit to another transgression. "Dunno," Clark replied. "Scraped 'em, I guess."

Marvin Redding leaned back into his chair, shook his head slowly, and stroked his graying beard. "I suppose you don't know what started the fight either," the principal mused, his patience wearing thin. Clark did not respond. "Clark," Mr. Redding urged, changing his tone, "tell us why. Your mother and I want to understand. Why did you bite Jesse?" Clark shrugged again. " 'Cause I did," Clark explained. "That's no reason!" Mr. Redding shot back, denying the boy's answer. The principal raised his voice to ensure that Clark had heard the actual question. *"Why?"* he questioned. "Why did you bite Jesse?" he asked, leaning forward to press the question further. *"I bit him 'cause I bit him!"* Clark screamed. *"I bit him 'cause I did!"* Katie reached out to calm her son.

Marvin Redding swallowed his anger. District policy would not allow a principal to lash out verbally at a student, especially the son of the PTA president, nor swat one when reason no longer worked. Reason never worked with Clark, and that was Marvin Redding's frustration. Clark refused to reason, simply refused, that's all. How could this kid ever become socialized, let alone civilized, when he refused to reason? Marvin Redding recognized that neither he nor his staff knew what to do with Clark to help him change. Worst of all, none of them could admit they didn't know. District policy would not acknowledge ignorance even though they knew it existed. At every opportunity, this district billed itself as the best in the state, leaders in education. How could they not know what to do with Clark? Marvin despised hypocrisy, especially in himself, but he dare not admit it, especially to such an ardent supporter. Marvin rose from his chair. "Come on, son," he motioned to Clark. "You know what the rest of the day holds for you." The principal escorted Clark to the door, opened it, and directed him to wait on the bench. Again Clark complied. He knew he was in trouble now, *real big trouble*, even bigger than before. Marvin Redding returned to his chair, and he and Katie sat in several moments of silence while she dried her eyes.

"Well, Katie," Marvin said, "what can I say? I can't explain his violence. Wish I could . . . " Marvin trailed off, about to admit what he might regret. "You know," he said, catching himself before the brink, "the staff here at Pacific Elementary has done everything possible for Clark, everything we could think of," he added, attempting to qualify his statement. "Remember?" Marvin asked. Katie nodded, trying to be polite. At times she hated herself for being so damned polite, but Katie knew that nothing would be served by criticism. She did not want to hear the litany of interventions again: how Clark repeated the first grade for reasons of social immaturity . . . how he was included in the resource room during his second year of first grade even though he didn't qualify academically . . . how the district made adaptations the following year by changing his handicapping condition from behaviorally disturbed to learning disabled, even though he really qualified for neither . . . how they always targeted him for the very best classroom teacher in his grade . . . how they did so very much but accomplished so very little.

Yes, Katie assured Marvin, yes, she knew the teachers had tried their best. All of them had all tried their best. "I only wish," Katie added, but then stopped, realizing that irritation would only lead to policy protection. "I need to take Clark home now," she said abruptly. "How long will he be suspended from school this time?" Katie asked. Marvin thought that the remainder of the week should be sufficient, but wait, he said, he wanted to talk about one thing more.

"You know I don't want to bring this topic up again, Katie, you know I don't," Marvin began, stroking his beard for wisdom. "But I have to say again, Katie, especially after another incident like today, that Clark will not be able to remain in school if this violence continues." Katie nodded. "I know, I know," she said sadly. "We can make it through the rest of this school year at Pacific," he added. "We only have a few more months, but next year, Katie, next year," he repeated, raising his hands to the heavens for emphasis. "I just don't think he'll make it in junior high, Katie, I just don't, too many variables, too many demands. You and your hubby, Jim, have to think about that, Katie."

Katie assured him that they already had, that she and Jim had anguished many hours late at night, long after Clark had gone to bed, talking and crying and trying to understand their son's behavior. They had consulted their physician. Yes, they had consulted professionals. Yes, they were frightened of the future. Katie stood up to leave, and Marvin followed her to the door. "I'm not implying anything, Katie," Marvin went on, "or suggesting you're doing anything wrong as parents. You and Jim are two of the finest parents I know, but surely, Katie, this violence is not strictly related to school. I mean, if Clark is violent like this at school, he must explode at home! Actually Clark's behavior was manageable at home. Katie could always soothe him, but she wondered for how long. She thanked Marvin for his concern and reached for the door. Katie met Clark at the trouble bench, touched him on the shoulder, and directed him to follow. Clark complied.

On the drive home, Katie uncovered the truth of the morning. She understood intuitively that demanding reasons would not dislodge them from Clark. Instead, she guided him to tell her who did what. "Tell me what Jesse did to you today, Clark," Katie encouraged softly. "Dunno," Clark responded. "Remember who I am, Clark?" she asked. "I'm you're mom. Talk to me, Clark. Tell me what Jesse did to you today."

In quiet times when he was contained in small, simple spaces, Clark talked, sometimes in an unbroken string of language, especially to his mother. "He looked at me funny," Clark answered, "all morning in reading, all morning he made faces at me, mean faces," Clark went on as he stuck out his tongue. "And he growled at me . . . grr . . . grr," Clark snarled while he looked out the car window. "And he wouldn't stop, he wouldn't stop, he wouldn't even stop at recess, and he called me a dodo bird," Clark added. "What's a dodo bird, Mom?" Clark asked. Not waiting for his mother's reply, Clark added, "And he hopped and flapped, and he flapped and hopped real dumb like and kept on sayin' all this weird stuff, dodo bird dummy stuff. I hate Jesse," Clark concluded.

"But you feel bad, don't you, Clark, that you hurt Jesse?" Clark nodded his head. "Yup," he said matter-of-factly. "Can you imagine how much Jesse's arm still hurts?" Katie asked. "Can you just imagine, Clark? Remember when the neighbor's dog bit you on the arm and you needed to have stitches? Remember how much that hurt you?" Clark nodded again, this time with his nose pressed against the car window. He spotted the church that he and his family attended. Clark liked that church. "Pray for his arm!" Clark announced. "Glory be to his arm!"

Clark frequently communicated on the edge of meaning. Passing the church and remembering how much he had hurt his classmate, Clark asked for forgiveness by directing himself to "pray for his arm, glory be to his arm!" Katie knew that Clark was sorry for biting, but she also recognized that sorrow would not prevent him from biting again the next time Jesse, or any other classmate, teased him. What would make a difference? Katie wondered aloud as she pulled into the garage. Clark could not respond to such a vague query. Instead, he got out of the car, walked into the house, and retreated to his bedroom, the place to which he was automatically sentenced whenever Mr. Redding suspended him from school. Katie reminded Clark of the rules for the day: no television or toys or coming out of his bedroom until dinner. She closed his bedroom door. Katie did not react when he threw something soft against it nor open it again when he yelled "poop, crap, shit" in a repetitive trilogy. "What else can I do?" she asked herself again. "What else, in God's name, can I do?"

Later that day Katie called the clinic. She might have done so sooner, a year or two before perhaps, had her support of schools not prevented her from doing so. Katie felt guilty for going outside the system, a feeling that several educators at Pacific reinforced. They were, after all, the best in the state, the leaders in education. How would they interpret her calling an outside agency? Katie wondered as she reached for the phone. Katie thought she knew the answer, but she believed that she had no other choice. Junior high was just a few months away. Katie dialed the number anyway.

A clinic assessment confirmed Clark's fine motor difficulties, which previous school testing had already uncovered. In addition, the clinic assessment pinpointed other difficulties, broad-based ones, which Katie and Jim long suspected but were never able to substantiate through the school assessment process. "Fine motor delays we knew about," Katie said the afternoon that she and Jim discussed the clinic assessment with a director. "Jim and I have known about Clark's fine motor difficulties since he was first assessed in the primary grades, which explains why writing is so difficult for him. But broad-based language difficulties, receptive and expressive language delays," Katie read quoting from the report, "getting meaning from language, and expressing meaning through language . . . of course," Katie said breathing a long sigh. Her shoulders dropped from the weight of a dreaded suspicion finally identified. "Of course," she repeated. "That's why he talked so late and used language so poorly as a toddler. Remember, Jim? Remember how often we asked the pediatrician if Clark would ever learn to talk, and each time he dismissed our concern?" Jim nodded.

"That's why Clark shuts down when we talk to him, Jim," Katie went on, a veritable avalanche of language pouring from her mouth. Jim continued to read the report, underline its key points, and write in its margins. "I explain and explain to him, all the time," Katie went on. "I tell him why he shouldn't bite, how he should act, over and over I lecture, but the poor kid gets lost in what I say!" Katie accepted the power of confession, embraced it as the precursor to forgiveness.

"That's the reason he misunderstands," she went on, "and that's why . . ." Katie paused to gather her sorrow. "That's why he still bites." For a moment, Katie fell silent. Quietly, she added, "He doesn't have the language to do anything else."

Katie was right, of course. Clark didn't have the language he needed to guide his thinking or to monitor his behavior.[1] When he learned a new skill in school, Clark promptly forgot it because he didn't have the language to attach to the learning. For three successive years, Clark relearned the process of division, each time as though he hadn't seen the skill modeled before. He had, of course, but Clark couldn't reduce the skill to an internal schema or summary.[2] He couldn't attach his language to it, and so he easily forgot, particularly in times of stress such as timed math tests. Insufficient language also explained his behavior.

At weekly staffings, meetings called to review the status of special education students at Pacific, Marvin Redding frequently raised the name of Clark Honeycutt. All the staff in attendance — the building psychologist, the special educators, the classroom teachers, and the principal — concurred that Clark did not "think through" his actions. What they meant was that Clark did not predict the consequences of his behavior. He did not weigh and measure. Instead, he reacted, often disproportionately to the triggering event, like Jesse's teasing. As Katie observed, however, Clark didn't have the language to do anything else. At one level, Katie understood the importance of language. It is the primary vehicle that parents use to socialize their children, to pass on to them a set of values, to teach them a template for conduct. Modeling is critical too, of course, but language is the bridge to reason. It is the medium of interpretation. Language allows us to interpret actions, to understand how an object or event is transformed in space and time, and to understand the relationships between the actions.[3] Hence, language is the system that leads us to recognize cause and effect. Clark did not. He would bite his classmate and never know the reason why, a fact that incensed the principal and disgusted the teachers. What they did not understand themselves, however, is that knowing the reason for an action, understanding its cause, assumes that the actor has language. Clark did not.

Katie berated herself for not identifying the problem herself and for not doing something sooner. "I've known this all along," she said shaking her head in disbelief. "Yes, in a way I have." Katie recounted all the times that she had questioned Clark's classroom teachers, educational specialists, even the principal. Do you think Clark could have a problem with language? she asked them. No, they assured her. Equating speech with language, the educators concluded that Clark couldn't have any problems with language. His speech was just fine.[4] Katie apologized for doubting them. "I should have persisted," Katie continued, "I should have...."

Jim interrupted his wife's confession by reminding Katie that she was the most responsible person anyone had ever met. If Katie had known what to do, she would have done it. She didn't know. Neither did he. Simple as that. Comforted by the certainty of facts and figures as well as the promise of the future, Jim observed, "There's enough blame here for everybody, Katie. Anyone who has ever taught or tested Clark shares a little piece of negligence. Let's not waste time blaming or going over all that's already happened," Jim concluded. "Let's just get on with this and figure out what to do next. What does Clark need?" Jim asked the clinic director.

What Clark needed, of course, was intensive language work. Throughout the remainder of that spring and the summer months that followed, Clark received language instruction twice a week at the clinic. He rehearsed imagery activities. He learned to capture the essence of the image that language conveys and to learn new vocabulary by categorizing and sorting their meaning into images. He rehearsed asking questions of images and of spoken and written language. What Clark most wanted to learn, however, was how to play TurnAbout, a board game that his family played on weekends and vacations. Clark could not master the rules. No matter how often he and his clinic tutor rehearsed them, Clark could not grasp the rules of TurnAbout.

Nor could he learn, in the short time available, the language skills needed to cope with junior high. They were simply too numerous and complex. District policy would not allow Clark's language instruction to continue as a class at the clinic. Katie requested that that happen, but the district refused. After all, the administration reasoned, Clark did not qualify for language work. His speech was just fine. More importantly, the junior high had its own program, one of the best in the state. Unfortunately, Clark did not have sufficient language to succeed there. Once seventh grade began, for example, Clark had to sort through the language of five different teachers rather than two. Not only did the classroom rules and expectations differ from his former sixth-grade teachers, they differed from one another. In language arts, for example, the teacher expected Clark and the other seventh-graders in her class to work independently and quietly, raising their hands in silence when they had a question. The metal shop teacher, on the other hand, expected Clark to work with a partner and to ask for help by making a verbal request that was louder than the din of the humming machinery. The physical education teacher expected yet a different response — that Clark and all other seventh-grade P.E. students comply immediately to any command given by his ninth-grade student assistant.

In addition, each of Clark's teachers used a unique vocabulary. The math teacher spoke of "quotients" and "dividends" and "denominators," for example, words that Clark thought he had heard before but whose meaning he did not yet understand. The earth science teacher, like the metal shop teacher, spoke a completely foreign vocabulary. They said words like "sediment," "tectonic plates," and "lathes," and Clark could not keep the categories straight. Where did a "techtonic plate" belong? Was that the project he was making in metal shop? Clark was not certain. Peers spoke novel vocabulary as well and conveyed social cues in a different way than they did in elementary school. Clark's classmates were no longer direct, either in their actions or their language. Seventh-graders seldom are. Instead, they conveyed messages indirectly, always assuming that others understood. Often Clark did not. In fact, he frequently missed the message, and his behavior deteriorated in relation to his confusion.

As expectations became more complex and social cues became more subtle, Clark's anger escalated to rage. When the ninth-grade P.E. assistant, who happened to be black, blew a whistle at his seventh-grade charge, Clark called him a "nigger boy, a dirty, smelly nigger boy." Clark was suspended from P.E. for the remainder of the semester. When students refused to make room for him at the lunch table, Clark scooped the spaghetti off his tray and hurled it at the nearest classmate, an unsuspecting eighth-grade girl. The vice principal caught Clark with the evidence hanging from his fingers and suspended him from school for a week. When the language arts teacher assigned Clark to write one hundred times "I will not make clicking noises with my teeth," he stopped outside her classroom window at the end of the day. The language arts teacher informed the vice principal that she would not soon forget Clark's devious smile as he threw the rock at her window, shattering it as well as any chance he had of succeeding in her seventh-grade classroom. The vice principal catalogued the threat. She moved Clark to a different language arts class when he returned to school after another week's suspension.

Suspensions increased to such an extent that Katie resigned all her committee and volunteer work. She dreaded to hear the phone ring, especially during the middle of the day. She knew that Grace Bloom, the vice principal of the junior high, was likely to be at the other end. "Katie?" the vice principal would begin, "Grace here." Grace liked to keep things simple — no fuss, simple and straight. "I've got your boy in my office, Katie. Right, Clark?" Grace asked. "We're lookin' across the desk at each other again, Clark and I." Clark smiled his half smile. Grace smiled back. "Clark knows he has to go home for the day," Grace went on. "He bit somebody. Clark knows that biting is not acceptable. Right, Clark?" Grace asked. Clark nodded that he understood. Clark liked Mrs. Bloom. He could understand her.

Each of his outbursts at junior high spilled over into his conduct at home. For the first time, Katie worried whether she could control Clark. He was not as tall as his mother, but when enraged, Clark was stronger than anyone else, even stronger than Jim, whose job demanded more and more time away from the home. Katie felt her resolve of motherhood slipping. She entertained the unthinkable, finding another school for Clark, a private school for learning disabled students, but she soon discovered that none existed within or even near their community that matched his needs. With the assistance of an educational advisor who located private schools for learning disabled students, Katie and Jim searched outside their community. Yes, if need be, she and Jim would consider sending Clark to a private school away from their home, even out of state. They went to observe several. "If we must send him away to save him," Katie reasoned, "we will do it." Whatever the cost, Katie would bear it.

Before making a final decision, however, Katie met with Grace to solicit her view. Katie knew that Grace would give an unguarded opinion, even if it conflicted with district policy. Grace paused less than a moment before answering Katie's question. "Do we have a program within this school or within this district for Clark?" Grace repeated. "Tough question, Katie, very tough . . . I'd like to tell you that we do, but I can't. . . . Just can't tell you that, Katie. Know why?" Grace asked. "Tell me," Katie requested. "The reason I can't tell you we have a program for Clark is that we don't have one. . . . Simple as that," Grace continued. "I know we're supposed to have one. . . . By law we're supposed to, but we don't, just don't. . . . Simple as that . . . but if we admit we don't, then we have to provide one . . . so we pretend we do . . . that's why Clark can't have his classes at the clinic . . . it'd be an admission."

Katie knew why Clark liked this stony little woman. Grace kept a candy dish on the edge of her desk as a token of friendship, which she offered to any student, even the worst behaved one, before she meted out punishment. Grace was the school disciplinarian. No, Katie, thought. What Clark liked about Grace Bloom was more than the candy. It was her deep-down simplicity, her straightforwardness, her predictability. Clark needed that.

"Want a piece?" Grace asked. Katie declined. "Nothin' like a dish of candy to break the ice with a kid, even the meanest one," Grace explained. She returned the dish to its corner. "Sorry we don't have a program," Grace apologized, "or teachers who are able to adapt. That's all I can say. Doesn't seem like much of an answer, does it?" Grace asked. Katie reassured this unorthodox administrator that the answer was heroic. Not only did it release Katie from guilt, it also launched Clark upon a journey that transformed him. He would leave his home and the junior high and attend school elsewhere, out of state.

Clark helped his parents select the school that he would enter in the fall of his eighth-grade year — Baker Academy in Arizona. Even though the vice principal was supportive of him, Clark did not want to return to his junior high, the only one within his community. "They'll whop me," he complained, referring to the students who threatened his safety. He thought that finding a new school designed just for him was a good idea, "real good," he said. He and his parents spent most of the summer selecting the ideal school. Clark liked Baker Academy the best. "Warm weather and horses," he noted. "Like 'em."

Clark was not able to enjoy either one — the weather or the horses. By the end of the first month of school, the director of Baker Academy called the Honeycutts. Clark refused to cooperate, the director said. Clark would not dress for dinner. He would not follow the rules. He would not even talk! Clark simply climbed into himself and would not participate. Katie reminded the director of Clark's language difficulties and of the staff's reassurance that they could teach through those difficulties. They just taught kids, the director reminded Katie. They did not make miracles. That afternoon Katie flew to Arizona to retrieve her son.

For the next few weeks Clark remained at home, where he spent most of his time in his room. No, he did not want to come out for dinner! No, he did not want to eat! No, he did not want his mother in his room! No, he did not even want to *be* at home! No! No! No! Frantically, Katie and Jim renewed their search. The day before Thanksgiving, the Honeycutt family — Jim, Katie, Colleen, and Clark — flew to southern California to investigate another school, Rolling Hills. The warm weather renewed Clark's spirit. "Yup," Clark answered when Katie asked, at the end of the

Thanksgiving weekend, if he thought he wanted to enroll as a student. Within a few weeks, however, the Honeycutts received a long-distance call from the director of Rolling Hills.

Sorry, the director informed them, but Rolling Hills was definitely not the school for Clark. Yes, they did teach learning disabled students at Rolling Hills. Yes, of course, they recognized Clark's language difficulties. That was not the problem, the director explained. Clark's behavior was the problem. He was behaviorally disturbed, at times even violent, the director continued. Last night Clark shattered thirty windows after one of the counselors reprimanded him for spitting in a classmate's dinner. Once confined to his room, Clark ripped his bedding to shreds, punched holes in his mattress, and urinated on the carpet! No, Rolling Hills was definitely not the school for Clark Honeycutt. The director recommended another school in Maine, a very specialized one named Pine Mountain. That afternoon Katie and Jim flew to California, met Clark, and proceeded on together to the East.

The director of Pine Mountain admitted Clark to the school for a trial period. A clinical psychologist herself, she believed that Clark was not really learning disabled but instead that he was retarded. That's why he had such limited language, she reasoned. Clark didn't have the intellectual equipment to acquire it. In addition, he undoubtedly needed medication to control his behavioral outbursts. She would speak to the attending physician. The Honeycutts protested that medication had not worked with Clark in the past. Why did she think it would work now? Undoubtedly the wrong dosage, the woman explained. The physician prescribed a stimulant medication. Clark's behavioral outbursts increased in intensity and scope. Violently he struck out against the world — objects, animals, people — anything in his path.

At the end of the two-week trial, the director of Pine Mountain called the Honeycutts. No, Pine Mountain was definitely not the place for Clark Honeycutt. The previous evening Clark beat a classmate bloody and tried to choke him. All the kid did, the director explained, was call Clark a dodo bird! If the counselor hadn't been right there, Clark would have killed the kid . . . killed him! Clark definitely needed an institutional setting, more structure, greater control, the director continued. She knew of just such a place in Idaho, a small, well-staffed, highly structured facility for children who were out of control. Clark was definitely out of control.

Katie wondered how a facility differed from a school. The amount of structure it provides, the director answered. That's basically it. The director also urged Katie and Jim to have Clark transported to the facility in Idaho.

"Do not transport him yourself! I must remind you," the director warned. "Clark is violent. I cannot guarantee his safety if you come back and get him. I will arrange for two of the strongest counselors at

Pine Mountain to escort him to the facility in Idaho. Once he is settled there and under control, you can go visit him, of course." Reluctantly, Katie agreed. As Jim pointed out, the two of them had already made three lousy choices. A professional would have to make a better one, he reasoned.

Clark and his escorts arrived at the Idaho Institute the following day. Mel Gilling, one of the counselors at the institute, met Clark at the gate. That was not standard procedure, of course, especially in a high security plant for violent delinquents, but Mel relied upon kindness and other simple truths rather than rules, regulations, and legislated beliefs. Mel also relied upon common sense. Within a few weeks of working with Clark on a daily basis, Mel realized that this boy was not delinquent. Common sense told him so. Yes, Clark could be violent, but only when he was cornered. Frightened, Clark lashed out in an attempt to survive. Mostly, Clark was hungry, desperately hungry.

Mel reported his finding to the participants of the daily staffing. The supervisor laughed aloud. "So that's why this damn kid bit so hard that he drew blood! Hungry, is that it? Hungry?"

Mel tried to explain what he meant by Clark's hunger — his isolation, his separateness, his deep desperate loneliness. During the past few weeks of work with Clark, Mel recognized his hunger.

"You did, did you? Well, try to explain that to the poor kid Clark bit!" the supervisor hooted. Dismissing Mel's interpretation of Clark's latest outburst, the supervisor turned to the attending physician, who recommended that Clark be taken off the stimulant medication and be put on an immediate course of Haloperidol, an antipsychotic drug that slows physical agitation as well as the thinking process of the patient.[5]

Clark did not waken for days. He heard the sound of keys unlocking a door. Clark knew he was in a room. He could touch its walls, but they were soft and padded, shiny like his mother's robe. Where was the window? He couldn't find the window! A man in a white uniform tapped him on the elbow. Clark could not decipher what the man said. A funny noise echoed from his mouth. Did he have a mouth? Where was the man's mouth? A hand motioned Clark to follow.

A long stream of people, all of them faceless, walked through the hall. Who were they? Clark squinted to bring the faces into focus, but they seemed to fade before his eyes. The man in the white uniform guided Clark into an office, led him to a chair, and helped him to sit. The chair felt familiar. "Morning, Clark!" a voice beckoned. Clark wondered where he'd heard that voice before. He struggled to remember. "You awake?" the voice called again. "I said good morning!" Clark recognized the sound of Mel. "Morning," Clark replied. Mel extended a dish. "Like one?" Mel asked.

"Huh?" Clark answered.

"Candy...this is candy, Clark...the kind you like the best. Want a piece?" Clark knew he'd heard that voice before. "Want a piece?" Mel asked again. Clark felt the vast emptiness inside, a hole so large that he thought he might disappear into himself.

"Here, take one," Mel urged. Clark reached across the desk and took the chocolate sustenance.

Mel and Clark talked all morning. Mel mostly talked, and Clark mostly "yupped" and "noped," except now and then when he emitted a long string of language. The two of them ate malted milk balls as they talked. Mel told Clark that he had spoken with his parents many times over the past several weeks and many hours over the past days. Mel Gilling didn't believe that Clark belonged at the facility. Didn't need medication either. He told his wife Laura so. Clark wasn't a delinquent. He was a hungry kid, a real hungry kid. Laura understood. She suggested that they bring Clark home. She realized that Mel would have to quit his job as a counselor at the institute, of course, but she argued that he had a lot of work on the ranch to keep him busy. Besides, he could spend more time on his garden, grow some of his famous corn. Mel agreed and called Katie and Jim to make the offer.

"It's simple here," Mel explained when he called the Honeycutts. "Not real fancy...just plain and simple...predictable too...horses wake up at the same time every day, chickens too...get real testy if they have to wait too long for their breakfast...good for a kid to have something as simple as a chicken to need him...chickens never notice much...only notice if nobody shows up....Real quiet here," Mel went on. "No TV...a little radio now and then...loudest sound is the crickets humming at night...boring, some folks might say, but it's good for kids," Mel argued. "We've raised five of 'em...a real fine batch. ...They still come home for dinner, every Sunday except the youngest, of course...she's away at college, our last college student."

Katie was uncertain about such a change. "Clark'd do just fine here," Mel went on. Yeah, he knew all about Clark's behavior..."read his file...real thick one." Mel didn't think that Clark would have that kind of trouble on the ranch though. "Not too much trouble a kid can get into out here...lot safer too," he said.

Katie still was not convinced, but she liked this man, and she liked his wife, Laura. Jim reminded Katie of the cost she was willing to bear: giving her son up in order to save him. Katie and Jim accepted the Gillings's offer.

"What do ya' think, Clark?" Mel asked that morning. "Ya' want to come home and live with Laura and me?" Clark nodded. "Yup," Clark said. "Yup, I do. I like horses. Not so sure about chickens, though." Mel laughed. Two malted milk balls remained in the dish. Clark and Mel reached for them at the same time, opened their mouths, and tossed them in, like basketballs into hoops. Mel smiled, and Clark smiled back, savoring the sweetness of communion.

That was more than two years ago. Clark now attends high school at Noble Ridge, the small senior high in the Idaho community. During summers and other vacations, Clark returns to his home in the Northwest. Each time they see him, Katie and Jim marvel at Clark's changes. He laughs at jokes and tells them. He gives hugs and returns them. He initiates conversation and communicates effectively. He still misses some of the nuances of meaning, of course, but clearly his language has improved. So has his ability to understand relationships. Clark now understands actions. Last vacation, for example, Clark accepted his father's reprimand for driving the car to the store and back without permission. Clark understood that ranch rules differed from city ones. He even suggested an appropriate punishment for himself — no pizza party with the neighborhood kids. Clark loves pizza. "I'm a real hog," Clark explained, "when it comes to pizza."

Mel relies upon the "corn principle" to explain Clark's changes. "Raisin' kids is kinda' like plantin' corn," Mel has always said. "Nothin' fancy ... just plant 'em and water 'em so they get well anchored ... weed 'em now and again, then leave 'em alone so they can grow ... but mostly," Mel added, "never try to talk 'em into growin' ... never try to reason with a stalk of corn," Mel grinned. "Just won't work, that's all ... just won't work." Mel and Laura subscribed to the corn principle with all of their children and recognized that some took a little longer than others to ripen.

Last week Clark called his mother to tell her the big news. Clark calls home every Sunday as well as other times during the week when he has something to share. "I beat 'em at TurnAbout!" Clark laughed when he called. "I really beat 'em, Mom ... Mel and Laura and their oldest sons, Matthew and David ... I mean I really beat 'em ... fair and square. Do you believe that, Mom?" Clark wondered with joy. "I'm gonna' beat you and Dad and Colleen too the next time I come home. You just wait, Mom, you just wait until I come home. I'm awesome at TurnAbout."

Katie said that she and Dad and Colleen were really looking forward to their next vacation together in a few weeks. They'd plan to play TurnAbout.

"Make sure to tell 'em at the clinic," Clark went on. "Be sure to tell them that I learned how to play this game." Katie said she'd call the clinic that very afternoon. "No, Mom, no!" Clark pleaded. "Go over and tell 'em, face to face," he said, "so I'll know how they looked and what they said. Please, Mom, just drive over there and tell them." Katie said she would. Such a small cost to bear, Katie thought, such a small cost for the life of a son.

Part 2

THE
SPATIAL
SYSTEM

Some concepts are best understood by comparing them to what they are not. That is the case with the spatial system. It is neither neat nor tidy, singular nor static. It is real but not concrete, evident but not directly seen, unlike the language system. The spatial system is an abstraction that can only be understood as a rich pattern of relationships, a mosaic of connections that our brains construct. Using the input from all our senses, our brains weave an integrated system that allows us to pilot our bodies within and through space as well as among, over, and around the objects and people who occupy it.

Developing a functional spatial system begins simply enough. Once they discover their hands and learn to use them as tools, babies conduct an endless profusion of experiments. What is that colored shiny thing? they wonder, as they try to pick the stenciled animal pictures from their bumpers. How far away is that bottle? Can I reach it? How can I get that interesting looking toy? Babies learn to measure the world by the standard of their body. Are my arms long enough to reach the glass? Am I tall enough? Long after infancy, the child continues to conduct experiments that support the developmental process of perceiving space and acting within it. If I can jump down from this curb, the child says, I betcha' I can jump down from that tree, easy! What does the world look like when I hang upside down from the top bar of my swing set? Sudden growth spurts momentarily convert the most agile of children into unguided teenage missiles who crash into furniture, tip over lamps, and stumble over their feet until they have adjusted to their new size and scale. Both developmental and learned information blend to shape a system, a marvelously complex integrated system of body and mind.

Language, of course, plays its part in the developmental process. The spatial system wraps around language, which reciprocates by penetrating back into the heart of the spatial system. Although the systems can act separately, as in the case of the deaf-mute artist who produces sensitive sculptured forms or the uncommunicative athlete who brings home Olympic medals, the systems typically act in tandem. In its vocabulary and its structure, language incorporates spatial elements: a vocabulary to convey position such as "between" and "adjacent" and an ordering convention to signal meaning. Language enhances children's understanding of space and their spatial understanding enhances their language. Each system reinforces the other.

For a few reasons we do know and for many reasons we do not know, the spatial system does not always develop or operate efficiently.

Problems can center in more than one area, but they tend to cluster in one of the following: the visual-spatial area, the motor-spatial area, or both the visual-spatial and motor-spatial area. Each of these areas is related to an individual's academic performance.

Visual-spatial performance refers to the process of using sight to discriminate differences like size, scale, position, or orientation. Individuals with visual-spatial confusion have difficulty constructing reliable images, particularly visual ones, unless, of course, they use language as a guide. They have difficulty with visual-spatial tasks like recalling how a word "looks." Hence, they have trouble with spelling. They cannot recall where to place punctuation marks, the visual marks that note the natural spaces within language. They have particular difficulty knowing how a three-dimensional object, like the neighbor's house, looks along a two-dimensional plane. Hence, they have trouble drawing it accurately and resort instead to stereotypic renditions of "houseness." Individuals with visual-spatial confusion also have difficulty imaging how a two-dimensional form looks in the three-dimensional world. Hence, geometry is a nightmare. Typically, all of math is difficult for them. Of all subjects, math is the most dependent upon the spatial system. Number is, after all, a mechanism for keeping track of mass in space. Our place value system is based on relative position. Relative means relational, which means arranged in space. Carrying, borrowing, decimals, percentage, and, most of all, fractions, rely on spatial position for their correct solution. Each math operation has its own set of relational rules.

Motor-spatial performance refers to the process of using one's body and the movement of one's body to discriminate differences. Problems can occur within the fine motor area, the large motor area, or both areas. Individuals with fine motor delays have difficulty taking on fine motor tasks like handwriting. Individuals with large motor delays have difficulty maneuvering their bodies in space. They trip over the lint on the rug. They crash through the world or bump into others, accidentally of course. Unless they are vigilant, individuals with large motor spatial difficulties are menaces on the road. They have difficulty constructing reliable images too — not necessarily those that are visually based but rather the images that are body based. They do not have a good sense of their bodies. Hence, they cannot re-create the image of a motion — like how it feels to write a sequence of letters, how it feels to connect the swinging bat to the ball, or how it feels to ride a bike.

The individuals whose stories follow have difficulty within the spatial system itself or with its linkage to their language. Elizabeth, for example, has tremendous difficulty with the visual-spatial area. Elizabeth, Liffy for short, begins this section not only because she is one of the most fascinating but also because her spatial confusion is the result of a missing chromosome, a disability that cannot be changed, merely accommodated. In the process of her learning, Liffy instructs the reader in the meaning of "disability."

A handsome young man follows. Steve has difficulty with motor-spatial tasks, those that call upon his fine motor system as well as his large motor system. Like Liffy, he also teaches us. Steve shows us the ways that motor planning impacts upon a student's performance. He also shows us the price that definition exacts and the freedom that responsibility affords.

Rollo comes next. He has spatial difficulties too, primarily because he has not integrated language into his guidance system. However, Rollo's difficulties seem whimsical in comparison to Janine's. She is a strange girl with dark, distant eyes. Her spatial difficulties encompass the visual area as well as the motor area. She has no other avenue to turn to except her talk. Of all the characters in the book, Janine is the most inflexible. In fact, without instruction, she bordered on the edge of being crazy.

John ends the book with an apparently simple learning problem but a complicated message. For the life of him, John cannot recall what a sequence of letters looks like. Never could, no matter how hard he tried. He knows them when he sees them on the page, of course, but his visual memory for words is vague, "like mush" his teacher explains. John cannot image them in his mind's eye, and for that reason, he cannot spell. He learns to do so, and like so many of the other people in this book, John teaches us too, a metaphysical lesson much grander than spelling. "Everything's related to everything else," he tells us. That's true of the spatial system, of course, but John suggests that connections extend far beyond that. Perhaps every event is connected to every other event. Perhaps our efforts do matter, even to those we cannot immediately touch.

- 7 -

PATCH FOR A MISSING CHROMOSOME

The Pacific Northwest is noted for its November winds, which can rip branches off the trunks of trees and uproot them from the ground. The sound of breaking branches woke Dorothy that night. She could not return to sleep, especially when so much work faced her at the clinic. Rather than submit to slumber, Dorothy rose several hours before dawn, quietly, so as not to wake her husband. She reached into the darkened closet for her terry cloth robe and wrapped herself within its whiteness. Hoping that the weariness might leave her, Dorothy paused a moment, only that, before sentencing herself to several hours of work at her desk. So much to do, so many tasks to complete, Dorothy thought as she approached it, one of her favorite spots in the house.

Her solid walnut desk sat like a sentinel in the family room. It faced a long wall of windows that looked out upon the Narrows Strait, the deepest and most dangerous waters of Puget Sound. Dorothy never tired of looking at the waters. Sometimes she studied them. A long cedar deck stretched across the front of her house, and a cluster of maple trees, cluttered now with brown aging leaves, obstructed portions of her view. Dorothy could not see the Sound that morning, for light had not yet penetrated the sky, but she could hear the storm raging outside and autumn dying on the deck. Torrents of rain beat the maple trees into submission, and wind stripped them of their leaves, tossing them helplessly, like broken angels, round and round upon the deck. The anguished sounds made Dorothy shiver.

Dorothy disliked cruelty of any kind, even cruelty against the leaves, but, sadly, she did not extend the same compassion to herself. Never considering her work ritual to be the least bit unkind, Dorothy expected herself to rise before dawn and work even through exhaustion. Rather than turning up the heat to remove the morning chill, she sat down at her desk and tucked one flap of the terry robe far underneath the other. She cupped her cold hands around the mug of tea she had prepared and sipped from its edges, allowing herself that much kindness, a moment of warmth, before the dawn broke.

Morning appeared without Dorothy's recognition, her attention focused upon the mound of work that seemed to grow in proportion to her efforts. A glance at her watch startled Dorothy into action. She wakened her husband, dressed hurriedly, and returned to the kitchen for a dry piece of toast, which she ate on the way out the door. Dorothy called to her husband and blew him a kiss down the hallway. No, dear, she dare not wait, though she wished she could. So much to do. A hectic day, a frantic one. Secretly, Dorothy wanted to protect him from the disquiet that brewed beneath her flurry of activity.

Dorothy arrived at the clinic, as usual, long before the other staff appeared. She made coffee for them and tidied the staff room as well as her own. At times like these, when she had more to do than what she could master, Dorothy minded untidiness in her environment and any hint of absent discipline within herself. She examined again the state of her readiness. Dorothy reviewed her day's schedule, a long list of clients that filled the first several hours, as well as a longer list of self-imposed "to do's" that filled her late afternoon. Dorothy looked for some measure of joy, some bright spot in her day. It appeared in the afternoon. Elizabeth Nettleson, Liffy for short, appeared in Dorothy's two o'clock spot.

Of all the students she had ever taught, Dorothy was fondest of Liffy. She demonstrated so many of the qualities that Dorothy valued most, especially courage, a willingness to battle limitations against all odds. Dorothy taught Liffy in elementary school and then again in high school. Liffy would be a senior now. Her name triggered a flood of memories.

Elizabeth Nettleson first came to the clinic in the fourth grade. She was unusually tiny as well as unusually verbal. Liffy's verbal skills convinced her primary teachers that she was one of the most capable students in the classroom, and indeed she was. Liffy understood the printed word without instruction or clarification. She talked with the facility of a much older child and memorized lengthy complex language such as poetry and famous speeches during the time she spent riding the bus from home to school. Some of her performances perplexed her third-grade teacher, of course, like her inability to compute with accuracy and her inability to draw, but Liffy's academic difficulties did not really concern her teachers until the fourth grade.

That was the year that Liffy's mother, Ruth Ann Nettleson, then a single parent, noticed her daughter brooding about school. Initially, Ruth attributed Liffy's distress to the recent divorce, but as the fourth grade continued and her daughter's dislike of school increased, Ruth was not so sure that divorce was a key factor. She asked for a school conference with her daughter's fourth-grade teacher, Miss Leeson.

Liffy's reading skills and her verbal ability convinced Miss Leeson that this mite of a child was not trying. In fact, she suggested that Liffy was a little bit spoiled. "Ms. Nettleson," the teacher began, "I'm wondering if Elizabeth has any chores to do around the house ... you know, like make her bed, or feed the dog ... take out the garbage ... tasks like that?" An educator herself, Ruth Nettleson anticipated the reasoning of teachers. As a philosophy professor at a local university, she taught several teachers in her classes. Ruth predicted the direction that Miss Leeson's reasoning was headed but listened politely as the teacher continued to grasp at irrelevant variables. "You know, Ms. Nettleson," the teacher continued, "sometimes we don't expect enough of our children when they are so cute and tiny ... that's why I asked about the chores."

Ruth Nettleson assured the teacher that not only did Liffy have household chores but that she took responsibility for other chores her brother neglected. "Well, Liffy acts ... well, how can I say this," Miss Leeson fumbled, "a little ... well, a little irresponsible. She doesn't seem to care about the mistakes that she makes on her papers, and most every one of them is caused from sheer carelessness. See what I mean?" she asked as she pointed to one of Liffy's papers. "Now just look here," Miss Leeson directed, "look how many mistakes Liffy made in copying directions from the book to the paper! She was very careless here."

Ruth Nettleson did not define her daughter as irresponsible or even as careless. In fact, she defined Liffy as quite the opposite, overly cautious.

"Hmm," Miss Leeson pondered and then tried a different tack. "You realize, of course, that fourth grade is a great deal more demanding than the primary ones. I didn't realize that myself until I moved up to fourth grade many years ago. Fourth grade," Miss Leeson continued, "introduces some very difficult intellectual requirements. Much, much more is expected of fourth-graders than of the younger students. The children who are not ready for the intellectual challenge of fourth grade just don't do well, and even though Liffy is older than most of her classmates, perhaps she just is not. ... "

Ruth Nettleson stopped her. "I expect you're correct about fourth grade," she replied, diplomatically trying to prevent Miss Leeson from making the ultimate judgment. "Fourth grade is certainly more demanding than the primary ones. I have no doubt of that. I also have no doubt, and her previous teachers have never had a doubt, that Elizabeth is quite a capable girl. Her language, after all, is a measure of her intellect."

Like other philosophers, Ruth Ann Nettleson esteemed language, valued it not for its own sake but rather for what it accomplished. In her philosophy classes, Ms. Nettleson defined language "as a vehicle that helps people actualize their humanness." What makes us human, she argued, was not our ability to use and understand language but rather our need for intimacy, our drive to be known and spiritually familiar with others. Language was a shared gift that signaled that need. Understandably, then, Ruth Ann Nettleson reinforced language and its development within her own children and measured their intellectual growth against it. "Elizabeth's ability to use and understand language," Ruth Nettleson said to Miss Leeson, "illustrates how very capable she is!"

"Oh, of course, of course," Miss Leeson agreed. "I didn't mean to imply that Liffy isn't capable," she said, changing directions again. "Liffy is quite a capable little girl," she acknowledged, "but she cannot manage math, not at all." Miss Leeson was absolutely certain of that. "Elizabeth has no grasp of mathematics whatsoever. I sometimes wonder if math is taught sufficiently well in the primary grades," she offered, preparing herself for a different direction in case this one failed. "Teaching Liffy to multiply has been a nightmare, a sheer nightmare... and her ability to make change, estimate numbers, and tell time... well, " Miss Leeson added, "those objectives have been nothing short of horrendous... and even though she has this abundant amount of language, Liffy simply cannot solve story problems... not at all!"

Ruth Nettleson learned what she had wanted to know. She had asked for the conference in hopes of understanding her daughter's dislike of school since fourth grade began, Liffy's worry over not doing well, and the number of assignments that came home with unfriendly red words written across the top of them: *You must try harder! Sloppy work! Too many careless errors!* To the inexperienced listener, Miss Leeson's words may have indicated dislike. Ruth Nettleson interpreted them as frustration. She philosophized that most teachers would have felt the same, angry at themselves. Miss Leeson had given her best, though her best was insufficient. Miss Leeson recognized that she failed to reach one of her students, and anger was the result.

The professor thanked Miss Leeson for her time. "I'll work on this problem with my daughter, Miss Leeson, and I'll encourage her to check her work. Thank you for seeing me this afternoon."

Ruth left, drove back to her office, which she shared with another faculty member, and said to her colleague, "You won't believe what I just heard." Ruth recounted the school conference and Miss Leeson's frustration. Her colleague not only directed Ruth to the clinic but suggested a staff member named Dorothy. "Ummmm," Ruth said warily. "Our pediatrician needs to evaluate Elizabeth first." She trusted his diagnostic skill.

Ruth Nettleson really did not expect anything to be wrong with her daughter. After all, Liffy was so linguistically capable. Still, she could not draw. Her drawings, in fact, resembled a preschooler's, not in their pencil control but in their accuracy and sensitivity to form. When she had to draw a dinosaur to accompany her fourth-grade science report, for example, Liffy disassembled the creature, drawing its head and its feet, its tail and its body as separate, disconnected pieces. Odd, Ruth thought to herself when she saw it. Even though occasional doubts nagged her about Liffy — her immature drawings, her anxiety in unfamiliar places, her mathematical confusion, which seemed to grow in proportion to her grade level, even her size — Ruth found ways to explain them. I'm not skilled at drawing either, Ruth reasoned. I dislike math too. I'm not very tall, Ruth said to herself; that's why Liffy is so short.

Ruth Ann Nettleson was not prepared for the pediatrician's diagnosis, which lab reports confirmed. Elizabeth Nettleson had Turner's syndrome,[1] a rare chromosomal abnormality[2] that occurs only in females, restricting their stature and, in odd ways, skewing their performance because of a missing chromosome.[3] Liffy's performance was definitely uneven, the pediatrician explained. Her language was disproportionate to her spatial skills. See, he said, as he showed Ruth Ann some drawings that he had asked Liffy to make. Ruth Ann's heart stopped momentarily. Moreover, he said, Liffy's language was disproportionate to her size. Liffy was tiny, so small, that she wore toddler-size clothes when she entered kindergarten. The depth of her daughter's difficulty stunned Ruth to near silence. "What can be done?" was all she could ask.

Well, the pediatrician went on, growth hormones might increase Liffy's stature. Learning was another matter, however. Another stop. Turner's syndrome restricted, probably prevented, Liffy's ability to understand spatial concepts, like drawing and math and finding her way around, the pediatrician explained. Turner's girls can't find their way in space and time, he added. They just can't manage spatial tasks.[4]

For a moment, nothing else existed except a mother's grief. Finally, she posed a question. "Can't?" Ruth Nettleson asked. "That's so definite. Why can't Liffy understand spatial concepts?"

The pediatrician explained that besides limiting the child's stature, Turner's resulted in the early and rapid development of the girl's left hemisphere, and therefore her language skills, at the expense of her right hemisphere, and therefore her spatial thinking.[5] That's what my fellow pediatricians conclude, he said. The limitation is built in.

"Something must be able to change this!" Ruth pleaded. The pediatrician recommended the clinic. Ask for Dorothy, he said. She has a particular interest in spatial thinking. Ruth stopped at the clinic that very afternoon. Dorothy had an unexpected opening. "Two professionals whose opinion I value highly recommended you to me," the philosophy professor told Dorothy. Dorothy's insides turned over a little. Yes, Dorothy said, the pediatrician had just called and referred Liffy.

"I would be indebted to you if you would teach my daughter," Ruth Nettleson said. "You specifically," the professor added. Dorothy's insides fluttered again. She wondered if she could meet the professor's expectations. "I would also like your help in explaining Liffy's difficulties to her fourth-grade teacher. She doesn't have the vaguest understanding of the reason for Liffy's difficulties," Ruth Nettleson added, "nor does Miss Leeson have an appreciation of Liffy's capabilities."

Capabilities intrigued Dorothy almost as much as limitations. She liked finding ways of circumventing limits and liked even better defeating them. Still, the thought of teaching a Turner's girl frightened Dorothy. She had read the research articles on Turner's syndrome and understood their bleak conclusions. Because of their apparent inability to understand spatial concepts, most Turner's girls performed very poorly in school. In fact, several of them were institutionalized. Dorothy wondered what made *her* think she could teach Liffy. What made her think she could do anything at all to make a difference with a child who was born with built-in limitations. Dorothy agreed to try, not because of heroism but because of fascination. Dorothy recognized that Liffy would stretch her intellect and demand the very best from her teaching. Liffy would not only instruct her, Dorothy thought, but she would lead her to a level of understanding she did not yet possess.

For the remainder of that fourth-grade year and for portions of the fifth-grade year, Dorothy instructed Liffy in spatial skills. She began by teaching Liffy to measure with her body.[6] Ruth wondered if such a skill was actually necessary, but she was too polite to question. Anticipating the professor's doubt, Dorothy explained to Ruth that number is a concept we arrive at through our bodies, using it as a measuring stick to comprehend quantity, size, and distance. "Hmmm," the professor wondered. By learning to measure with her body rather than to make wild and inaccurate guesses about height and length, Liffy would internalize a more accurate sense of number. "Hmmm," Ruth Nettleson pondered again.

Dorothy poured water into a clear glass until it reached the first inch mark on a ruler. She added several drops of red ink, stuck her index finger into the glass, pulled it out, and asked Liffy to do the same. Teacher and student compared their inch-long marks. The red stain extended nearly to the second joint in Liffy's finger. "My!" Liffy exclaimed. "So that's an inch. My goodness, I never realized that an inch is this little. Is it the same size every time?" she asked Dorothy, who nodded with a smile. Both she and Liffy predicted and then measured a number of items in inches, then constructed larger units of measurement and repeated the same sequence — predicting then measuring items in feet and then yards.

"You know," Liffy reasoned late in fourth grade, "common sense should have told me that a door stands between six and seven feet high. After all, I am four feet tall myself," Liffy reasoned, "but I really didn't know how tall a door was, or a foot was, until I measured it that way against myself."[7] Dorothy wondered why Liffy learned so easily, without the struggle that authority predicted. Dorothy concluded that she must not be asking enough of her student. She was not teaching her enough. Dorothy introduced a more difficult skill.

She taught her how objects penetrate and occupy space, one of the building blocks of imagery. Dorothy taught Liffy to construct them three-dimensionally in cardboard and examine the shape verbally with her language. "So a box actually has six sides, does it? Look at that, Dorothy, a box has a top and a bottom and four sides. My goodness, look at that!" Liffy directed. Dorothy taught Liffy to discover the relationship between three-dimensional objects and their two-dimensional forms by disassembling the cardboard objects, laying them flat so that they appeared along a two-dimensional plane, and tracing around them using language all the while. "You mean to tell me," Liffy asked Dorothy, "that when I push this pyramid down flat with my finger, it is actually a square? My goodness!" Liffy wondered in amazement. "And look at this!" she exclaimed as she rotated a rectangular box in different positions behind a window and drew, with one eye closed, the contours of the rectangle on the window. "Look how this rectangle changes shape when I move its position!" Liffy exclaimed.[8]

Liffy learned spatial skills so easily that Dorothy questioned, was Turner's really present after all? She called the pediatrician, who confirmed the diagnosis. "Absolutely no doubt," he said. Well, Dorothy concluded, the fault was hers. She wasn't expecting enough, not doing enough, not teaching enough. Dorothy always accused herself of falling short of expectations. She must teach Liffy more difficult skills, academic ones that depended upon spatial thinking. She must teach Liffy math.

Numbers confounded Liffy. What did they mean, and what did they ask her to do? Liffy was not certain. Measuring with her body and building her own number system out of beads helped Liffy gain a more accurate sense of number, but she had no concept of action. A numeral represents a chunk of mass in space, and a math problem identifies the actions to take with that mass. A minus sign, for example, says to reduce the mass; a multiplication sign says to add identical groups of mass together.

Liffy did not understand that math calls for an action. "What does this problem really want me to do here?" she asked Dorothy, "take the bottom from the top or the top from the bottom?" Liffy did not know. Hence, during fifth grade, Dorothy taught Liffy to understand computation as a series of actions that occur in the three-dimensional world. They added, subtracted, multiplied, and divided with legos, described the action in Liffy's language, and reduced the action to symbols. Dorothy reasoned that her student understood the operation when Liffy could compose a story problem that matched its computational counterparts. When shown the problem "5 x 6," for example, Liffy said the following, "Well, let's just see now, if the classroom has five rows of desks with six desks in each row, how many desks does the classroom have? Would that work, Dorothy?" Liffy asked. Dorothy nodded. "Of course, dear," she said. "You've got the hang of it. See?" Liffy thought she did see.

Dorothy used the same procedure to teach Liffy fractions, decimals, and percents: observe the action with three-dimensional objects in the real world, describe the action in Liffy's language, and reduce her language to symbolic form. Liffy learned so easily. Why? Dorothy questioned.

Somewhere toward the end of Liffy's fifth-grade year, Dorothy thought she understood. She thought she knew the answer to the question that haunted her, often in the middle of the night. Liffy learned so easily, slick as silk in fact, because of her abundant language. If Liffy attached her own language to the action, she understood the spatial concept. For Liffy, language was the patch for a missing chromosome. Dorothy was absolutely certain of that. If Liffy translated actions through her own language, Dorothy explained to Ruth Nettleson, she understood spatial concepts. The professor seemed to understand.

Liffy's performance during her middle school years affirmed Dorothy's belief. Occasionally, Liffy returned to the clinic for help on an assignment that had a spatial component — map assignments, for example. "I simply cannot remember what state goes where," Liffy complained when she returned for some assistance in sixth grade. Dorothy taught Liffy how to construct her own map of the United States, out of foam core and talk her way through its construction as well as the relationship between the states.

"This method certainly works!" Liffy proclaimed when she brought in the map test she had taken at school.[9] Liffy earned an "A" and wanted to share the triumph with Dorothy. Liffy liked to affirm others. She also liked to achieve. In fact, she expected herself to achieve, and when she could not do so or feared she could not, she returned to the clinic to solicit Dorothy's assistance.

"Now tell me, Dorothy, how am I going to be able to learn to drive?" Liffy asked when she returned to the clinic as a sophomore in high school. "How will I know where I am in relation to other cars on the road? How can I find my way to new places or prevent getting lost?" Liffy asked. Dorothy returned to the same principles that worked so well in the past: translating the concept or the action through Liffy's own language. She rehearsed with Liffy how to talk to herself when she rode in the car, to look for identifying landmarks along the route, to describe them to herself aloud into a tape recorder, and to speak of their relationship to other points along the way. Liffy would bring in her recording, and she and Dorothy would draw a map from the taped description and then compare it to reality. "Let's drive to your school using the map we've drawn, Liffy," Dorothy said. "Let's see how accurate your description is or if you omitted any important landmarks." Liffy seldom did.

Liffy learned to judge the distance between cars in the same way she first rehearsed measurement in elementary school. She measured distance against her body and talked her way through the action. When her car was parked in the driveway, for example, Liffy walked next to it to gain a sense of its length, then estimated how many times her car could "fit" in the length of the block. She had to describe other spatial aspects of driving as well,[10] telling herself aloud, for example, that when she saw the brake lights appear on the car in front of her, she must reduce the speed on her own car by pushing her foot down on the brake. "Well," Liffy announced when she stopped by the clinic one afternoon to share another triumph with Dorothy. "The method worked again! The examiner didn't exactly understand why I talked so much during my driving test, but who cares? I passed my test," Liffy announced as she dangled her car keys in the air.

Although she did not care what the driving examiner thought of her method, Liffy definitely cared about what her teachers thought of it, as well as her need of it. "You know, Dorothy," Liffy wailed near the end of tenth grade. "They just don't understand. They try to be helpful, I know they do, but my teachers really don't understand my method of learning and my absolute need of it. Math teachers seem to be the worst. I absolutely dread geometry next year," she moaned. "I need it for college, and I absolutely must get a good grade in it to maintain my grade point," Liffy worried, "but Dorothy I've already looked at the geometry book. It's a nightmare! Designs and imaginary points that appear along a vanishing plane. Postulates and theorems," Liffy added. "How in heaven's name will I learn geometry?"

Dorothy suggested that Liffy take it for credit at the clinic the following year. She would be her teacher. "Oh, I don't know, Dorothy," Liffy replied. "If my teachers don't understand my method or my need of it, why would they allow me to take a special class in geometry here? I don't know if it's possible to make my teachers understand, especially my math teacher," she added.

Dorothy suggested a school conference so that she and Liffy could explain her learning profile and her difficulties to her teachers as well as her need for specialized math instruction. Dorothy remembered Liffy's courage, how she sat amid a group of educators, all of them authorities in their field, and explained and answered questions until finally they understood, even her math teacher.

"You should be a teacher, Liffy," Dorothy whispered to her on the way out of the conference. "You're very skilled at helping others understand." The following year Dorothy taught Liffy geometry using the same principles: observe the action with 3-dimensional objects, describe the action in Liffy's language, then and only then reduce her language to symbolic form. Liffy learned easily. Her language was the patch that bridged the hemispheres.[11] Dorothy was absolutely certain of that.

Her certainty as well as her fondness for Liffy explained why Dorothy felt such joy when she saw Liffy's name appear on her schedule that November day. They met in the waiting room, each anticipating the appearance of the other. Dorothy waited at the window and watched Liffy rush up the walk to find shelter from the rain. The November wind nearly blew Liffy through the front door and into Dorothy, who stood waiting for her a few steps away.

The two of them greeted each other in gestures of friendship. "It's so good to see you," Liffy exclaimed as she hugged Dorothy hard, her blond head bobbing just a notch above Dorothy's waist. Water dripped from her raincoat. "Oh, look at that will you," Liffy apologized, "I've rained on your dress." Dorothy laughed. She liked her so.

On the short walk down the hall to Dorothy's office, the two of them chatted freely. Liffy took off her raincoat, sat down in the chair adjacent to Dorothy's desk, and crossed her legs. Her feet did not reach the floor.

"Well," Liffy began, identifying immediately the reason for her appearance. "I'm thinking about college." Dorothy nodded, "Well I should hope so! You weren't thinking about not going to college, were you?" Dorothy asked.

"Oh, I'm not questioning if I'll go on or not," Liffy explained. "I've always planned on going to college, but that's just the point, Dorothy. I want to make certain that I go to a really good one, not just any college. What would you recommend?"

Wanting to dispel any concern for limitations, Dorothy replied, "Liffy I hope you realize that you can go to any college you want. You have the grades, and you surely have the intellect to attend any college you want!"

Well, Liffy wasn't certain about that. She wished and needed to be selective about a college. Not only did she want a challenging school, but she needed a responsive one, especially in light of her learning disability. She had to learn in certain ways, study in certain ways, take tests in certain ways. She had Turner's syndrome after all.

"But Liffy," Dorothy pleaded, "you're so skilled at using language to talk your way through tasks that... well," she said, "You're not handicapped at all, not at all!"

Liffy sat back and thought a moment in preparation. She realized that her teacher did not really understand the meaning of the word. "Dorothy," she said, "I realize I am not the person I'm supposed to be." Liffy paused, allowing silence to emphasize the meaning of her statement.

"Do you know what I mean?" Liffy asked when she recognized that her teacher did not fully understand. No, Dorothy was not certain. "I mean that I can do what I'm not supposed to be able to do, if research is any measure of the truth. I've read those research articles about Turner's syndrome too, Dorothy, and I think that they are appalling, absolutely appalling."

Dorothy was about to agree, but Liffy stopped her as she raised her small hand to the halt position. "However," Liffy added, "I *am* learning disabled." She paused again. "I *do* have limits, and frankly I'm a little miffed when others suggest that I don't. Actually, I'm offended when people tell me that I'm not learning disabled, as though it's a ploy . . . just as offended when researchers predict the outcome of my handicap, as though they already know who I am and what I can do or what I might be. I've already proven them wrong long ago."

Dorothy concurred. Yes, Liffy had done that. Not only had she surpassed any of the academic and intellectual limitations that researchers predicted, but Liffy had shattered them. "That's what I mean," Dorothy said. "You're not handicapped at all!"

"But that's just the point, Dorothy," Liffy went on. "I am handicapped. For heaven's sake, in one way or another all of us are. That's what's so wonderful. Don't you see?" Liffy asked, "Limitations create possibilities that would not otherwise exist!"

Dorothy had not thought of that. Truly, she had not, and she felt as though she had been jolted suddenly to a new perspective.

"I don't deny my limitations," Liffy concluded. "They make endless variations possible, like the universe which is continually unfolding. Well," Liffy said, "so much for my philosophizing. That's part of my tradition," she winked. "When you've had time to think about the colleges that would be best, call me," Liffy said, "and we'll talk again."

Yes, Dorothy said, savoring the realization that possibilities are borne from limitations. Of course she would call her. "Good," Liffy replied, "I need to hurry home now and finish reading a book for one of my papers. Oh, I just love stormy days like this," Liffy added as she peeked through the blinds to assess the weather. "Rainy afternoons like this make reading a good book all the more delightful. I absolutely love wrapping myself in a blanket and curling up on the couch with a good book. Don't you, Dorothy?" Liffy asked.

Dorothy nodded, still struck with the wonder of being led to a spot she would not otherwise have gone, at least not on her own. "Yes, I do dear," Dorothy answered, "I do love to read a good book, especially on a rainy afternoon, though I seldom give myself permission."

"Well, today's the perfect day to do so," Liffy observed.

"Yes, I suppose so," Dorothy replied. After Liffy left, Dorothy reviewed the long list of tasks she expected herself to complete by the end of the work day. Nothing that can't wait, she thought. Instead, she would follow her student's advice and enjoy a good book, a warm blanket, and a comfortable spot.

Dorothy returned to the place that brought her greatest comfort: her solid desk in the family room and the long row of windows that looked out upon the Sound. She brewed herself a cup of tea, and while it steeped, she looked out upon the strait. A hint of sunlight threatened to dispel the storm. For a moment Dorothy hoped that the storm might continue, at least the rain. Somehow she felt nourished by the rain.

As she wrapped herself in the blanket and opened her book, Dorothy felt a quiet settle over her. The winds had stopped, the storm abated. The waters of the Sound no longer churned into a frenzy. All that remained was the steady sheet of rain that cleansed the deck.

– 8 –

COACH'S CHOICE

Larry Reichert, one of the fifth-grade teachers at Elmhurst Elementary, yelled at his offensive line. "Wait for the snap of the ball! The snap of the ball," he repeated. "How many times do I have to tell you guys?" Coach Reichert questioned. "Huh...how many times?"

The fifth- and sixth-grade boys, members of the intermediate football team from Elmhurst Elementary, dared not answer. A response would only escalate Coach Reichert's tirade. The veins in his neck protruded. Blotches of red splashed across his face. "Huh...How many times?" Larry Reichert asked. "You're wigglin' your butts like a bunch of rag dolls," the coach scoffed as he mocked the movement of his players. Coach Reichert grumbled something unintelligible, then commanded his troops, "Come on, let's get this right. Wait for the snap!"

Coach Reichert did not mean to bully, of course. He simply wanted the best for his boys. He believed in their potential, said they were capable of excellence, but professed that the only way to reach such a lofty goal was to demand it. He did so, demanding excellence of himself and of his students, daily. Physical fitness, self-discipline, and goal setting were all part of his plan.

Twenty years ago Larry Reichert formed the football team for a reason: excellence, a quality he thought was absent in America's youth. Then he was a young, idealistic teacher, just out of college, intent on doing what he could to change society's slovenly youth. He formed the Elmhurst Brigade so that his fifth-grade boys could learn about goal setting, self-discipline, and excellence. His girls would learn by observation. No team of his would have a girl on it!

Not only was it restricted to boys, the Elmhurst Brigade was also composed exclusively of fifth- and sixth-graders. For the first year, the Elmhurst Brigade played intrasquad games, but by the following year, Larry Reichert convinced schools from the Elmhurst district as well as schools from the surrounding ones to participate. Unlike higher level football programs, tryouts for the elementary teams began in the spring, and games continued throughout the summer. Larry Reichert wanted to nurture excellence as long as possible.

Nearly as quickly as it was formed, the Elmhurst Brigade became one of the most prestigious groups at school, and its coach the staff member with the most personal power. Students valued Reichert's word over that of any other adult at school, even the principal. Every spring, the fifth- and sixth-grade boys from Elmhurst Elementary tried out, hoping to earn the coach's acceptance.

Mr. Reichert encouraged Steve Schneider, one of his fifth-grade students, to try out. As he watched him participate halfheartedly in P.E., Larry Reichert decided that Steve was just the kind of kid for whom his football team was designed. Intelligent, sturdy, but slothful. "Schneider!" Mr. Reichert yelled as Steve ran around the track. "Push yourself. Come on, come on... Push!"

Steve Schneider stood well above most of his peers. His broad shoulders, large frame, and strong jaw convinced most adults that Steve was athletic, but this gentle giant of a boy was an athlete in size only, never in motion. He stumbled up and down the basketball court, his arms and legs flailing in all directions. "Keep it together, Mr. Schneider," Reichert yelled along the sidelines. "Make your arms and legs work *for* you!" he hollered as Steve lumbered through the game of basketball, struggling to control his appendages.

Steve performed no better at individual sports than at team ones. He could not run the mile without stopping several times for breath. In fact, he could not even walk the mile without pausing to regain his strength! Coach Reichert interpreted Steve's lethargy as a sign of laziness. He did not realize that Steve's clumsiness and sluggishness stemmed from motor planning difficulty. Had he realized that and understood the significance of "motor planning difficulty," Reichert may have understood... perhaps. At least he would have been more cautious about the criticisms he leveled at Steve out of sheer frustration.

One day during a class run, for example, Coach Reichert spotted Steve resting on a stump. Incensed by Steve's laziness, Reichert stormed across the field, his anger building with each step. Long before he reached his fifth-grade target, Reichert spewed out his disgust. "Schneider!" Reichert hollered halfway across the field. "Schneider!" he hollered again, trying to capture Steve's attention. Breathing hard and trying to regain his strength, Steve raised his head from his hands. "Yeah, coach?" Reichert loomed over him. "Schneider," the coach said, "You are a wonder...yes sir, a real gutless wonder."

Later, Coach Reichert apologized to Steve for his careless words. Steve accepted his teacher's apology and tried to dismiss the hurt. "That's okay, Mr. Reichert," Steve replied.

Mr. Reichert simply could not believe that this blond lumberjack of a kid whose feet and hands were bigger than his own could not excel in sports. Steve could, Reichert believed, if only he chose to do so, if only he demanded excellence of himself. Larry Reichert's goal that year was to motivate Steve to achieve in sports, and therefore in life, even if he had to shame him into the accomplishment. Mr. Reichert made a special point to invite Steve to try out for the prestigious team. "I need a big smart kid like you on the team, Steve." Steve valued smart. "Now I know you're smart. You show me that every day in class. It's obvious you're big. So you're it, fellah! The team needs a big, smart guy like you."

Steve's size belied his age. He would not be eleven until the late summer, yet at the age of ten, he was one of the largest students in his fifth-grade class. Steve was also one of the last students in the class to be chosen for any team. Understandably, then, he could not imagine why Mr. Reichert courted his participation. The invitation affirmed him, however, and increased his stature in the eyes of his peers. Steve decided to try out for the team. He announced his decision that night at the dinner table.

"I've made a momentous decision, folks" he said to his parents, Nancy and Bill Schneider. An only child, Steve usually conversed with his parents in adult language, which he spiced heavily with drama. "I don't want the two of you to become alarmed or to think that I have lost my senses," he said, crafting a reaction, "but I have decided, upon the urging of my teacher and future coach, to try out for the football team. I repeat, the football team!"

Nancy and Bill responded in simultaneous disbelief. "What? You have? You're kidding! No, you're not kidding? Well, what prompted this decision?" they asked. For years Nancy and Bill endured several painful seasons watching their son trip over his feet on the soccer field even though no other player was near him. They watched him miss the ball by several inches even when it rested stationary on the Tee stand. Once softball began, Nancy worried for the safety of her son and of his classmates. "He's either going to kill himself or one of his teammates with that bat," she told her husband Bill. "He has no sense of his body or how to control it."

At the end of Steve's fourth grade, Bill abandoned the notion that his son would ever be an athlete. "Sad," Bill often remarked, "I would have given anything to be as big as that kid's gonna' be." Bill loved the competitive challenge of sports, particularly of football. Whenever he got the chance, he reminisced about his high school football days and how, even though he was the smallest end in the entire state, he scored the most touchdowns. When his son, his only son, announced that he too would try the sport, Bill could not contain his joy. "Wow! That's wonderful, Steve! Wonderful! What position are you going to play?" Steve replied that the coach recommended him for tackle.

Nancy was less enthusiastic. She worried that another athletic failure would wound Steve's self-esteem, and the likelihood of failure was great. Steve's clumsiness was not deliberate but rather the result of broad-based motor delays — that is, difficulty with both the fine motor as well as the large motor systems. Steve could not write, cut, or draw with accuracy or ease. He knew where he wanted his pencil to go, of course, but often it did not arrive at the place he intended. His writing looked like scrawl. He had to carefully *aim* his pencil at the line, but as his attention waned, his writing wandered. In fact, he really did not learn to write until late in elementary school. The reason was that in addition to his large and fine motor delays, Steve was also dysgraphic.[1] In other words, his motor recall for letters was vague and inaccurate. Steve could not recall the motor sequences involved in forming letters. "Let's see, how do I make a 'g,' a 'z,' an 'f'?" Steve asked himself. Often he could not recall, and as a result, handwriting was simply awful for him, even now in fifth grade.[2]

Maneuvering his body was equally difficult. Steve knew where he wanted his body to run or where he wanted a baseball to land, but he could not organize his motor system to comply. As a result, he would bump into a doorway, fall up the stairs, even fall out of his chair! Maintaining his body upright, standing, or even sitting in a chair required great effort from him.[3] So did moving it. When he tried, he fatigued quickly or he missed the mark entirely. Hence, he could not sustain physical exertion, and when called upon to tackle, he missed his man.

"Gee, Steve," his mother responded, "have you really thought about what this asks of you? If that's what you *really* want, Dad and I are for it, but dear," Steve's mother implored, "think for a minute about what this demands! I hear that Mr. Reichert's spring football practice is pretty grueling...every day after school and all day on Saturday...rain or shine...that's quite a commitment, Steve."

"Don't discourage him, Nancy," Steve's dad chided. "Steve knows all about commitments. He honors his commitments, don't ya, son?" Steve nodded, trying to ignore the vague uneasiness in his stomach. "See, Nancy, he'll do fine, just fine. Let's go out after dinner, Steve, and get you some cleats." Mr. Reichert would provide the uniform.

For the next three weeks, every day after school and all morning on Saturday, Steve turned out for practice. As the days wore on, Steve shared less and less with his parents. "How was it today?" his dad would ask at dinner. "Okay," Steve responded. "Okay!" his father repeated, "Only okay? Did you hear your son?" Bill asked his wife, Nancy. "Did you ever think Steve could say so little?" Nancy and Bill urged their son to explain, but Steve responded in monosyllables or shrugs. That concerned them. Steve was prone to verbal excess. Nancy sensed her son's discouragement, but he would not acknowledge it. "Aw, Mom," Steve said, "I'm just tired, that's all."

The next day, just before practice, a spring storm hit. Throughout the day a strong wind, menacing clouds, and occasional thunder warned of the storm's arrival. As the boys donned their football uniforms, its fury hit. Mr. Reichert looked out the window of the gym onto the practice field. In minutes, a relentless sheet of rain turned the play field into a muddy soup of ooze. "Perfect day for football," Larry Reichert thought, recognizing that the day's weather would prevent any of his boys from keeping a clean uniform. "Let's go," he hollered. "Let's see how tough you guys are!" he challenged his team. Pulling on their helmets, the boys followed, echoing noises in unison. Unwilling to submit to the weather or any other difficulty, Mr. Reichert and his troops ran through their drills.

Nancy was concerned when Steve did not arrive home at the expected time after practice. She wanted to drive to the school to look for him but remembered her obstetrician's orders. "Bed rest. If you want to carry this baby to term," he advised, "quit your job, avoid strenuous activity like vacuuming and lifting, and don't expose yourself to any unnecessary risk. Stay out of the car!" Nancy waited instead on the living room couch and hoped that Steve would soon arrive. Finally, she saw him approaching the crest of the hill. Covered completely with mud, even his hair, Steve was recognizable only by his walk. She met him at the door.

"Steven, what in heaven's name happened to you?" his mother asked. "I quit!" Steve said rattling off his anger nonstop. "Old man Reichert called me a gutless tackle, a gutless tackle, can you imagine that? A Gutless Tackle!" he repeated for the third time. The words curdled in his mouth like vomit. "He said I wasn't pushing myself hard enough, that I was bein' a sissy, and he had me run the ball against the whole defensive line, with no protection, so I'd know what bein' tackled felt like ... like I didn't know how it felt ... like I missed tackles on purpose or something! Stupid! That guy doesn't know the first thing about being a coachthreedotsa warden, maybe." Steve's storm of words shielded his vulnerability.

"Three times he had me run the ball with no protection! Three times. Tres," he shouted while he waved the appropriate number of muddy fingers in the air for effect. "Three times the whole grimy defensive line piled on top of me! It woulda' been four except I finally came to my senses. I stood up, slammed my helmet in the mud, and yelled at Reichert, 'What do you think this is? The army? *I quit!*' " Steve pried his feet from his cleats and stripped off his uniform. He left them on the front step and slammed the door behind him. "Leave 'em there," he ordered. "Maybe the neighbor's dog will steal the filthy things and rip 'em to shreds." His verbal excess could no longer diffuse his pain. Tears ran down the mud on his cheek. Steve ran up the stairs, tripping on the top one, his mother following slowly behind.

No amount of reason would change his mind. "No!" Steve yelled. "I'm through with it, finished. I wouldn't go back to that ridiculous-mud-slamming-craziness for anything! Forget it! Besides, the dog down the street would feel cheated. I promised him that he could have the clothes!" Besides dramatic, Steve was often unyielding, especially when he felt he was right.

Later that evening Mr. Reichert appeared at the door of the Schneider home. He wanted to talk to Steve, who by now had forgotten his rage. Just as he was quick to forgive, Steve was quick to dismiss his anger. Mr. Reichert wanted Steve to reconsider his decision. Quitting, he said, could affect Steve's entire future. The next time he met a difficult challenge, Mr. Reichert went on, Steve might give himself permission to quit again. Steve listened, his parents sitting on either side of him. He resisted the urge to call his teacher a jerk. "Well, Steve," his dad asked. "What do you think?" Bill Schneider quietly hoped that his son might return to the team. He regretted that the coach needlessly backed his son into a corner, but he hoped that this one event would not sour Steve on the sport of football.

Steve paused long enough to swallow his irritation. "Thanks for your concern, Mr. Reichert," Steve replied, "but I can't think of one reason why I should return to your team. I really can't do what you need. Thanks anyway. I'll go get your uniform." Steve hoped that the neighbor's German shepherd had not taken him up on his offer.

After Mr. Reichert left with the mud-caked uniform, Bill Schneider cautioned his son that quitting might produce more severe consequences than his teacher's disapproval. "Consequences?" Steve asked. "What other consequences?" His dad pointed out that his peers might not approve of his quitting. "David... Robert... James, you mean? They saw it. They saw what Reichert did. He tried to humiliate me. The guys will understand why I quit!"

Unfortunately, they didn't. The next day Steve arrived from school quieter than usual. Normally he burst through the front door, nearly ripping it off at its hinges, and bellowed a greeting to his mother. Today he arrived quietly. In fact, Nancy hadn't realized Steve was home until she heard whimpering from the family room. "Steve?" she called. "Steve, is that you?" she asked again and tracked down the sound of sorrow.

Steve was stretched out face down on the family room couch. He buried his face into the cushions to muffle his crying. "Steve, what's wrong?" his mother asked. Steve hid himself deeper into the crevices and released heaving sobs. Nancy sat on the edge of the couch. "What happened, dear? Tell me what happened," Nancy said as she rubbed her son's back, a maternal reflex designed to ease a child's pain. Reluctantly, Steve turned around to show his shame. He had been beaten. His eye had already blackened from the fist that crashed into it on the playground after school. Dirt and pebbles were lodged in his scalp as well as his elbows, the penalty of being thrown to the ground. A small cut on the side of his mouth dripped blood down his face and neck. His shirt was ripped and his glasses broken.

"Oh, Stever," his mother said, calling him the name of greatest endearment. "Who did this to you?" Steve shook his head, not wanting to acknowledge the deepest shame that could befall a boy in Mr. Reichert's class yet unable to bear its burden. "My friends!" Steve sobbed. "David and Robert and James . . . I thought they were my friends . . . they waited for me after school . . . and then they. . . . " Steve could not be understood through his tears. The taunting and name-calling that his dad had feared triggered the fight, and four boys, all of them friends, lost something dear: one of them his pride and three of them their compassion. "I'm not goin' back to school!" Steve went on. "I can't go back to school . . . ever . . . never!"

That evening at dinner Steve would not eat even though Nancy prepared his favorite meal. He refused to leave his room. In an effort to regain some measure of emotional control, Steve organized his drawers, cleaned his closet, and found all the stray pieces to his science set. "Steve," his mother exclaimed when she went in Steve's room to check on him, a plate of cookies in her hand, "you've never cleaned your room unless I threatened you with your life!" Steve could not yet smile. "Yeah," he said. "You'll feel better tomorrow, dear," she said as she hugged him hard. "This kind of hurt doesn't last forever." His dad had made the same observation, but Steve did not believe that the pain would ever leave him. It only intensified when the lights went out.

Steve could not sleep. He relived the event, David and Robert and James and what they said . . . they really meant what they said, really *meant* it . . . that he was a wimp, a stupid little wimp . . . he couldn't even tackle Jerry Swanson, the biggest baby in fifth grade. . . . Jerry Swanson knew better than to try out for football, how come baby Stevie did, huh, how come, how come? How could they say that? How could they do that? He thought they were his friends.

Nancy heard Steve's tears. They woke her from her pregnant slumber. She went into her son's bedroom, asked him to make room for a mom and a growing baby, and lay down on his bed. She did not speak of the day's shame. Instead, she asked Steve to remember the past and to consider the future. Pain is only unbearable when time is confined to the present.

Nancy patted her son gently and asked, "Well, Stever...what do you suppose we should call your baby sister?" The question shocked him upright. "Sister?" Steve asked incredulously. "Who said anything about a sister? I was countin' on a brother!"

"Fifty-fifty," replied his mother. "So what do you think about a name for her?" she asked. "Ohhhhh," Steve sighed as he returned his head to the pillow. "I dunno'...Susan maybe...that's a good name, or Kathy...what do you think of Kathy?" Steve asked.

"Hmmmm," his mother answered, "not quite the right sound... close all right, but not quite the right one. Stever," she said, "what do you think...Daddy hasn't even heard me say this one yet," she said, piquing Steve's curiosity. "What about the name...Eudora?" A few anxious moments of silence hung in the air before the two of them broke into uncontrollable giggles.

Laughter helped Steve move beyond the hurt of the day. His mother reminded him of the qualities that made him special, the gifts that made him unique. "Who else in your class knows how to take a carburetor apart?" she asked. "Who else in your class wonders about the workings of the universe? Or understands the birth of stars?" Nancy would not allow Steve to demean his talents by defining himself from the events of a single afternoon. Instead, she detailed all the talents that were uniquely his until he drifted off to sleep. Before it overtook him, Steve asked, "Could you think about havin' a boy, Mom? I'd like a brother...Mike...Mike's a good, strong name."

The next morning Steve decided that he would return to school. Neither Bill nor Nancy assumed he would do otherwise. They merely affirmed his decision. "This is not going to be easy," Steve announced at breakfast, "but I'm going to do it. I'm going to forge ahead and *do* it. Besides, I only have a month, well maybe a month and a half left of school." Had he realized what those six weeks held, Steve may not have returned.

After the lunch count and morning announcements, Mr. Reichert explained the project that he expected from his students. Every spring Mr. Reichert's fifth-grade class studied butterflies, caught them, mounted them, read about them, and wrote a report on a classification of their choice. For fifth-graders the report was demanding: eight to ten pages of composition, their *best* handwriting, ink, no misspellings or punctuation errors allowed, normal margins, no double spacing. Once Mr. Reichert mentioned the word "handwriting," Steve's interest waned, but he knew that catching, mounting, and studying butterflies would be fun. He already knew the butterfly he wanted to write about: the monarch.

Steve had read about it in a natural science magazine that he received monthly.

Catching butterflies was not as easy as Steve had imagined. "You gotta' be fast to catch these little buggers!" he complained at dinner. "Fast and sneaky. Since I'm neither one, I gotta be persistent." Steve's approach paid off. Within a few weeks he compiled an impressive collection, enough to give some of his duplicates to Robert and David who by now had shelved the fight into a dim memory.

Mr. Reichert encouraged the class to begin the task early, but Steve avoided writing the report. He hated to write! He asked Mr. Reichert if his mother could be his scribe. That's what his fourth-grade teacher, Mrs. Abramson, recommended. Mrs. Abramson was the one who suggested to the Schneiders that they take Steve to the clinic. "He's so capable," Mrs. Abramson reasoned, "but he just cannot write! It's such a struggle for him. That's why he's often behind in his schoolwork and frankly, Mr. and Mrs. Schneider, unable to demonstrate how capable he really is. He can't translate his wonderful ideas onto paper. Something must be getting in his way!"

Mrs. Abramson was right, of course. She knew at the intuitive level what the clinic assessment documented: broad-based motor delays. One of the recommendations that the clinic made was to allow Steve, in fact to encourage him, to demonstrate his knowledge in ways other than writing.[4] Mrs. Abramson complied. She had him dictate his reports, even his math assignments, into a tape recorder, and she never, ever, asked him to copy from the book to the paper. "For heaven's sake," Mrs. Abramson said, "that's what copy machines are for, Steve! You just go walk yourself down to the office and ask the school secretary to run us a copy!" Steve did so with glee. He loved Mrs. Abramson.

With adaptations that she and the clinic devised, Steve had a successful fourth-grade year. One of the adaptations was to provide a scribe. Steve talked, and someone else wrote down what he said. Mr. Reichert would not allow such pampering, however, believing instead that Steve's illegible penmanship was due to carelessness. "Motor delays!" he scoffed in the staff room. "Who ever heard of such nonsense? What that kid suffers from is a large dose of laziness!" Mr. Reichert also believed that Steve's penmanship would improve with additional practice, even though it had not done so to this point with six years of practice. Steve dreaded what lay ahead. Only three weeks left of school and an eight-to-ten-page paper to produce, handwritten in ink, no spelling or punctuation errors, normal margins, no double spacing. God.

Every night after dinner Steve worked on it. For several hours on the weekend he worked on it, reading, composing, and amending his copy. He also asked his mother to edit the final draft for spelling and punctuation errors. "You know how bad my spelling is when I write,

Mom," Steve confessed. Although he always knew how to spell a word aloud, even very difficult ones, he frequently misspelled them when he wrote. His motor memories for words were inaccurate. He could not rely upon how it felt motorically to write them; instead, he had to rely upon his visual control of the pencil, forcing it to go where he aimed it. When that control lapsed, as it often does in the mundane act of handwriting, Steve misspelled.[5] "Mr. Reichert will flunk me for that!"

Nancy corrected all the spelling errors, added the punctuation marks that were missing, and commented, "This is a pretty good paper, Steve! Really it is. You should earn a high grade for it." Steve's confidence increased. His mom should know, Steve thought. After all, she taught high school English . . . well, she used to teach it before all this baby stuff happened.

Steve dreaded the final stage: copying the final draft in his best penmanship. For three successive days after school he worked on the final copy until late in the evening. He tried to keep the pen under control by writing in tight tiny strokes, but he soon realized that his paper would be four pages short. He began again. "I'm just gonna' take my time," Steve told himself, "take my time," but by the middle of the first paragraph, he had misspelled several words. Steve tried to correct them but pushed so hard on the ink eraser that he ripped the paper. He paused again, trying to control his anger. He began again. By the end of the first page, Steve thought that he might finish the report on time until he looked over the page to discover that he had omitted three lines. He ripped up the paper, slammed the pen on the kitchen table, and announced, "This is impossible! I can't do this!"

Mom and Steve decided that the only way through this was for her to sit beside him, give him another pair of eyes, and read the copy to him as he wrote it. Still he made mistakes, which he tried as best he could to correct, but smudges, wrinkles, and occasional crossed-out words dotted his eight-and-a-half-page paper. "That's the best I can do," he announced, and indeed it was. "This is great, Steve," his dad announced, admiring the document. He drove his son to the local drugstore to buy a cover, which Steve decorated with a monarch butterfly. Steve placed the report in its cover and added a title sheet. "There," he said on the morning it was due. "I hope I get an A."

Steve wondered why he didn't get his report back as quickly as the other students. David and Robert and James got theirs back days ago. They all earned B's, James a B+. "I bet I get an A," Steve thought. "Mine's better than James's. That's why I didn't get my paper back. Mr. Reichert really likes it." At the end of the day, Mr. Reichert called Steve up to his desk. Steve recognized his report by its distinctive color. "Before I give you this back," Mr. Reichert began, "I want to tell you something, Steve." Steve could hardly wait for the words of praise he expected to follow. "Had you worked as hard on your paper as you did on your collection, you would have earned an excellent grade, but your paper shows how little effort you exerted." Steve couldn't believe what he was hearing. "It is messy, smudged, and wrinkled. I can hardly read this!" he said. "I graded you accordingly."

Steve looked inside the cover and saw a D— written in bold red marks across the title page. He refused to show his feelings. He took the paper back to his desk and smoldered through the remainder of the afternoon. Steve walked home alone. He threw the paper on the top shelf of his closet and slammed the door. "Jerk!" he muttered. Not yet rid of his anger, Steve opened his window to make an announcement to the world. "Old man Reichert's a *jerk!*" Steve hollered. "Are you listening old man? You are the biggest jerk in the world!" and he slammed the window with finality.

That night Steve rummaged through his closet to look for a "gift" for Mr. Reichert. Students customarily gave them to him on the last day of school. "I bet it's still in here," he said to himself as he sifted through the pile of dirty laundry, comic books, leftover model parts, and sundry junk. "Hah!" he said as he retrieved the prize from a shoe box: a broken stopwatch he had found one day on his way home from school. "Missing its insides," Steve announced. "Perfect," he said. "It's gutless." He scoured the closet again, found a small box the appropriate size for a stopwatch, placed the gift inside, wrapped it, and placed a crumpled ribbon on top. Steve chuckled as he crawled into bed.

The next day in school Mr. Reichert called for order, collected the remaining books, and gave his yearly speech. He was hard on his students, each and every one of them, some of them more than others. "You got that right," Steve muttered to himself. If he was too hard, Mr. Reichert continued, he apologized. He never expected more of a student than what he could produce. He cared for each of his students. He wanted the best for them, and as a result he expected the most of them, more than any other teacher at Elmhurst. Before they left for the summer, Mr. Reichert went on, he wanted to say a personal word to each of his students as he handed out report cards, the traditional time of gift giving.

Steve watched Mr. Reichert move through the rows. For once, Steve didn't mind being at the end of the alphabet. In those extra moments of observation, he could see his teacher from a different point of view. Small, light-framed, almost frail. Last September, Steve thought, old man Reichert seemed huge, his strength and stature giant-sized. Strange, Steve thought, he didn't remember Mr. Reichert being fragile in September.

Steve fingered the box that held a pretense of friendship inside. He felt the edges of its prejudice. What Mr. Reichert thought of him really didn't matter, not because the grades were already recorded and the summer was about to begin but because his teacher's definition bore no truth. It carried no weight. What mattered was how he responded to it. Steve freed himself from his teacher's control, defiantly at first by slamming his helmet onto the muddy field, but compassionately now, by stuffing the gutless stopwatch into his pocket.

As teachers often do, Mr. Reichert lowered himself to one knee as he approached Steve's desk. The coach extended his hand. "Well, Steve," he said, "we've had quite a year together, you and I. Me pushing you to do your best and you thinking that I'm a jerk." For an instant, Steve wondered if Mr. Reichert had heard yesterday's announcement.

For once unable to think of what to say, Steve simply grinned. "What are your plans for the summer, Steve?" Mr. Reichert asked. Steve stammered for a moment longer. "My plans? Ahhhh...well...my plans," he said, "I plan to get a baby brother! My mom's due any day. That's why I didn't have time to get you a gift, Coach."

"That's not necessary, Steve, you know that," Mr. Reichert responded. "A brother," he repeated, "what happens if you have a sister, Steve? Would a sister be all right?" he asked. "You know you have a fifty-fifty chance."

"Yeah, a sister would be okay," Steve replied, but he really wanted a brother. He really *really* wanted a brother. "Why a brother?" Mr. Reichert asked. Steve thought for a moment and then replied. "I could teach him things, a lot of things, but I couldn't teach a girl anything...ever! Besides," Steve went on," I'll be a lot older than him, and we'll be really different. He'll be good at things I'm not, and I'll be good at things he's not. That's okay," Steve reasoned, "that's how we'll learn to teach each other. I'll teach him, and he'll teach me."

Once again Mr. Reichert was bewildered by this big blond kid he sensed he had failed. "What will you teach your brother, Steve?" Mr. Reichert asked, genuinely wanting to know. The word "football" nearly escaped his lips, but Steve caught it at the "f." "Fishing," he said. "I'll teach him how to fish and camp. I'm a good camper, you know, almost as good as my dad. And I'll teach him how to repair things like clocks and how carburetors work and how to build model steam engines, and I'll teach him...." Mr. Reichert appeared to lose interest, and he stood up preparing to bid Jerry Swanson, the biggest baby in fifth grade, farewell. Steve was glad he didn't mention the word "football." The coach never would have understood.

The following week Steve's brother, Mike, was born, and as predicted, he was good at things that his brother was not. From the time he was little, Mike not only looked like an athlete, he moved like one. Smacking the softball off the tee, hurling his body against the soccer ball to prevent a goal, or racing around the track, Mike owned the sport he played. Steve didn't mind. In fact, he was proud of his brother's accomplishments on the field.

Except for one season of softball in the spring of his sixth-grade year, Steve no longer participated in team sports. In junior and senior high he learned to ski and to golf, and in college he became the best basketball shot in his fraternity, although he never could play the game. Steve shoots with accuracy, but he still cannot make all his parts work together when he has to move his body up and down the court.

Handwriting is no easier for him now as an adult than it was as a child. He still misspells when he writes, although never when he types. Like other dysgraphics, Steve's motor memories for words are not dependable, and no amount of rehearsal over the years has improved them.

In spite of his motor planning difficulties, Steve became an exceptionally strong student. Recently he graduated near the top of his class from a large university noted for its academic challenge. Learning to type and to use a computer as a communicative device alleviated Steve's difficulties with handwriting.[6] As the grades advanced and the learning demands lined up with his linguistic skills, Steve was able to demonstrate his intellect. Good grades followed. What made the difference for Steve, however, was not the machinery nor even his abundant language but rather his discovery that year in fifth grade of the awesome power of definition and his ability to escape its boundaries.[7]

– 9 –

THE SUN SINKS IN THE WEST

Except for his size, the most striking characteristic was his skin. Rollo Polen was pasty white. From his belly up, Rollo resembled a corpulent dumpling, a soft lump, moist from the sweat that oozed through his folds. Laughter was the other feature that distinguished him. When Rollo Polen laughed, his belly rolled, and so did his flesh. In waves it rippled.

Rollo Polen liked to laugh, ostensibly at his name, perhaps at himself. "I just kind of grew into it," Rollo said, explaining his calling. "What else could I do?" he asked Nelda Fellers, the one tutor at the clinic who had an unusual name herself. "Others have suggested that I change my first name or take on a nickname, but," he added nonstop, "how could I deny my heritage?" Not waiting for a reply, Rollo continued. "I am the only child of aging parents who themselves are a generation away from the old country. The name 'Rollo' comes from my mother's side, and 'Polen,' of course, comes from my dad's. So what else was I to do?" Rollo asked again, his stubby hands raised and opened, prepared now to receive Nelda's answer.

"I like your name, Rollo," Nelda replied. "And besides," she added, "do you realize who *you're* talking to?" Nelda asked, poking fun at her own. "My very own kids call me Nellie Fellers!" Nelda and Rollo chuckled in unison.

Referred to the clinic by a vocational counselor, Rollo lacked the educational training, the physical stamina, or the appearance to be employable. Rollo dropped out of high school in his junior year. He worked at a few jobs here and there, but by the time he was twenty-seven,

Rollo still lived at home tending his aging parents and they him as he ballooned into obesity.

"What finally made you decide to venture out into the world again?" Nelda asked Rollo. "I've run out of pants," Rollo replied. "What?" Nelda asked incredulously, choking down a laugh. "Pants," he repeated. "You know," he said, pointing to his own, "these leg wrappers with a zip-lock fly." Rollo certainly had a way of turning a phrase. "These are my last pair," he said, holding a pant leg up for Nelda Fellers to see. "It's quite a challenge to find pants this large," Rollo continued. "I thought I might have to learn to sew before I finally found these. Can't you just see me sewing these stubby little pork chops together?" he asked as he wiggled the fingers on his free hand. "So I said to myself, Polen, get on with your life or do battle with a sewing machine!"

Rollo's equating a pair of pants to a zip-lock bag and his holding the leg of his trousers up in the air struck Nelda as absurd. She burst into laughter, and Rollo laughed too. Tears streamed down as each of them struggled to regain their composure, then lost themselves in another round of hilarity. Nelda offered Rollo a tissue, wiped her own eyes dry, and asked him a question. "Well," she sighed, releasing the leftovers of heeing and hawing, "what can I do to help?"

Math, Rollo answered. "I'm going to enroll in a G.E.D. program pretty soon here," Rollo explained, "and I don't know enough about math to get me across the street. Math prevented my graduating from high school you know." Nelda didn't know. "I either had to pass a basic high school math class or a competency exam, and I couldn't do either one," Rollo explained. "I failed any math course I ever took," Rollo went on. "Numbers never did make any sense to me. I can add and subtract, of course. After all, I have a full set of fingers and toes. Multiplication is a little shaky, however, and division," he said wobbling his hand to illustrate the point, "all I can say about division is that's why God gave us calculators!"

Language streamed from his mouth without attention to pause. "Fractions, forget it," Rollo went on, waving them away with the flick of his wrist. "What's bigger, the top or the bottom? Who knows?" he answered. "Just when you think you've got it figured, you're wrong sure as anything. Decimals are worse, though. Actually, I've always doubted their existence. Anything as small as a decimal can't possibly exist," Rollo surmised.

Was this guy a comedian or what? Nelda Fellers asked herself. What had she gotten herself into? Why had she ever told Ralph Wilson, the referring counselor, that she would see this fellow who was down to his last pair of trousers. She must have been asleep when she agreed. Ralph Wilson lived next door to Nelda and Bob Fellers. For the past twenty years the Wilsons and the Fellerses shared the heartaches and the joys of a close neighborly friendship. Ralph, who called himself Wilson, liked to roust Bob out of bed early on Saturday morning to go fishing. "Fish on!" Wilson hollered as he walked through the front door several hours before dawn. Sometimes Nelda cooked Wilson and Bob breakfast. "Why not?" she asked, coming out from the bedroom in her most comfortable robe. "I'm awake now. Who could sleep with you two kids making so much noise?"

Nelda kind of liked Wilson. Something about him was irresistible. That's why she must have agreed. One particularly early Saturday, Ralph convinced Nelda to see Rollo. "I'd like you to meet this rolly-polly guy," Wilson said, "just one time, Nelda girl, just one time, as a favor to your old neighbor. I don't think he's learning disabled, just fat that's all, but if you think he's got some kind of learning problem, let me know, and I'll find a way to fund his program." Nelda wasn't sure she should do that. "Ah, come on, what are neighbors for if not to help each other out? Besides, you'll really like this guy," Wilson predicted. "He likes to laugh as much as you do."

She should have known better, Nelda thought to herself. No assessment. No plan of action to follow. "Now what am I going to do?" she asked herself, as she listened to Rollo berate mathematics. "As far as percentages go," Rollo observed, "all I have to say about them is, who do they think *they* are? Little princely figures insisting that attendants follow close behind them. Percentages are definitely snobs. But story problems, story problems, story problems," Rollo reiterated to emphasize his disgust, "they are the nastiest creatures that have ever roamed the face of this earth. You simply cannot trust them. They lie to you every time."

Nelda used the only armor she had available to stop him. She began to question. Nelda wondered if Rollo had difficulty with spatial tasks other than math. Difficulty in math and spatial confusion frequently accompany one another. That's why she looked for other markers of a spatial disorder. "Do you drive?" Nelda asked. "Oh, God, no," Rollo answered, "I don't drive. I can never tell which side of the road that cars are on, even oncoming ones. Besides," Rollo added, "cars always look like they're too close to the road. God no," Rollo repeated, "I don't drive. I'd undoubtedly kill myself, or someone else, if I did. I take the bus." Pausing only for breath, Rollo added, "Sometimes I get on the wrong one, though. Nothing's ever a sure thing with me. Nothing. One day I went to the dentist's office, and I ended up at the zoo. Can you imagine that?" he asked, not waiting for a reply. "The zoo! Took the wrong bus, I guess," he explained nonstop. "When I got off the bus, I looked around and saw a sign that read 'ANIMALS THIS WAY.' Whoa, I thought! Wait a minute here! Dogs and cats and other furry creatures see this guy too! Time for me to find myself a new dentist I said to myself! Didn't realize what happened 'til I got back home."

"Stop!" Nelda begged, a case of the giggles nearly immobilizing her. "You're killing me, Rollo," and the two burst into another episode of laughter, this one more raucous than the last.

Nose blown and tears wiped, Nelda continued. Did he tell time? "Call me Mr. Digital," Rollo smiled. Did he like to draw? "Does connecting dots in coloring books count? No, I didn't think so," Rollo said, answering his own question. "Let me put it this way," he went on. "After my one and only art class in high school, the teacher walked up to me and suggested, quietly of course, that I never, I repeat never, take art again, at least not from her. Try choir she suggested."

"Well, whatdaya' think?" Rollo asked, "am I hopeless or what?" Nelda assured Rollo that he was neither hopeless nor terminal. "You have spatial problems, and that's why math is so difficult for you! You get lost in time and space." Rollo thought for a moment and then announced, "So that's why I went to the dentist and nearly ended up in the gorilla cage!" Nelda smiled at him, not in joy but in sadness, struck by the cruelty of his criticism. She wondered if Rollo consistently inflicted himself with wounds that way.

"So what does that mean?" Rollo asked again. "Can you help me learn math or not?" Actually, Nelda thought that math instruction was premature. "Oh, God," Rollo responded spontaneously, "it's worse than I thought." Nelda paused and looked directly at the young adult who protected himself with mounds of flesh. She smiled but did not laugh or even giggle as she was often wont to do. She did not want to reinforce his self-flagellation.

"Rollo," Nelda explained. "I have a hunch that you could be very good at math, but math is not the problem." Rollo tossed his head back and chortled, "Boy, I should have brought my checkbook along! Maybe I could introduce you to the tellers at my bank," he went on.

Nelda clarified her meaning. "I don't doubt that you have difficulty with math, Rollo, but the reason you have trouble is your imagery system. What I mean to say is that your underlying problem is imagery, not math."

"Huh?" Rollo asked. "You mean I don't image either? I'm empty-headed after all?"

"No," she said, ignoring his criticism. "Of course you image. You couldn't tell such wonderful stories if you didn't image. What you don't do, Rollo, is make them accountable."

"Neither's my checkbook," Rollo explained.

Nelda continued. "Well, I could be wrong, Rollo, but what I think you need to do first, before you learn math, is learn how to make your images accountable — in other words, learn how to make them better approximate the actual environment." She stopped, then added, "You can do this, Rollo. Yes, you can."

Rollo did not yet understand the meaning of Nelda's words, but he did not question, longing for the confirmation that she offered. Rollo traded wisdom for humor. "Well, whatever you suggest," he replied. "Remember my alternative," Rollo said verging on a wink, "it's either on with my life or . . . " Nelda nodded. Rollo knew she understood. Nelda promised to call the vocational counselor that very afternoon and explain his needs to Wilson. "He's my case worker, you know," Rollo added. "He didn't have to say it, no one ever does, but Wilson thinks my problem is just this." Rollo held his arm out straight and jabbed at the flesh, which hung in globs.

"Wilson?" Nelda asked when she called on the phone that afternoon. "Guess whoooo?" Nelda sang, "your dear old neighbor." Wilson suspected a setup.

"Rollo came into my office today," Nelda went on. "Yeah . . . " Wilson said waiting for her findings.

"And I'm going to hold you to your promise, Wilson," Nelda threatened. "Rollo needs work at the clinic." Wilson thought he could arrange that if, indeed, she'd found a learning disability. "What is he," Wilson asked, "dyslexic?" Not exactly, Nelda said.

"Dysgraphic?" he offered. Nelda didn't think so.

"Well, he can't have any language problems!" Wilson huffed. "That guy talked my leg off for three whole hours." Nelda agreed, no language problems either. "So what's his problem then?" Wilson asked.

"Spatial," Nelda answered in one word. "Come on, Nelda, don't get fancy with me! I'm your neighbor! Remember? I'm the guy who refuses to shave on the weekend or take my baseball hat off when I come to the dinner table. I'm that guy who goes fishing with your husband. Remember? Make sense, Nelda girl, it's Wilson you're talkin' too, a common man."

Nelda laughed. She apologized for using the term, explaining that Rollo did not image accurately. "You mean he's empty-headed?" Wilson asked. Nelda chuckled again. No, she argued. Rollo wasn't empty-headed. In fact, she thought he was quite intelligent. What he had difficulty with, however, was constructing mental images that were accurate.[1]

"Hmmm," Wilson mused, "you mean he doesn't remember where he's been or know clearly where he's goin'." Well, in a way that was true.

"I'll have a real hard time sellin' this one to my boss, Nelda. Employability is the name of the game here, dear. If I try to get this case funded with the information you're tellin' me, I'd be laughed right out of my office. Nelda, you expect a lot from me," Wilson moaned. "What's a dear old neighbor for?" she asked, then added seriously. "He needs the work, Wilson." Wilson promised to fund it, but he'd write the proposal up as math work. "If anybody from the vocational office ever calls and asks," Wilson whispered into the phone, "keep the rest of this stuff quiet, will ya'?" Nelda promised that she would. Rollo was given funding for four months of clinic work. Employability was the goal.

Nelda believed that Rollo did not link imagery and language. In other words, he did not attend to the images that language triggered within him nor did he link his own spoken or written language to his abundant imaginings.[2] Her goal was to teach him to link the two. She also believed that Rollo needed more than rehearsal. He needed to do more than listen to someone talk and mentally picture what was said, for instance. Rollo needed first to shape the accuracy of his images, particularly the images of his environment. She realized that shortly after he began his clinic work. Her belief was confirmed easily enough. For his first three lessons at the clinic, Rollo entered the wrong office. He walked into the one that was adjacent to Nelda's, sat down, and continued to talk nonstop. Rollo did not realize he was in the wrong spot until he looked up to see the wrong staff person sitting across from him. "Oh," he said at the beginning of each lesson. "I must be in the wrong office," he said, stood up, and moved next door.

Rollo and Nelda mapped the clinic and other places that were important in his environment. They mapped his home, for instance, inside and out, and its relationship to significant landmarks. Direction was a huge problem, however. Rollo did not know what direction his house faced or how other landmarks were positioned in relation to it. He did not know what direction he headed when he left his house to walk to the nearest grocery store. Nelda reminded him of one of the most basic of markers: the sun. "Use the sun as your guide," she urged. "The sun sinks in the west. Where is your house in relation to the sun?"

A look of wonder crossed Rollo's face. "The sun sinks in the west?" Rollo said with the inflection of a question. "Are you sure?" he asked. Nelda nodded. "Absolutely certain?" Yes, she was certain. "Every time?" Rollo asked. Nelda nodded again. "You can count on it, Rollo," Nelda replied, "every time. The sun sinks in the west."

Rollo sat back and heaved a huge sigh, as though unburdening a lifetime of uncertainty. "God," he exhaled. Rollo fell silent and closed his eyes worrying Nelda, for an instant, that he might have died. "God," Rollo said as though to himself, "It feels so damned good to have one sure thing, just one sure thing," he said again, acknowledging the certainty and the freedom that an anchored image provides. For the first time, his images felt real.[3]

Rollo flourished from the freedom. In the weeks and months that followed, he looked for ways in his daily life to put his imagery system to work. He looked for ways to move mentally within space and time and to examine, in his mind's eye, places, events, and ideas. "I listened to the radio last night!" Rollo announced to Nelda. "I listened, and I imaged to what the announcer had to say. You know," he said, "I never used to be able to remember a thing of what I heard. Now I just listen and turn on my mental tube. I can remember everything, even little details," he smiled, delighted with himself.

"I hate to admit this," Rollo went on, shielding himself from unwarranted criticism, "but I didn't used to remember anything of what I read either. In fact," he said as he dropped his voice a notch as is to guarantee privacy, "once I read a novel five separate times and never recognized I had until I looked at the signature on its library card. 'Rollo Polen,' the name appeared in five different spots on the card. Isn't that sad?" he asked. "I never recognized where I'd been before."

Over several months Rollo and Nelda practiced a variety of activities to link imagery and language:[4] listening to conversations, discussions, even lectures, and taking picture notes to the language;[5] later, asking questions of the picture notes;[6] reading a variety of print and imaging to the meaning of the language conveyed; memorizing a list of items through the pegword system and other imagery techniques;[7] looking at a picture until he could remember it in his mind's eye; later, writing a description of the picture and comparing his response to the actual stimulus; imaging a remembered person or event and capturing the idea in writing. Rollo rehearsed a number of activities, each one designed to make his images known and anchored in the real world.

With his ability to mentally manipulate his images firmly in place, Rollo learned the fundamentals of math, even the solution to story problems. "You realize, of course," he informed Nelda one day, "that story problems are simply little events that happen in space and time!" His goals accomplished, Rollo decided to challenge the G.E.D. exam rather than take a series of courses. "Why not?" he asked. "I should be able to pass it. After all," he concluded, "I already know how to do anything the exam will ask of me." Nelda concurred. Their predictions were accurate. By linking his images to his language and his language to his images, Rollo blended two pools of his intellect that formerly were isolated and, by themselves, insufficient.[8]

Rollo not only passed his G.E.D. exam, he received one of the highest scores ever earned. He was so delighted with himself that after informing Nelda, Rollo called Wilson up for a conference. "I'll no longer need vocational assistance," he informed Wilson over the phone, "but I want to see you in the flesh to shake your hand." Few of Wilson's clients ever thanked him, and so he agreed, even if that meant a long afternoon.

Rollo arrived in a fresh shirt and tie as well as a new pair of trousers, many sizes smaller than the last. "I'll just take a few moments of your time," Rollo said as he walked into Wilson's office, extended his hand, and sat down. "I appreciate your seeing me so promptly." Stunned into silence by Rollo's confidence as well as his slimmer appearance, Wilson affirmed the appreciation with a nod. "I want to thank you," Rollo went on, "for taking a chance on me. You didn't have to, I realize that, but I want you to know, sir, that I appreciate your kindness."

Wilson fumbled a few moments to find the words. Rollo did not look at all the way Wilson had expected. He was different somehow, not merely thinner, but settled somehow, settled and certain. Wilson asked Rollo his plans now that he had completed his high school degree. "Well, Mr. Wilson," Rollo explained as he folded his arms across his chest, "I'm thinking about college." The prospect of such a leap startled Wilson. Secretly he thought of school as a series of locks and the student as a ship that passively moves through them, floating on top of the curriculum in one lock before being passed onto the next. Rollo, like many other students, learned much more than he was ever told, or taught, in school.

"Yes, actually I am thinking of college," Rollo went on. "I've become quite good at dreaming you know. I learned that at the clinic." Wilson nodded but did not question. He hoped that Nelda would honor her promise of secrecy.

"To support myself as well as save money for my education," Rollo continued, "I've just taken a job as a groundskeeper at the zoo. A little part of me still lives there you know," Rollo added, a twinkle in his eye. Wilson was not certain what Rollo meant but decided not to ask. He had another client waiting. Besides, Wilson thought, he could find out. He'd call Bob Fellers tonight and set up a fishing date for early Saturday morning. Maybe Nelda would fix them breakfast.

- 10 -

I'M TALKING AS LOUD AS I CAN!

Janine Nevitts waited until her mother turned on the afternoon soaps. Even though she was nineteen, a common age for melodrama, Janine disliked watching them. She preferred a different ritual, a seemingly simple one that always ended in the same confusion. Every weekday afternoon, with the sound of the daytime dramas playing in the background, Janine slipped unnoticed from the house and headed for the mailbox, which was located no more than forty yards from the front door. Janine walked a few steps and promptly became disoriented, unable to find the mailbox or retrace her steps back home.

Understandably, her mother pleaded with her not to leave the house alone, but Janine was not dissuaded even though her search for the mail ended the same way, in frenzied confusion. Fortunately, Janine was never lost for long. Clarence Gurtsen, the kind old gentleman who lived next door to the Nevittses, saved her. Every afternoon, even in the suffocating heat of August, Clarence unobtrusively stood guard, anticipating the need to rescue his nineteen-year-old friend, who appeared lost and confused.

Clarence watched in silence, hoping that Janine might find her way home unassisted. After all, he was getting on in years. Eighty-one this fall. He would not be around forever, and how would she find her way then? Clarence did not want to rush to Janine's aid too soon. Still, he did not want to witness another loss. Last week on one of her confused searches for the mail, Janine crushed three of his best dahlia plants.

Clarence stood over his prized beauties as Janine walked up and down the driveway, back and forth across the yard, and cautiously around its edges. She examined the flowers and the shrubbery as though for the first time, talking to them all the while. Loudly, in flat repetitive monotone, Janine talked. "Why does she persist on sending me? Insist on sending me. Why does she fuss and muss and cuss about the mail . . . always, always sending me . . . sending me after the mail?" Janine complained to the greenery. She stopped, stymied by the large rhododendron that she could not get beyond. Confused and frustrated, Janine shuffled her feet back and forth. Her voice rose on the cloud of dust created by frenzied feet digging into a dry August flower bed. *"Why does she persist? persist!"* Janine asked again. *"Always always persist, persist after the mail!"*

Not wanting to startle her nor lose his own precarious balance, Clarence walked toward Janine, cautiously. How beautifully peculiar, Clarence thought as he approached. Her translucent skin glowed white like a pearl from within. Her deep dark eyes, frightened and haunting, seared the landscape or anyone in her path until another set of eyes caught her gaze. Then she darted to an interior place, distant, silent, and safe. Long brown hair graced her shoulders, bony and protruding, the result of a diet that followed Janine's rigid specifications.

"Good afternoon, Janine," Clarence called. "It's a hot one today, isn't it?" he asked. Janine did not respond to Clarence's question directly. Instead, she repeated her complaint in lowered tones, "Can't find it . . . Can't find it . . . Can't find it, Clarence." For a moment, Clarence caught her gaze, and instantaneously Janine dropped her own. She renewed her frenetic complaint. "Always, always sending me . . . sending me . . . fuss and muss and cuss about the mail . . . no mail."

Clarence wondered how Janine could say that her mother sent her after the mail when in reality she pleaded with Janine not to go? Strange, Clarence thought, but he never questioned her behavior nor asked her to explain her statements. He did not ask Janine why she blamed her mother or, for that matter, why she constantly lost her way, even in her own front yard. Clarence knew that questions would only escalate Janine's frustration. Instead, he accepted this strange young woman as she was and neither demanded nor expected a response. Clarence soothed Janine with his talk. He narrated their way back to the front door of the Nevittses' home, described the sweeping grounds, the brick lining the walk, the long, low colonial house that wrapped this way and that, and the front door — solid, stained, and adorned with brass. Clarence rang the bell.

In the same moment, Gloria Nevitts, recognizing that her daughter had disappeared again, flung the door open to see Janine standing next to Clarence, the guardian of dahlias as well as lost souls. "Janine! Janine!" Gloria exclaimed, shouting her relief as well as her anger. She grabbed her nineteen-year-old daughter by the wrist and swooped her inside while Clarence stood at the door, abandoned for the third time in a week. Had she known, had she only known, Gloria derided herself later, she never would have been so rude.

The wooden portal, closed tightly against the world, did not muffle Janine's loud protest. "The mail is *never* in the mailbox! *Never* in the mailbox! Go get the mail. Go get the mail. How can I get it when it isn't even in the mailbox?" Janine asked. Gloria Nevitts did not answer her daughter's question. She recognized that it was not directed at her. Instead, it was directed at the self that eluded Janine, the self that lived just beyond her grasp.[1]

Janine was neither blind, unbalanced, nor retarded even though casual observers believed her to be so. Her eyesight registered 20–20, yet Janine became lost, confused, bewildered even on familiar grounds. Last summer, for example, she lost her way in the produce department of the local supermarket, a place she went almost daily with her mother. A cluster of shopping carts abandoned in the aisles blocked Janine's path. She stopped, her mother browsing ahead, unaware of her daughter's confusion. When a barrage of talk boomed through the store, Gloria Nevitts realized what had happened. Her daughter was lost.[2]

"The onions... and the lettuce... and the lettuce and the onions... the radishes and the cucumbers all in a row... in a neat little row," Janine announced in loud, homogeneous tones. For the most part, the local citizenry knew Janine. They respected her private ranting by diverting their eyes and closing their ears. They moved on by her, not wanting to intrude. Family and neighbors intervened only when the pace and the loudness of her talk increased to a frantic pitch, as it did that day in the supermarket.

"The cauliflower and the peppers... who eats green peppers?" Janine asked herself. "And the potatoes.... Where are the potatoes? I can't make clam chowder without potatoes! Don't they know chowder must have potatoes? Potatoes and bacon and clams! There are no clams here.... No clams.... Where are the clams.... I can't find the clams! I'm talking as loud as I can," she wailed, "But I still can't find the clams!"

To the relief of the shoppers who were wary from the clamor in the produce department, Gloria Nevitts rescued her daughter. "Here I am, Janine," Gloria called. "Here I am, dear," she called again. Come with me, and we will find the clams." Janine followed, talking to herself as she went. "No clams here!" she said. "No clams."

Janine's parents, Gloria and Dave Nevitts, could not define the reason for their daughter's continual dialogue, but they no longer tried to stop it. Years ago, in fact, they stopped believing that Janine's behaviors would normalize because of the external forces that shape most children. This beautiful child with the dark, distant eyes seemed to mature and to learn in spite of her parents' and teachers' efforts, not because of them.

Strangely, she appeared to grow in isolation, like a moth in a cocoon, removed from the pressures of the environment.

In an effort to better understand their daughter, the Nevittses consulted numerous experts throughout her childhood years. Pediatricians, neurologists, psychiatrists, psychologists, a long line of professionals. Dave Nevitts was a no-nonsense, brusque sort of a man, the chief executive officer of a large manufacturing firm. When problems cropped up on the manufacturing line, Dave expected his employees to fix them. He realized that neither he nor his wife could fix Janine, but at least, at the very least, they could try to understand her. Gloria and Dave could not pinpoint the reason for the terror that seized Janine as a very young child or why she reacted in bursts of wild, uncontrollable screams. "WHOOOOOO, WHOOOOO, WHOOOOO," she would scream, like an alarm signaling danger. Why did seemingly innocuous threats, like an open door or a new piece of living room furniture, trigger her rage. "Bad," she would yell when she was just a toddler. "Bad, Bad," she would growl as she crouched in the corner of the living room and pointed at the new couch. Why did she insist on sleeping with all the lights blazing in her room or with one of her parents tucked closely beside her? They could not understand the fluctuations in her moods or the unevenness of her learning. Was she autistic? Mentally disturbed? Retarded? Or worse? Dave's mother, Esther Nevitts, implied that possession happened in families of mixed faiths, particularly if one of the parents was orthodox.

As best they could, Gloria and Dave ignored the guilt conveyed intentionally or otherwise by concerned family members. Instead, they chose to listen to the words of experts. No, Janine was not autistic, although she did indeed demonstrate autistic-like behaviors. No, she was not retarded, even though she had huge gaps in her learning, and although she demonstrated inexplicable behaviors, she did not fit the pattern of mental disturbance. Gloria and Dave followed the recommendations of these same experts — behavior modification programs, family counseling, trial periods on medication, even drastic alterations in Janine's diet. Still she raged. Still she cowered at the change of a room or the alteration of a routine. Still she misunderstood the simplest of concepts like "under" and "on" and "around" and "through."

Once school began, the advice from experts increased. From the time she was in kindergarten, Janine attended special education classes. Classification: learning disabled. "What the hell does *that* mean?" Dave Nevitts asked at one of the elementary school conferences. "Learning disabled. Of course she's learning disabled. Any damn fool knows that, but what exactly does that mean?" he asked the school specialists. No one could supply a definition that made sense to the Nevittses. No one could explain why Janine's aberrant behavior continued in spite of all that Gloria and Dave tried. Why? they asked. Why? No organic dysfunction. Normal intellectual abilities. An understandably stressed but intact family unit. Yet a daughter with bizarre behaviors and erratic academic performances. Why? Secretly, her teachers thought Janine was a little crazy. The Nevittses struggled to understand.

Janine's behaviors fluctuated so widely that her disparate achievements caught her parents as well as her teachers by surprise, confirming to educators their unspoken suspicions. At the age of eleven, for example, Janine's tantrums, which had raged daily since she was a toddler, simply disappeared. The methods that her parents and teachers used to diffuse her outbursts never seemed to have an effect. Janine's tantrums took on a life of their own, consuming her being until the violence ran its course. Yet, soon after Janine celebrated her eleventh birthday, the tantrums vanished, replaced instead by a steady stream of talk.

Janine's reading was equally as mysterious. Previously unable to read even the simplest of stories, one day in eighth grade Janine picked up a story and read it. Before that she was illiterate. After it, she read newspapers, magazines, and books, any type of print, to the amazement of her parents and her teachers. She read as she talked, words falling out of her mouth, one after the other without attention to tone or pause. She could even read college-level print; yet seldom could she understand a whit of any author's meaning. No one could explain why. Nor could anyone explain another puzzling behavior, which did not become evident until high school: Janine's getting lost. Until that time, Janine clung to the adult who happened to be nearest — her parent, her teacher, the bus driver who picked her up at the front door, or the duty on the playfield. Janine refused to leave their side. However, once she entered high school, Janine tested boundaries, especially when she was at home or with one of her family members. She remained in a self-contained special education classroom throughout high school, and she followed her teacher's orders: *never* leave the room alone, not even to the restroom! However, when she was at home or at the grocery store with her mother, Janine ventured forth. Each time she lost her way.

"I have to watch her like a hawk," Gloria reported at an annual school conference in high school. Many of the high school staff attended: Janine's teacher, the district psychologist, the school counselor, the nurse, the vice principal, even the principal. "Like a hawk!" Gloria sighed. "I feel like a jailkeeper imprisoning my very own daughter," Gloria continued, fighting back the tears. "Both of us imprisoned in the house." Her anguish turned to anger. "Janine wants to go outside...on her own...like other students her same age...but I can't trust her...I can't even trust her to go to the mailbox! She gets lost...on the way to the mailbox!" Gloria poured out her pain like a confession too long avoided.

"We have a neighbor, Clarence Gurtsen ...a gentle old man who brings her back safely when she escapes my sight...but my God, Clarence won't be around forever. Who will save her then?" The school personnel remained silent. Some looked away, unable to face the mother who repeated her question, this time in despair, "Tell me...who will save my daughter then?" No one knew. Nor did any of them know what to save Janine from, except from getting lost, of course, or for that matter how to save her.

Janine's teachers did not understand the reason for her strange behavior; they merely regarded her as strange. Secretly, they thought she was a little crazy. They did not understand that Janine's odd demeanor and her unpredictable performance stemmed from profound spatial confusion, both motor-spatial and visual-spatial confusion.[3]

Janine could not move her body easily or fluidly in space nor image objects or events in space and time. As her grandmother observed, Janine "was without grace or imagination." She lumbered rather than walked, lurched rather than ran, crashed into doorways rather than moved through them with ease. The net effect of Janine's motor-spatial problems was her inability to form accurate images of the world through the active exploration of it the way most young children do. Repetitive motor patterns such as riding a bike, swimming, even a simple motor pattern such as jumping up and down were not easy or automatic, no matter how often Janine practiced them. As a result, she could not rely upon muscular imagery to impose order and control upon the world.[4]

Neither could she rely upon visual imagery.[5] She could not image what an object looked like in its absence. That is why as a younger child she reacted so violently when a stranger or a new item, like a living room couch, appeared in her environment. Anything new was an invasion of Janine's space. She could not recall where she put an object, unless of course, she used cues to remind herself. That is why, as an older child, she talked continuously as she placed objects in their proper location. Janine could not mentally map her environment — the route through the local supermarket, for instance, or the route to the mailbox. As a result, whenever she traveled outside the boundaries of her house, she risked disorientation, like a perpetual traveler condemned to arrive in a foreign port.

Not only was she unable to recall how objects or events were arranged in space, Janine could not mentally transform them. She could not take another point of view — imagine what a cup would look like from the top down, for instance, understand why her older sister became enraged with her behavior, or comprehend why her mother was fearful when she insisted on searching for the mail. Her inability to take another viewpoint contributed to delayed social development. In social skills, Janine lagged a lifetime behind her peers. She ignored the boundaries of social exchanges. She stood too close or too far away. She seldom established eye contact and then only fleetingly. She blurted into conversations and ignored the pace of give and take.[6]

Janine's spatial confusion also affected her academic performance. The visual form of print did not appear constant to her until the eighth grade. She could not recognize a word (or a form) as being the same the next time it appeared.[7] As a result, she could not read — could not, that is, until the form of print stabilized in eighth grade, and suddenly, spontaneously, she read. Many other tasks, seemingly simple ones like knowing her height and weight, eluded her as well. When she took her physical exam required for high school, for example, the nurse asked, Janine, "How tall are you now?" "Eleven," Janine answered. "Eleven?" asked the nurse, knowing that the gangly teenager could not be referring to age. "Did you say eleven, Janine?" the nurse repeated. "Yes," Janine confirmed matter-of-factly. "I'm eleven." "Eleven what," the nurse continued, trying to impose some sense upon Janine's guess at height. "Eleventy hundred," Janine replied. The nurse shook her head in disbelief, suspecting, again, that Janine was a little crazy. The nurse did not understand that her question imposed spatial demands upon Janine.

Spatial confusion also explained Janine's compulsion to talk. She could not image an action or an event without talk attached to it. In fact, in the absence of talk, the image did not exist for Janine, and so she talked and talked and talked. Incessantly she talked in language that lacked melody.[8] No contour, shape, or inflection. Janine talked for a reason: to orient herself in space, to remind herself that she was in the produce section of the supermarket or on her way to the mailbox. Without such self-talk to guide her, Janine lost her way. Her verbal navigational system was fragile, however, subject to unanticipated objects, like the shopping carts gathered in the aisle, or unexpected events, like a change in routine.[9] Turning up the volume of her talk or quickening its pace were the only methods Janine had to attempt to regain control.

Janine's profound spatial confusion also explained why she did not monitor the effect of her continual talk or even the effect of her behavior. She behaved as though others did not exist. One summer afternoon, amid a bed of dahlias, an event happened that triggered a series of changes.

On her daily search for the mail, Janine ran into Clarence. He stood a few protective steps behind the dahlias that divided his property from the Nevittses. Today they bloomed splendidly, rainbows of petals stretched forth like arms waiting to embrace a homecomer. Clarence and Janine met at this same spot every afternoon — he behind his delicate soldiers and she a short distance away from destroying them. Yet Janine always expressed surprise at their meeting, as though she hadn't expected him to appear. "Clarence! Clarence!" Janine boomed, not pausing for breath. "I can't find the mailbox! I can't *find it. I've been looking and looking, but I can't find it,"* Janine repeated, her voice rising as she continued. Clarence smiled, as he smiled every afternoon, extended his hand, and spoke reassuringly to his young friend. He paused, stood frozen for a moment, then suddenly collapsed. Clarence slumped to the bed of dahlias that waited below. He died so easily. Gone, his breath simply swept out of him.

For a moment, Janine looked at him and then crumbled to the ground. "Clarence!" she hollered, shaking him so furiously that the dahlia stalks underneath his frame snapped like tender bones breaking. "CLARENCE! CLARENCE!" Janine screamed. The rise in Janine's voice always brought her old friend near. Not so today. Janine changed her appeal. "Clarrrrence!" she called, but he lay limp amid the broken stalks and scattered petals. "Clarrrrence!" she called for the last time. Gloria Nevitts and several of the neighbors, one of them still in slippers and a robe, rushed breathlessly to respond to the mournful siren.

"Oh, dear God," Gloria cried as she saw the dead man sprawled in the flower bed. Gloria tried to coax her daughter away from the body, but Janine would not be moved. She rocked back and forth. Gloria touched her daughter on the shoulder. Janine looked up at her and asked sadly, "Where did he go?"

"Clarence had to leave, dear," her mother answered. "He was old, very old, and he . . . " Gloria stopped, surprised by the significance of Janine's question. Gloria realized that unlike all the other ones her daughter asked before, Janine posed this one directly to her mother, not to the void beyond, as though acknowledging that she existed in relationship to another human being.

Gloria Nevitts offered her hand and led her daughter, who fell silent, back to the house. For the next two days, Janine remained mute and firmly planted in the house. She did not look for the mail. The third afternoon, when her mother turned on the soaps, Janine appeared and asked directly, "But how will I be able to find the mailbox?" Her sense of self had awakened.

Clarence's death and the questions that followed were the triggering events that brought Janine to the clinic. "Can you teach her to find the mailbox?" Gloria Nevitts asked. "Janine really wants to be able to find the mailbox. She has asked both her father and me for days now to help her find the mailbox."

Had Janine still attended school, Gloria would have asked her special education teacher the same question, but Janine had graduated the previous spring and remained at home, both she and her mother imprisoned. Over the years, Gloria witnessed her hopes die. The only wish that remained was for Janine to be able to find the mailbox. Gloria dare not hope for more. Dave, however, remained the incurable pragmatist. "Maybe this is an impossible request," he said when the three of them came to the clinic, "but I'd sure like my daughter to be able to hold a job. Could you teach Janine the skills she needs to do that?"

The clinic teacher, Adele Gray, wasn't sure. In fact, Adele thought to herself, she wasn't even sure why she was assigned this case! Adele preferred neat and tidy ones, the kind that were predictable, not realizing that she did her very best work when students challenged her to teach just beyond the edge of her control. Janine was anything but predictable!

"I'm not sure about teaching Janine to find a job," Adele responded to Mr. Nevitts. "What are *your* goals, Janine?" she asked, turning to the strange young woman.

"To find the mailbox!" Janine replied loudly. "Teach me to find the mailbox!"

"Ohhhhh Kay!" Adele answered. "Let's just see what you and I can do to help you find the mailbox," and Adele asked the parents to wait for their daughter in the waiting room.

Adele recognized that Janine needed to map her environment to prevent becoming continually lost within it. Janine needed to construct a more accurate mental map of her immediate world. Hers was vague, like a surrealist dream, diffuse and disconnected. For the next several weeks Adele taught Janine to build crude, three-dimensional maps of her immediate environment as well as her extended environment — large maps out of butcher paper with items stuck on them. Janine built a map of her home, for example, which not only located the rooms within the house but also the most significant items within the rooms — the kitchen table, the dresser by the side of her bed, the chest at the end, the closet on the wall opposite the window.

Through mapping, Janine learned the meaning of directional or positional words such as "adjacent," "between," "beside," "ahead," and so forth. Janine also built a map of her community and placed the significant landmarks on it — the elegant old cedar at the edge of the driveway, the row of rhododendrons lining the beds, and Clarence's dahlias. They bloomed long after he died. Janine used colored balls of clay to represent the dahlias on the map. Carefully she placed them in rows on her map. After each of her outings, she added other features — the mountain to the west of the city; the freeway that ran through its middle; the domed stadium where, to her mother's horror, Janine wanted to go to watch a rock concert.

As she constructed each map, Janine predicted where the landmarks went. She then checked her predictions by comparing her map to the real world. Janine's inner world became more integrated, and her observational powers increased as she confirmed or rejected her predictions. She began to see the world that had been present all along but that previously went unnoticed or remained disconnected. She added to the map as she began to venture forth and deliberately explore her world, reporting back to Adele each of her new discoveries. *"Did you know,"* she reported one day in her loudest voice, *"that all fir trees are green? Did you know that, Adele?"* she asked incredulously, not yet waiting for a reply. *"I didn't,"* Janine answered. *"I certainly didn't."*

Adele responded with an equally loud comment, *"Janine, all fir trees are green!"*

Janine looked at her teacher quizzically and asked, "Why are you yelling?" Adele responded, "because you were." She taught Janine to modulate the tone of her voice. On a scale of 1 to 10, Janine tried to speak at a 4, certainly no louder than a 5, and to talk at the speed of a sailboat but not the speed of a jet. Janine understood.

Janine also learned to use scripts. That is, she learned how to use her talk to strategically guide her behavior.[10] Instead of talking diffusely at whatever happened to be in her path, Janine learned to be led by her talk. She and Adele wrote scripts, and Janine tried them out in the real world: "I'm going to find the mailbox," she directed herself. "Walk out the door and step off the curb. Face the street and walk toward it. Walk past the light post. Walk past the big old cedar. Walk toward the ivy. Look for the row of posts with the mailboxes sitting on top. Our mailbox is red, white, and blue."

Janine always reported back to Adele on the effectiveness of the scripts. *"Hey, it worked, Adele . . .* I mean it worked, Adele," Janine reported one day at the clinic. "I got to the mailbox and back. Janine wrote her scripts down on small white index cards. She said the appropriate script as she performed the task, and whenever necessary, she and Adele amended the language to prompt the correct action. When the family got a new pet, for example, Janine added, "Don't let the puppy escape!"

Janine carried her scripts with her and used them as needed. When she went to the mailbox, for example, she referred to her "mailbox cue card." When she used the washing machine or loaded the dishwasher, Janine pulled out the appropriate cue card and said the language aloud as she performed the task.

Through mapmaking and scripting, Janine gradually built reliable internal images for actions and events. She internalized those images by rehearsing them, refining them, and attaching language to them. As her instruction progressed, Janine's personality unfolded. She communicated her needs, asked questions of others, and listened to their response. She learned to laugh, tell jokes, and appreciate humor. Her learning not only changed her personality, it changed her angular appearance. Her face softened. The sharpness of her jaw and the fear in her eyes faded. Her strangeness almost disappeared.

Janine's learning made her want to know more. After several months of instruction, Janine exploded with requests for autonomy. She wanted the freedom to move within her environment and the power to be in control of it. She wanted to walk to the store and buy the groceries without her mother hovering nearby. She wanted to take the bus to town, all by herself. She wanted to spend an afternoon at the library and choose her own books. Maybe even go to a movie. Janine liked movies.

With each new territory, Janine's parents expressed joy and terror. "The store! That's wonderful! Are you certain she's ready?" Gloria asked. "That's so far," she moaned. Gloria and Adele struck a compromise. Gloria would walk a block behind her daughter, no closer. Janine used her cue card to lead herself to the store. She talked all the way.

As she gained greater control over her environment, Janine wanted to expand her territory even further. "I don't know how to multiply or divide. I can't even make change," she went on. "How can I get a job if I can't make change? Do you think I could ever get a job?" she asked Adele.

"Oh, yes," Adele replied, "but I think you and I have a few more scripts to write. What do you think, Janine?" Janine agreed. The two of them wrote and rehearsed many more scripts for a variety of actions and reduced the scripts to cue cards.

With sufficient rehearsal, Janine was able to give up her cue cards, but she was never able to give up her talk or even send it underground. Janine continues to talk to herself out loud. She talks when she divides. She talks when she multiplies. She talks on the bus and on her way to the store to remind herself of the markers as they pass. She talks when she dresses for work and on her way to work, her most recent accomplishment. Janine sets and clears the tables at a large local restaurant. Janine talks all the while. Unfortunately, not everyone understands why.

The restaurant manager, Ralph Owens, does not yet understand the meaning of his new employee's continual self-dialogue. When Janine's parents stopped at the restaurant one day for lunch, Dave asked Ralph how their daughter was doing. "Well," the manager replied, "she's a fine worker . . . no complaint there . . . a real fine worker. You can be proud of that."

Ralph lowered his voice as he sat at their table. Ralph fiddled with the salt and pepper shakers, folded and refolded the unused napkin in an effort to dislodge the question he longed to ask. Dave recognized the symptoms of worry.

"Do you have any concerns about Janine?" Dave asked the manager.

"Well, not any concerns exactly," Ralph replied, "but now that you mention it, I do have a question."

Here it comes, Dave thought. Dave hoped he could accurately explain the reason for his daughter's strange behavior. "I've been meaning to ask you," Ralph went on. "Did you know she talks all the time . . . to the dishes, and the napkins, the silverware too. Why do you suppose she does that?"

Dave asked the young manager to have a seat. For the next hour,

Dave and Gloria explained the meaning of their daughter's odd behavior. Ralph listened intently, asked a few questions, and at the end observed, "Ya' know," he said, "I got a cousin, he talks all the time too. Drives us all nuts. We always thought he was a little crazy, but maybe...."

- 11 -

EVERYTHING'S RELATED
TO EVERYTHING ELSE

After his divorce, John Sammons moved to the family farm, which stood empty and still, just at the edge of exile. Located on the rim of the Ohop Valley, the Sammons farm backed up to the foothills of the Cascade Mountains, whose white peaks penetrate the sky. Even as a child, John preferred living out there. Now twenty-eight, in debt and alone, he returned to the Sammons farmhouse to find its windows and its doors sealed tightly as a tomb. Some years earlier when his grandparents died within a week of each other, John's father, Jonas Sammons, wrapped the homestead with boards to prevent intrusions. John removed them and moved in.

John's grandparents, Gunner and Ollie Sammons, homesteaded the land when they were the age that John was now. On the promise of rich soil, they immigrated to this country from Norway, and until they died in their late eighties raised the finest herd of Holstein cattle ever seen in the Ohop Valley. Gunner and Ollie wanted the land to remain in the family. They willed it to their only child, Jonas Sammons, who became a physician rather than a farmer.

Jonas hated farm life. He disliked its crudeness, its distance from civility, and the cruelty of its relentless demands. A dairy farm imposes unspeakable demands. As the only child of a dairy farmer, Jonas was assigned an unending burden of responsibilities, particularly the Holsteins. Whether he was sick or well, Jonas rose early every morning and helped his father milk the cows, then repeated the same cycle in the evening. Every single, solitary day the cows demanded Jonas's attention. He minded their demands almost as much as he minded their stupidity. Just when it arrived at the point of being a valuable animal, the cow would do something stupid, like stray into a patch of fresh clover, eat it, and die from a bloated belly.

Jonas could not abide the futility of cows. He wanted his efforts to matter. That's why he chose medicine as a profession. Jonas wanted to do some good in the world. So did the woman he married. She was blond and beautiful, her skin delicate like a flower. Still, she was sturdy. Given her nursing profession, she had to be. She put Jonas through medical school, and when he completed his residency, the two of them moved to the big city to begin life's important work.

When his parents died, Dr. Sammons sold off the herd of Holsteins, but he could not bring himself to sell the homestead, recognizing that in a real way the farm had prepared him for the rigors of his chosen profession. Jonas boarded up the house and allowed the seasons to take their toll until his oldest son, John, met another failure.

In his father's eyes, John Sammons was a disappointment. John bore his father's name, but with the exception of a few physical characteristics, the resemblance stopped there. They both had a ruddy complexion and a thick crop of bronze colored hair that curled at the edges, but in their faces John and Jonas were dissimilar. Like his Grandma Ollie, John had a wide-open face that burst into an easy smile, a trusting common face that always mirrored his emotions. John could not hide them nor did he even try, realizing that the more he attempted to conceal his feelings, the more separated he was from himself. Unlike his oldest son, Jonas had a poker face, just like his father Gunner.

What disappointed Dr. Sammons about his namesake was not John's looks but rather his academic achievement. Unlike his younger brother, who graduated from medical school, and his sister, who graduated cum laude from Rutgers University, John did not excel in school. He took college prep classes in high school, and he earned occasional A's and B's. For the most part, however, John earned C's, and he had to study hard to do so.

Dr. Sammons blamed John's lackluster performance on the psychological trauma that befell the family when the children were young. John was in fourth grade and his siblings in second and first when their mother's car careened off the winding single-lane road that led back to the city from the farm where she went weekly to check on her aging in-laws. She crashed into a tree and died instantly.

For the next few years Ollie and Gunner helped raise their grandchildren. During the summer months, in fact, all three children lived on the farm. John wanted to live there throughout the year and return to the city on the weekends, but Jonas refused, reasoning that a rural education was far inferior to an urban one. Had she been alive, Jonas explained to his eldest son, their mother would have agreed. Above all else, she wanted her children to have a good education as well as a cultural appreciation. John couldn't acquire either of them on the farm, his father reasoned. Jonas only wanted the best for his children. He reminded them of that, frequently. He urged them to study hard in school. He monitored their homework and exposed them to culture but believed that it stuck to only two of them.

When John entered junior high school, Jonas married again, but by then he no longer hid his dissatisfaction with his eldest son. Jonas attacked John's academic imperfection, picking at it like weeds in the garden. He nagged John, often unkindly at family gatherings, to study harder, threatening that "he would never amount to a damned thing without applying some cold, hard discipline."

Never able to pronounce her "j's," Grandma Ollie urged Jonas to be kind. "Yonnie's not liken' ta books, so much like his papa," she said with a lilt. "But Yonnie's a good boy, a fine boy. He likes ta farm, like his grandpa, yah?" Gunner nodded but did not smile as he reached for his third helping of mashed potatoes. Even though he made all the decisions, Gunner never said much and shared even less emotion, which Jonas interpreted as disapproval, the driving force behind his own achievement.

John's grandparents, his skill on the sports field, and Louise, one of the prettiest girls in high school, saved his self-esteem. John's father and stepmother never approved of Louise. She was the wrong kind of girl, they said, but John saw in Louise a pulsing, passionate, suffering human being who had been mistreated by her alcoholic parents and life itself. John despised injustice. He believed that the truths of life could not be found in ordered classrooms or on surgical wards disinfected of all human filth but rather on the streets and down the alleys, even the long, dark, dank alleys, of human existence. John liked to nourish people even more than he liked to tend the garden on his grandparents' farm.

In spite of his father's protests, John and Louise married soon after high school and rented a small home several miles out of town. Jonas loaned them the money to begin their life. He did not want his son to live like a peasant. He only wanted the best for him. John dreamed that one day he and Louise might eventually buy some acreage a little further out, a plot large enough for a few dairy cows. He found a job in a large electronics manufacturing plant where he worked the graveyard shift driving a fork lift and filling orders. To make extra money, John worked all the overtime he could, but the graveyard hours, the distance from the city, and three babies born one after the other made Louise break her vows. One morning John returned to an empty house. Louise took the girls and, as the note read, went to visit a friend in California. A week later she filed for divorce. Whatever little money he had saved, John spent trying to retrieve his girls through the courts. He lost them as well as the high school sweetheart he longed to save.

Before she left, Louise ran up large sums on their charge cards, so large that John could not honor his financial commitments even though he continued to work long hours at the electronics plant. When he asked his father if he could live on the vacant family farm long enough to climb out of debt, John endured another one of Jonas's endless lectures. "Any clear-eyed kid would have realized that she was a tramp," Jonas said, "ready to take you for all you were worth. Why in the hell couldn't you see she was a slut?" John shrugged, unable to demean her memory so soon after his loss.

"You never would listen to me! Never would," Jonas repeated, his voice rising as he paced the floor of his office. "All I ever wanted was the best for you, but you never listened. Now you expect me to bail you out again. Why the hell didn't you ever study, try, at least try to get an education?" John said that he didn't need to be important like his father. John had a way of cutting to the heart of things. The exposure enraged Jonas. "You ungrateful...," Jonas stopped, reached into his top desk drawer, which he reserved for valuables, and grabbed the ring of farm keys. He threw them at John. "Here," he said. "That's all! That's all I ever owe you. I don't want to see you in here when I get back." Jonas stormed from his office, leaving his son to face life's perils alone.

Part of Jonas's anger stemmed from his son's marital failure, of course, but only part. Most of it stemmed from a vague sense of disapproval. John was attracted to a life of farmwork rather than a profession, as though he longed to return to the very place that Jonas hated. Jonas never understood the meaning of his son's reasoning. "On the farm," John explained during the years his father still tried to listen, "everything is related to everything else." Dr. Jonas Sammons could neither understand nor tolerate such circuitous reasoning. He was a neurosurgeon. For Dr. Sammons, reason ran in a straight line.

Alone in his father's office, John reached for the farm keys lying on the top of the desk. He stuffed them into his jacket pocket and left. John neither heard from his father nor called him again. For the next two years John slept very little, choosing instead to cleanse himself with work. He spent the weekend and late afternoon hours painting and hammering and mending the farm. He spent the graveyard hours driving his fork lift, picking electronic parts from long rows of bins, filling orders, and communing with his co-workers during scheduled breaks. During lunch breaks they played hearts, told jokes, and saw who among them could down a can of pop the fastest. John always won. "It's the Pepsi," he claimed whimsically. "Pepsi has the softest bubbles."

John was the best worker on his shift. He consistently exceeded his quota and taught his co-workers how to do the same. John's work did not go unnoticed. In late March his supervisor handed John a note that asked that he report to Bob Chapman in the human resources department. John hoped he had not failed again. Mr. Chapman explained to John that he had been recommended for a promotion to a floor supervisor of the swing shift.

"Me?" John asked, his face blushing bright red. "You sure you got the right guy?" Mr. Chapman nodded and listed the reasons why. Not only was John an exceptionally hard worker, he also got along well with all the employees, the management and union employees alike. He seemed to value each and every person at the company and never missed an opportunity to help any of them solve a problem. John definitely showed leadership potential. That's why he was recommended for a promotion. Mr. Chapman continued to explain that to be a supervisor meant more responsibility and more pay, of course. It also meant being part of the management team. John would have to leave the union and participate in the company's training program. He had to become familiar with the manuals, the forms, and the written requirements of the job.

John's easy smile died on his face. The thought of returning to school, let alone having to write, horrified him. John could read sufficiently well, although he didn't like to, but he surely could not write. His inability to transcribe his thoughts to language that was correctly spelled and properly punctuated lowered John's high school grades from B's to C's and prevented him from earning more than a D in a foreign language. John could not spell. Given a list of twenty words, John would misspell eighteen of them and never know which two he spelled correctly.

"You don't need to give me your answer just now," Mr. Chapman said, seeing the horror written across John's face but unable to acknowledge it. "The promotion would not be effective until late in the summer, and so your training would not begin until the end of August. Think about this decision, John. It's an important one. Come back and give me your answer some time this week."

John stood up straight and wiped his hand on his jeans before extending it to Mr. Chapman. "Thank you, Mr. Chapman. Thank you very much, sir," he said, penetrating the human resources man with his eyes. "As you can see," John acknowledged, "your offer caught me a little off guard. I appreciate your giving me the time to think on this decision, Mr. Chapman."

On the way back to the farm, John turned the car radio to the only classical station on the FM frequency and belted out the melody to the Italian aria that played. Like most opera amateurs, John could not remember the lyrics, but he could surely sing the tune. As he drove his truck up to the restaurant, John turned off the radio. He did not think his neighbors who frequented the restaurant would understand.

Almost every morning after work and even on the weekends, John stopped at the RoundUp Restaurant a few miles from the farm to have breakfast and converse with his neighbors. They shared their fears, their hopes for the harvest, and their need for one another. John believed that faith was more alive at the RoundUp Restaurant than it was during most church services. It was there at the restaurant that John met Sally. She was sitting at the counter. Her hair was blond and her skin so delicate and unmarred that he could not take his eyes off her. John introduced himself.

"Are you new around here?" he asked. Sally nodded. As a matter of fact, she was.

He thought so. He hadn't seen anyone so pretty around here in a long while. "When did you and your husband move to the valley?" John asked, his face hopeful.

Actually she wasn't married, not now, that is. She'd been married for a while during her last two years of medical school. He was studying to be a doctor too, but the pressures of healing tore them apart. Sally's speciality was family practice. She was the new doctor hired to run the Valley Clinic, which would reopen in a few weeks after several years of vacancy.

"Gosh," John replied, nearly dropping his coffee cup onto the counter.

"Oh, you needn't be impressed," Sally explained. "My family isn't. Both my parents are physicians, and they think I'm absolutely whacky to move to such an uncivilized part of the world. But I've always wanted to be a country doctor," she said.

"You have?" John asked. "Yes," Sally said, "out here, beliefs must be wedded to actions. I like that." John did too. "Yeah," he said, "out here, truth can't be separated from the person who lives it. Out here," John added, "everything's related to everything else." Sally agreed. She took an instant liking to this man with a wide-open face.

"What do you do for a living?" Sally asked.

John said that he was a . . . a . . . well, that he was a fork-lift driver at a large electronics firm in the city, but, he added, he was being promoted to supervisor in a few months. He'd just met this very morning with the head of the human resources department. Very soon now he'd become a member of the management team.

"Well, say now," Sally said smiling. "The management team, that's impressive!" John blushed a bright red. "About as impressive as my becoming a country doctor, huh?" Sally asked. "Yeah," John chuckled, "about that impressive," and for a moment, the two of them embraced each other with their eyes.

John asked if he couldn't be of help. "Moving into a place that's been vacant for a while can be tough," he said, "like reclaiming a patient from the dead. I've spent every spare minute on my farm . . . actually my father's farm," John added, "and pretty soon, now," he said, "the old gal will be blooming." Sally smiled. She agreed that medicine and farming were a lot alike.

"Tell you what," John said. "This afternoon I'll stop by the clinic to see how I can be of help. The old place needs a good coat of paint, I'm sure, and a few new cabinets here and there." He stood up to leave, reached into the pocket of his jeans, and pulled out money for the tip. "Let me buy your breakfast," John asked, as he held out his hand for the slip. "It's the least I could do for one of the most impressive members of our farming community." Sally smiled and placed the slip in John's hand.

After a long night of work, John usually fell right to sleep after breakfast, but after such a rich morning he knew that was impossible. On mornings like these, when he could not sleep for the tumult within him, John climbed to the loft in the barn, as he did as a boy, to look through the top window at Mt. Rainier, which stood stark white against the sky. As the morning light filtered through the streaked window, John imagined the chaos that must be bubbling deep within the mountain's belly. "Just like my insides," he said to himself.

John wondered why he wanted this promotion. He thought he was content with the simple, insignificant truths of helping his neighbors and witnessing the seasons pass one unto the other. But he wanted this promotion, surely he did, or he would not have shown his heart to Sally and blushed bright red when she caught him being self-important. Did he really want to join the world of certainty, conformism, importance, like his father? John listened to his feelings. That's why the mountain attracted him, a bubbling cauldron of energy that human beings could not suppress. John did not condemn himself for his feelings, believing that he would be all the stronger for embracing them. Yes, he would accept the promotion. He would thank Mr. Chapman and accept his offer the very next day. John leaned back and drifted off to sleep on the shoulders of the barn. He did not waken until later in the day.

John woke with a start, climbed down from the loft, and showered himself clean. Wanting to stop by the Valley Clinic, he left the farm late in the afternoon. Perhaps, John thought, he could take Sally to dinner. She'd like that after a long, gruesome day of tending the dead.

During the next few weeks as she prepared to open her practice, Sally saw a lot of John. Some days, in fact, he did not even sleep, traveling directly from the warehouse to the Valley Clinic. John helped Sally discard the records of patients long since dead, clean the cobwebs from the corners, paint, mend, and hoe the clinic clean. As the days passed, John's anxiety increased. What was he worried about? she asked. Her opening the office? Her becoming a resident authority? Didn't he know by now how much she liked him? That wasn't it, John said. Then what? What?

"I can't spell," John confessed, bracing for disapproval to greet him. "Uh, huh," Sally asked, expecting him to admit to something serious. "I can't spell," John repeated. "I mean . . . I really can't spell."

"So," Sally answered. "Have you ever heard of this guy named 'Webster'?" Sally asked as she sat on the floor, exhausted from a day of cleaning.

"I'm serious, Sally, I'm really serious. I can't spell! I never could spell, and here I promised Mr. Chapman that I'd enter the management program at work in a few months. They'll expect me to complete forms, write letters and memos. God, I don't know what I was thinking of when I accepted the promotion," John moaned. "I guess I was thinking of you."

Sally stopped, recognizing the severity of the symptoms.

"Well, dear," she said, "I'm sure you can learn to spell."

"You're sure are you?" John asked. "I can't imagine why. Never have been able to in all my thirty years. Do you have any idea how much spelling restricts an individual's performance?" John asked his blond admirer, "or how much spelling defines his worth?" John added. "My dad used to hover over my papers like a vulture hunting for dead carcasses. 'For God's sake,' he used to yell, 'don't you see this one, and see this one? Don't you see it?' he used to yell."

John was never short on words, merely on writing them. "I always had these terrific thoughts to write," John remembered. "I simply didn't know how to spell the words, and no amount of looking them up in the dictionary, writing them over and over again, or studying made them stick in my head. As soon as the test was over, the words fell from my head like these cobwebs from the air," John remembered with sadness.

Sally rose from the floor and embraced him. She promised that in the morning she would call one of her colleagues in the city for a reference.

"It won't help," John shrugged.

"Trust me," she said. "I'm the doctor." John smiled. "Meet me for breakfast?" Sally asked. "Ummm," John answered as he hugged her back and bid goodnight. John walked to his truck and drove the long winding road back into town. He met Sally the next morning for breakfast. She handed him a prescription with four words written across it: "Another Door to Learning."

"What's this?" John asked. "A course of action for your profile of spelling dysfunction," Sally answered, in her most professional voice. John laughed. "You don't waste any time, do you girl?" he asked. "Remember?" she said. "Out here beliefs must be wedded to action. My one and only patient, whom I'm very fond of I might add, asked for help. It's my job to provide it or find resources that can. The colleagues I spoke to last night assured me that the folks at Another Door can teach you how to spell. They're a little on the edge, I hear," Sally added, "as far as the unconventional teaching methods they use, but you'll like that," she smiled. "Yes, I suppose you will. You like living on the edge."

John called the clinic as soon as he returned to the farm. He asked for the soonest available appointment. It was now the end of April. The assessment indicated that John could not hold onto the image of a symbol. That is, when he imaged words, letters, and their position within words, John drew a blank. He recognized words and letters when he saw them, of course, but his visual memories for them were vague and inexact. John spelled all words phonetically, even though fewer than half the words in the English language are phonetically based. He spelled the word "conscience" as "conshunz," for example, and "tomorrow" as "toomaro." The spelling of small, seemingly simple words confused John as much as the larger ones. He spelled "lion" as "lien," for example, and "easy" as "ese."

"I never have been able to spell," John confessed to his tutor when they began working together in mid-May. Her name was Amanda. She hated her name. "It's just like my hair," she complained. "Can't do anything with it."

Amanda had a broad face and wide, thick hands, the kind that milk cows, knead dough, and make pies. "So, you never have been able to spell?" Amanda asked in return. "Well, you've come to the right place," she continued. "We have a lot of folks come here who can't spell. Yep, you're one of them," Amanda said, as she examined his writing. The pile of books stacked on her desk obstructed their work space. Amanda moved them as deftly as a farmer moves a bale of hay. "But," she added with a lilt in her voice, "you'll be happy to know you're not the worst speller I've ever seen, and I've seen a number of them. You're kind of in the middle, John, somewhere between poor and lousy." Amanda's commonness helped others feel accepted.

"This won't be so hard, John," Amanda continued. "I can read your writing," she said. "Lots of people who come here spell so poorly that deciphering their writing is impossible!" John felt a little better.

"Tell you what I want you to do here," Amanda said, as she reached for a handful of lower-case, plastic, "refrigerator" letters and threw them into a cloth bag. "Stick your hand in there, John," Amanda directed, "grab a letter, and identify it from feel alone."

John felt a letter for several seconds but could not identify it. "My God," he said as he held it in the bag, lines of worry wrinkling his brow, "why is this so hard?" Amanda explained that identifying a letter from feel alone required him to refer to his image for letters.[1] Apparently, she said, his images for letters and words were a lot like mush. "Mush?" John asked.

"What I mean," Amanda began, "is that you can't accurately see the letters in your mind's eye. Your image for them and for words is inaccurate." John wasn't certain what Amanda meant by an "image" for words. "Remember those standardized spelling tests in high school?" she explained. "You know, the ones that gave you several choices for a word's spelling, only one of them correct.[2] Your job was to figure out which spelling was right. Remember?" Amanda asked.

John nodded. "I always scored at the bottom," he said. "In fact, my dad accused me of sleeping through that portion of the test. He never could understand how I could score so high in math but so low in spelling. Yeah, I remember," John acknowledged. "So tell me . . . how come I scored so low in spelling?" he asked. Amanda answered, "The reason is that the image you referred to for words was so inaccurate that you couldn't figure out if a word was right or wrong. Does that make sense?" John thought it did.

Amanda continued, "For the same reason you got tired when you read. Didn't you have to fight the urge to fall asleep when you read." John smiled as he recalled how reading a book always put him to sleep. "Well, the reason for your fatigue," Amanda explained, unable to omit any portion of an idea, "was that your memory match for words was inaccurate, and you had to be very diligent, very attentive to the language structure on the page in order to decipher the meaning."[3]

"Hmmmm," John nodded, still feeling the same letter for more than a minute. "Any guesses?" Amanda asked. "I think I've got it!" John announced. "Tell me the name of that little creature," Amanda said. "Uh, uh, don't pull it out of the bag yet," Amanda urged. "First, tell me the name of the letter." John paused. "I'm sure it's a little 'a,' " he said. John pulled the letter out of the bag and placed it on the desk. It was a lowercase 'u.' He looked at it in disbelief.

Over the next several weeks, Amanda and John rehearsed a number of unconventional activities to improve his spelling. To help him form more accurate memories for the look of letters, for example, Amanda taught John how to identify letters by their visual features. In other words, she taught him to identify the visual characteristics that make each letter distinctive — the features that made an "e" an "e," for example, but not a "c" or an "a." For each letter of the alphabet, John drew a single feature card, spread the cards out on the desk, felt the refrigerator letters, and matched each letter in the bag to its correct feature card. Soon John could identify all the letters without any feature cards present. When he could do so quickly, under two minutes in fact, John progressed to other sets of lowercase letters, each of them flatter to approximate the two-dimensional letters that appear on the page.[4]

John practiced his letters daily, and he wrote daily as well, simple, nonthreatening assignments at first. Amanda and he set up a desensitization scale, that identified writing tasks that were the least frightening to the most frightening.[5] Lists were at the bottom. A letter to an employee was the worst. "No, wait a minute!" John added. "A letter to my father is the worst, the most frightening thing I could ever write." Amanda did not probe, recognizing that John's childhood wounds were far more serious than his spelling errors.

John rehearsed the assignments daily and came to the clinic twice a week after work to learn more. John doubted that something as unconventional as feeling letters could change the way he imaged words.[6] "You have to trust a little," Amanda urged one morning at the end of his lesson. "It'll come. Trust a little."

John drove straight home that morning. He did not stop at the restaurant nor even meet Sally for breakfast. She already had too many patients to see at the Valley Clinic that day. John and Sally had agreed to meet for dinner. As he turned into the gravel road that lead to the farm, John felt his weariness. Or was it doubt? John climbed to the loft and stared at the mountain, its top covered in a bank of clouds. "Sure sign of rain," he said to himself. Why did this matter so? John wondered. Sally didn't care about the promotion. Hell, she didn't even care about his spelling. So why did it matter? he wondered. Whenever he was troubled, John could find comfort in the barn. He curled up into its loft.

He woke with a bolt. He sat up so quickly that he banged his head on a rafter. He did not bother to shower or even to change. Instead, he raced his truck to the Valley Clinic, jammed it into park, and left the motor running as he rushed into waiting room filled with patients.

"She's in her office," the receptionist said. John ran down the hall of the Valley Clinic and bolted into Sally's office without knocking. She feared something terrible had happened. "God," he said. "I saw it! I saw it in my dreams! I've never seen anything like that before! Never! Ever," he said, as he sat down in the chair to at side of her desk. "What does it mean, Sally?" he asked. "What does it mean?"

Sally couldn't imagine what frightened John so. Calmly, she urged, "What, John? Tell me what you saw."

John looked at her and said, "I saw the word 'Pepsi' in my dreams. 'Pepsi' written right across that big white mountain, Sally, in big bold letters, right across that mountain! God almighty," John said. "I've never had a dream like that. I've never ever seen a word before. What does it mean?" John asked again.

Sally sat back and smiled a little. "I'm not sure, John. I don't pretend to understand the mysteries of learning. I'm a doctor. If I had to bet, though, I'd guess you're learning something. Why don't you go ask your teacher?" Sally suggested. "But I think I'd shower first."

John laughed out loud, slapped the barn dust from his jeans, and said, "You're right, but I'll ask her tomorrow. How about if you finish up here. I'll go home and shower, and we'll meet for an early dinner." Sally thought that was a good idea.

The next morning John recounted his dream to Amanda. "What does it mean?" he asked. Amanda wasn't sure. "What do you mean, you're not sure?" John asked incredulously. "You always know what things mean, even when I haven't asked. I've never ever seen a word before like that! I could never picture a word! Never! And you're not sure what it means? Don't you suppose it means my memories are changing?" John asked.

Amanda smiled her big, broad smile and said, "Probably so. Not all of learning is explainable, you now. It happens when we least expect it and at times we're least prepared. It happens even though we cannot necessarily measure it. If I had to bet, though, I'd guess you're learning something."

As the summer lengthened and August approached, John and Amanda discovered more about words and writing and reading. He continued to dream about words — those that appeared on the dashboard of his truck and the ones on the menu from the RoundUp Restaurant. He rehearsed ways to remember the difficult part of a word's spelling, choosing each of the words from the language he wrote. He never could remember, for example, how to spell "lightning" or "frighten" until he identified its hard part — "ight" — and drew a picture note that captured the sound of the chunk as well as its spelling. To signify the spelling as well as the name of the "ight" sound, for example, John drew four light bulbs on a card.[7] He rehearsed other cognitive clues to remember a word's spelling — saying all the sounds that a word makes, for example, or finding a word within a word — but nothing worked as consistently as the method of drawing an image note to capture the difficult part of the word's sound and spelling.

John continued to write daily. He was now at the level of writing letters to different people on his list. When he brainstormed beforehand and edited afterward, John produced eloquent letters that were correctly spelled and punctuated. He also continued to read the kind of print that would be required of him during his management training. One day Amanda showed John how to stop difficult sentences, the kind that appeared in manuals, in textbooks, or in a set of directions. "Didn't these kinds of sentences confuse you in high school?" Amanda asked. "Do you remember that," she asked again, "reading them over and over again and still not knowing what they said?"

Amanda had neglected to watch John's face. Tears welled up. "God," he said, "do I remember." John remembered how his father made him sit at the kitchen table at night and read and reread the directions from assignments or homework. Again and again he had to read them, out loud, even if someone else was listening, like his younger brother or sister. Suddenly, John understood why all this mattered, why the promotion mattered and the spelling mattered even more.

"Haven't you ever told your father about your work here?" Amanda asked. No, John said. He hadn't even talked to him in more than two years. "Well, don't you want him to know? Maybe you're ready to tell him," she said. "Write to him. Tell him about you," Amanda urged. "You may not ever want to *give* him the letter," she said, "but somehow you must tell him of your hurt. That's the only way you'll get rid of it." John agreed. He never was good at burying his feelings, he confessed. The more he tried to deny them, the more separated he was from himself. Yes, of course, John realized, yes, of course. He needed to acknowledge them, and for the remainder of the hour and into the next, John wrote and wrote and wrote.

John looked up and smiled his big, broad smile. "I wonder if I can find any spelling errors in here," he said, a hint of whimsy in his voice. "Probably," Amanda replied. "Bet you can if you look." John erased and edited the few he found and added punctuation to note the natural spaces in the language.

"There," he said.

"Well?" she asked. "Do you know yet what you're going to do with it?" John folded the letter, stuck it in his back pocket, and replied, "I think I'll save it for my kids, pass my heritage along," he said.

"And your dad?" Amanda asked.

"I'm going to go see him, talk to him," he said. "I need to see his face. Besides," John said, "I have something to give him. I've been carrying it around in my wallet for the past couple of years. Didn't know what to say, how to explain. Now I do," John said. John drove to his father's office that very morning after leaving the clinic.

"Dr. Sammons will not arrive at the office until noon," the receptionist said. "He has surgery this morning. He sees his first patient at one o'clock."

"That's okay," John replied. "I'll wait for him here," and he hunted for the most comfortable chair in the waiting room, sat down, and leaned his head against the wall. John was skilled at falling asleep in uncomfortable spots. He'd catch himself a little nap before his father arrived.

"John," Dr. Sammons called, as he shook his son on the shoulder a few hours later. "You can't sleep out here in my waiting room for God's sake. Stand up! Come on back to my office," and he turned around, John following behind. Jonas Sammons positioned himself safely behind his desk expecting to be asked for another handout. He put on his poker face.

"Well, John, this is a surprise," his father began. "What brings you here after these past two years? What do you need?" Jonas asked.

"I just wanted to see you," John replied. His son's honesty disarmed him. "I had one other reason," John added. His father stiffened again, protecting himself.

"I have something to give you," John continued, as he pulled an envelope from his wallet. "For the past two years I've carried this around. Every month I've put rent money in here, not a lot, but the maximum I could afford. Each month I exchanged the small bills for larger ones as the amount increased. It's all in here," John said, as he reached across the table to hand his father the envelope. "There's a little more than seven thousand dollars inside."

"My God!" Jonas cried. "You carry this kind of money around with you? Haven't you heard about muggings and people killing each other for less than that? Why didn't you put the money in a bank?" John shrugged, explaining that he placed more faith in people than he did in institutions.

"Besides," John added, "I hoped that someday I would have the courage to meet you, and I didn't know if I'd be courageous during banking hours. I figured, when the feeling struck, I'd act on it or else I might lose my nerve." Jonas's face softened, and he motioned the gift away with his hands.

"No, Dad, I want you to take this," John said. "Think of it as a gift," he pleaded. "I need you to accept it. You can understand that, can't you, Dad?" John asked. "I don't care what you do with the money," John went on, "but please don't refuse it. That's all I ask, Dad," John pleaded, "just don't refuse it."

Jonas nodded. He thought he understood. He reached for the envelope, placed it in the top desk drawer he reserved for valuables, and said, "Well, son," and paused a moment to check his emotions. "You've been busy since I've seen you last. Tell me what you've been doing, John. I want to know."

John told his father of the farm, how he'd fixed it up, the house and all and the grounds outside. "I'd like you to see it, Dad. I really would. I love it there. Out there, on the farm, I feel so . . . well, I feel so connected. You know what I mean?" he asked. He thought he understood.

John told him of this wonderful woman he'd met a few months ago. "Her name's Sally, and she's a beauty, Dad," John said. "She's so soft and delicate, yet she's sturdy. Sally's a . . . a . . . ," John stumbled, "she's a very hard worker," he said choosing to wait for Sally to tell him herself. "Sally wants to do some good in the world," John added.

John told his father about his job at the warehouse, his promotion, and about his work at the clinic. "I found out why school was so hard, why I read so slowly and spelled so poorly," John explained. "Remember all those mistakes you used to find in my papers?" he asked. Jonas nodded. "And how poorly I scored on standardized spelling tests. Hell," he continued, "I couldn't figure out which word was right or wrong. I might as well have been blind," John said, his father listening intently now. "And remember how I hated to read, and how I read so slowly?" John asked. "Are you still reading that same damned book you used to ask me? Well, I couldn't read any faster because I couldn't remember what words looked like, you know, in my mind's eye. I had to read and reread," he recalled, while looking out the office window, "and I'd get tired and fall asleep until you came by and slammed the book shut." John laughed as he returned his gaze to the present. He stopped, seeing sadness cross his father's face. Children forgive their parents the deepest wounds without hesitation, much easier than parents ever forgive themselves.

"You don't need to know all that," John continued. "I'll give you a copy of the assessment. You can read what it says yourself. I'll even show you what I've been doing at the clinic," John offered. "Real strange stuff," he said, "but it works. I wrote a letter," and he stopped, changing directions entirely.

"Why don't you and your wife drive out to the farm this weekend and I'll show you around?" John asked. John never referred to his stepmother directly by name. "I'll make dinner, and the two of us can walk around the place." Jonas said he'd like that, but he wouldn't bring his wife. She'd left him a few months ago.

Jonas Sammons turned his car into the long gravel drive that ambled up to the farm. The bark of the white birch trees was even starker than he remembered. As a child, the birches frightened Jonas. Like white ghosts they stood, their arms stretched out, their trunks heaving from the thick, green moss that suffocated them. Jonas remembered that fear and how, as a child returning home from school, he ran down the road as quickly as he could into the safety and security of the farmhouse.

"Yonas, yonas," his mother welcomed with a lilt. "Take off ta yacket before you run inta ta house!"

His eldest son greeted Jonas that day. John's broad, open face bore a smile as wide as the gate. A blond, delicate-looking woman stood on the porch. John introduced them, and Jonas understood why his son loved her. After dinner, Sally washed the dishes so that Jonas and his son could make the rounds, to the barn and the garden, through the land now healed from John's care. As they walked, John told his father of his dreams. He and Sally were going to marry within the year. She wanted to get her practice started first. They'd really like to live on the farm. Jonas thought that would be fine, just fine.

"Well, I want to make sure we understand each other, Dad. I want to buy the farm, so that I'll really feel the responsibility for it." Well, Jonas said, he thought they could work that out.

"Good," John said. "I mean, that's wonderful, Dad. I'm glad you understand. You know, I've been thinking," John continued as the two of them strolled back to the farmhouse, "I haven't told Sally yet, but one of these days, I'd like to buy a few Holsteins, not a lot, just a few. More than a few is too much to care for, but this farm needs a few Holsteins, don't you think?" he asked his father. Jonas agreed. Yes, the farm did lend itself to cows.

"Yeah," John dreamed aloud, "we can do a lot after I get the farm paid down a bit." Well, Jonas said as they walked up the steps of the porch, the two of them could work out a fair price. The seven thousand dollars would be a nice down payment.

"Dad," John stopped. "All I asked when I gave you the money," he said, "was just don't refuse it. It's a gift. That money's yours, Dad. I thought you understood."

Jonas nodded. "Yes, I did understand, John, but," he added, "that doesn't mean I remembered. Age you know. Memory's the first to go. You'll probably have to remind me again, son." The two of them laughed as they walked together into the house.

Later in the evening over pie and coffee, Jonas announced his idea. "I've come into some extra cash recently, an unexpected gift you might say, and I just thought of what I'd like to do with it. How about," Jonas asked, "if I bought a few head of Holsteins to put on the farm? This farm needs a few Holsteins, don't you think?" he asked Sally.

"I'm a city girl, Jonas," Sally replied. "I thought farms were supposed to have horses. How come Holsteins?"

"Well," Jonas replied, "Holsteins root you to the land. They connect you to it and to everything else, I suspect, even to your history." Jonas turned to look directly at his son. "Out here," Jonas added, "healers know that everything's related to everything else."

Epilogue

Ethan Groat, the angry sixth-grader who began this book, not only learned to read and write but also graduated from high school and later from trade school. Ethan now owns his own business, an auto parts store, where sales have doubled since he purchased it from his father.

Tyler's baseball team made it into the playoffs this year, and was he ever hot! During one game of the season Tyler pitched a nearly perfect game. Next year, next year for sure, he'll pitch the shut-out, Tyler says. Oh, yeah, he maintained nearly straight A's in middle school, where he was a student in classes for the gifted.

Frank is employed as a repairman, though not within the schools. District requirements demand a high school diploma or a high school equivalency, and Frank simply couldn't muster the courage to face another test. Perhaps next year.

In the spring, Bert graduated from a private four-year high school known for its high academic standards. He awaits college in the fall. Bert hasn't thought beyond that.

Lucille read a newspaper article the other day, and not "no little bitty one either," she wants to add. Even though she trusted that one day it would happen, Lucille was so amazed that she clipped the article out and hung it on her refrigerator to show to her grandchildren when they come by to visit.

Clark has a job as a carpenter's assistant for the summer. He will return to high school in the fall to complete his senior year. Adults still confuse him with all their talk, but he's not as angry as he used to be, even when the principal suspended him from school near the end of the year for using "inappropriate and disrespectful" language, whatever that means.

Liffy completed her first year at an Ivy League school and earned a commendable grade point average, higher than most of her classmates. Liffy is not yet certain what her major will be. She has several interests and wants, at least for another year, to keep her options open.

Before he graduated from college and accepted a job with a large public accounting firm, Steve took the CPA exam, a notoriously rigorous three-day ordeal. He passed it on the first try. Steve was delighted with his achievement, especially in light of what authorities predict. However, Steve was not surprised. He says that definition was the reason he passed the exam, that and preparation, of course. Like most aspiring CPAs, Steve studied rigorously and for months; he also believed. One of the biggest mistakes people make, Steve concludes, is restricting one's achievements to fit someone else's definition.

Rollo will complete his sophomore year of college next year. He continues to work at the zoo, where he has made advancements in position and wage. Rollo's major is political science. After completing his undergraduate work, he intends to go on to law school.

Janine found a higher paying job in a packing plant, and with the additional income was able to afford her own apartment, which is not too far from her parents' home.

Over the past few years, John built his herd of Holsteins to a respectable size and risked some additional capital to begin one of the prides of the valley: the Sammons Dairy.

NOTES

1 / The Giant with a Boy Tucked inside His Pocket

1. Based upon the frequency that they are observed within families, learning disabilities appear to have a genetic base. Quite commonly someone else in the family demonstrates a learning disability, often of the same type.

2. At the clinic, every member of the staff who teaches has a mentor. A mentor helps the teacher examine the way she is heading in the student's program. The teacher meets with her mentor weekly to review the goals, the progress, and the problems on each of her student's programs.

3. As a result of the split-brain operations, right hemispheric thinking has been observed as a real and very different process from left hemispheric thinking. Often referred to as the visual-spatial hemisphere, right hemispheric thinking is far more global and intuitive than its sequential and analytical neighbor. The right hemisphere recognizes input in patterns and gestalts rather than in isolated pieces. That is the way we recognize words, as patterns or as wholes, the same way that we recognize faces, which is also primarily a right hemispheric function.

4. However, some words are more visually distinct than others. The word "people," for example, is far more distinct than the word "on," "no," "saw," "was," "of," or "to." The word "people" has more meaningful semantic features as well as more visual features that distinguish it from other words. Not so for the small and supposedly simple primary ones just listed. For that reason, many primary words are terribly difficult for students to learn. Their features are simply not sufficiently distinctive.

5. For an exhaustive and entertaining argument that reading is not a matter of attaching sounds to symbols, see Frank Smith, *Reading without Nonsense*, 2d ed. (New York: Teachers College Press, 1985).

6. Learning a word involves recognizing its features of meaning. Whether spoken or written, words have a set of semantic features or attributes of meaning. The word "dog," for example, includes the following meaning features: four-legged, bark, tail, wag, furry, bone, dig, fleas, protect, and family pet, to name a few. We use a word's features to assign it to a semantic field or category. In the initial stages of learning the spoken word "dog," for example, we readily assign it to the category of animal. Our understanding of the spoken word

increases as we identify more discrete meaning features and their relationships to one another. Our understanding develops even further as we recognize the distinctions between a given word, in this case "dog," and other words that occupy that same category of meaning. Because meaning features crisscross with many other words, learning spoken words is neither a straightforward nor systematic process. See George A. Miller and Patricia M. Gildea, "How Children Learn Words," *Scientific American* 257, no. 3 (September 1987): 94–99.

7. Attaching language to the image of a word's meaning is as critical a part of learning to recognizing the word as identifying the image in the first place.

2 / The Meaning of Rhyme

1. The largest cost that illiteracy exacts is loss of self-esteem. Frank did not tell anyone he could not read, not even his wife, because he truly felt that he "was not as good" as those people who could read. Other people who are illiterate carry that same burden around with them.

2. In his book *Illiterate America*, Jonathan Kozol encourages us to avoid quibbling over figures of illiteracy and get on with the business of doing something to eradicate the problem. Still, he presents some alarming figures, which illustrate the size of the crisis in this nation. In 1984 the adult population in America totaled 174 million. Of that figure, 60 million adults were illiterate, and that, Kozol says, is a conservative figure. Kozol then places that figure of 60 million in perspective: "I have proposed the following minimal estimates for 1984: 25 million reading either not at all or at less than fifth grade level; 35 million additional persons reading at less than ninth grade level. Note that, in both cases, I am speaking of performance, not of years of school attendance." To be able to survive in this society, Kozol explains, "It requires ninth grade competence to understand the antidote instructions on a bottle of corrosive kitchen lye, tenth grade competence to understand instructions on a federal income tax return, twelfth grade competence to read a life insurance form. Employment qualifications for all but a handful of domestic jobs begin at ninth grade level. I have argued, therefore, that all of these 60 million people should be called 'illiterate in terms of U.S. print communication at the present time.'" See Jonathan Kozol, *Illiterate America* (New York: New American Library, 1985), 10.

3. For the visual note method of learning words, see the chapter "The Giant with a Boy Tucked inside His Pocket."

4. At this point, Frank could read portions of print *if* he had experienced what the print described. He liked to hunt and fish, for example; hence, he had a background for the subject. The same was true of the first aid handbook. In the past, he had volunteered at the county fire department.

5. What happens to our reading when we cannot, for whatever reason, produce language? Our reading stalls, and we remain stuck at a certain level that we never get beyond. We might be able to say the words that appear on the page, of course, but we do not understand beyond a certain level. We cannot make meaning beyond a certain level.

In his book *Seeing Voices: A Journey into the World of the Deaf*, Oliver Sacks illustrates the relationship between language production and reading comprehension. "A study carried out by Gallaudet College in 1972 showed that the average reading level of eighteen-year-old deaf high school graduates in the

United States was only at a fourth-grade level, and a study by the British psychologist R. Conrad indicates a similar situation in England, with deaf students, at graduation, reading at the level of nine-year-olds." Sacks says that "oralism," the insistence that deaf children speak like other children, and the suppression of Sign, the language that the deaf can master, result in the deaf child's academic achievement. He does not suggest, of course, that deafness condemns the individual to limited achievement. That occurs when an individual is not allowed or taught to produce and use language. See Oliver Sacks, *Seeing Voices: A Journey into the World of the Deaf* (Berkeley: University of California Press, 1989), 28–29.

6. Not only did Frank have difficulty producing complicated language, he had difficulty understanding it when he heard it. Hence, merely reading a test aloud to him did not help Frank because he could not control the structure of the language.

7. In other words, Maggie showed Frank a set of simple sentences or he said them himself: "The water fountain has water in it. A bird is taking a bath in the fountain." His job might be to combine those two sentences into one without using the word "and," "but," or "however." Joining the two sentences would necessarily result in a different and slightly more complex structure.

8. These shapes and their use are described in the chapter "Lucille, How Do You Do?"

3 / The Fisherman

1. Reading programs tend to fall into two different types: the analytic/phonetic program and the synthetic/linguistic one. Some reading programs within the first category are more phonetic than others, and some within the second category are more language-based than others. The point here is that each commercially produced reading program can be categorized along a continuum of types. Like a wide sweeping pendulum, enthusiasm for these programs swings over the years. One is in favor, and then the next. Unlike some of her colleagues, Edna believed that the way to teach her students to read was to link the print on the page to language. Hence, Edna was an advocate of "whole language instruction."

2. The traditional "whole language approach" to reading did not work for Tyler. Edna asked Tyler to dictate stories, and she recorded them so that he could later read them back to her. She labeled items in the room and encouraged him to memorize what the words looked like. She read to him, and his parents read to him. She taught him to memorize the words from poetry, song, and commercials and used that language in his reading lessons. Still, at the end of the year he could not read the print that appeared on the page.

3. Tyler could not read independently. That is, he could not read the language in the book or the message on the board unless he was first instructed in it. Even then he needed extensive assistance.

4. Miss Oldenkamp was an advocate of the analytic school of thought. She believed that in order to read, the student must be able to "decode" — that Tyler had to be able to say the sounds that letters make and blend those sounds into words.

5. Dyslexia is not a singular condition. Instead, it has many variations, but the most common markers of the condition are these: inexact memories for the

symbols of language, directional confusion, and difficulty with some feature of language. Some dyslexics do not make an accurate sound symbol match and, as a result, cannot remember what sounds to attach to a string of symbols (letters). Others cannot do the reverse process: recall what letters (or symbols) to attach to the speech sounds that they hear. As a result, their spelling makes no "phonetic sense." Some dyslexics, indeed many dyslexics, cannot recall what a string of symbols looks like from memory. Remembering the direction of a symbol and its position within a sequence of symbols is particularly difficult for them. Still other dyslexics cannot recall how to make symbols from memory, some because of their inaccurate visual recall, others because of their inexact motor recall.

Research indicates that the dyslexic's inaccurate coding of language symbols is rooted in the language system itself. Hence, dyslexics illustrate linguistic difficulties in addition to and other than the symbol problem just described. Some dyslexics, for example, demonstrate poor vocabulary development. Others have difficulty recognizing grammatical and syntactic differences among words and sentences. Others have difficulty with the phonological or sound aspect of language. Still others have difficulty with all the above. The point is that dyslexia can occur in a variety of patterns, and in some instances some of those patterns can be subtle and elusive.

For a review of the literature on dyslexia see Frank F. Vellutino, "Dyslexia," *Scientific American* 256, no. 3 (March 1987): 34–41.

6. The phonetic instruction, however carefully administered, worked no better for Tyler than the traditional language program earlier described.

7. Spoken and written language have a similar but not an identical form. In talk, for example, parts of speech are distributed somewhat loosely with gesture and "um's and ah's" filling the gaps. In print, however, the same grammatical categories are doled out much more precisely. For a discussion of the form of written language see Frank Smith, *Understanding Reading: A Psycholinguistic Analysis of Reading and Learning to Read*, 3d ed. (New York: Holt, Rinehart and Winston, 1982).

8. Most children learn to read not because of what or how they were instructed but instead because of what they discover. Without ever being told, most children discover the similarities and the differences between the spoken and the written word. They discover the link: that the marks on the page, like the talk, that they say and hear, are both language but language expressed in a different form. This is the discovery that kicks their reading into high gear and allows them to read books and stories they have never seen or heard before. This discovery also explains why all reading programs, no matter how ridiculous, work for almost every student. Human beings crave meaning...demand meaning...insist upon its presence even if the author did not intend to convey it. If meaning is not inherent in the print, the student will impose meaning upon it. Learning to read, then, like learning to talk is the natural outgrowth of our need for meaning. Learning to read, like learning to talk, is more a matter of inevitability and discovery than it is a matter of instruction or program. For a discussion of this subject see Frank Smith, "The Learner and His Language," in *Psycholinguistics and Reading*, ed. Frank Smith (New York: Holt, Rinehart and Winston, 1973), 138–46.

4 / Taming a Bully

1. He really couldn't recognize more than a few survival words, and he could not read books of any kind.

2. Not only does dyslexia occur in different variations (see note 5 of "The Fisherman"), it also occurs in different degrees. Al's form of dyslexia was severe not only because his visual memories for printed words were highly inaccurate but his auditory and motor memories for them were unreliable as well.

3. Broad-ranged dyslexics will not learn to read through casual instruction or even typical instruction. They appear to need atypical instruction — that is, teaching that not only is designed for their specific profile but also that is individually administered, at least for a time. Broad-ranged dyslexics do not fit neatly into existing reading programs or commercially prepared ones but need instead reading programs that are designed for them. Without such programs, the psychologist's prediction too often comes true. Al could easily have been one of those who never learned to read. Figures indicate that if students are not reading by the end of second grade, the likelihood is that they never will.

4. Reading is a labeling activity to the degree that it involves attaching names to configurations. True enough, we can and do substitute one name for another. We might substitute the word "ball" for "toy" or "rose" for "flower," for example, and if the substitution makes sense in the context of the language, it is acceptable. So why teach the labels of letters if names can change? The reason is that spelling out a word according to its letter names, not its sounds, often helps dyslexic readers recognize its meaning. "L-I-T-T-L-E...L-I-T-T-L-E," dyslexics might say again and again trying to arrive at the word. By spelling words in their names, they will not arrive at nonsense. They will not call the word "later," for example, or "litlee"; however, they may call it "tiny" instead. Hence, learning to call letters by their correct name helps readers recognize words by their meaning.

5. The way we recognize input is by identifying the features that make it unique — the distinctive feature model of perception. Some argue that letters have a standard set of features that all of us recognize. Others argue that we need not teach those features. Dyslexics, however, do not appear to attend to a consistent set of features. Hence, by teaching them to identify what makes a letter unique — by teaching them what makes a letter that letter and only that letter — and teaching them to sift those features through their language system, dyslexics appear to form more accurate and reliable memories for symbols. For a discussion of perception see Anne D. Pick, ed., *Perception and Its Development: A Tribute to Eleanor J. Gibson* (Hillsdale, N.J.: Lawrence Erlbaum Associates, Publishers, 1979), and Robert B. Livingston, *Sensory Processing, Perception, and Behavior* (New York: Raven Press, 1978).

6. For a description of this method see the chapter "The Giant with a Boy Tucked inside His Pocket."

7. Once they learn how, most readers have a level at which they can operate independently — that is, without instruction, prompting, cuing, or preparation. However, that is not the case with broad-ranged dyslexics. They can learn to read, and they need not have someone else present to help them read. However, broad-ranged dyslexics must take certain actions before and while they read

and continue those actions during the reading process, or they will quickly lose meaning.

8. The idea of artistry and childhood suffering is expressed in P. D. James, *Innocent Blood* (New York: Warner Books, 1980).

9. For most students, continued practice produces better readers. That's the reason teachers often recommend on spring report cards that the student "practice his reading over the summer." For a broad-ranged dyslexic, however, more practice does not necessarily produce a better reader. Specialized instruction is required.

10. For the rationale behind this method and a description of it see the chapter "The Giant with a Boy Tucked inside His Pocket."

11. Reading does not happen in the absence of comprehension. We do not arrive at a sense of closure with print, in other words, unless we understand it, unless we abstract its meaning. Frank Smith, an educator and author who has written numerous books about reading, defines comprehension as the state of getting our questions answered. However, if we do not bring questions to the content, how much do we understand? Asking questions precedes the answering of them. Hence, in order to understand print, to make it our own, we must bring questions to it. See Frank Smith, *Reading without Nonsense*, 2d ed. (New York: Teachers College Press, 1985).

12. In order to understand print, we must also be able to formulate questions of it as the language unfolds — that is, questions that are sensitive to the structure of the language, questions that are sensitive to its form. For a description of the cuing process, see the chapter "The Fisherman."

13. Typing relies upon the motor channel too, of course, just as a written response does. However, once learned, typing one's language is much easier than writing it down, particularly for a dyslexic who has an inaccurate motor recall of symbols. Sticking the letter "k" on the keyboard, for example, is much less demanding than reproducing the strokes required to write the same letter.

14. Bert preferred to think in images rather than in words or signs. He arrived at conclusions holistically, in a sudden burst of aha, rather than in a logical, analytical sequence that traditional outlines demand. Hence, he first learned to write for the purpose of capturing an image rather than posing an argument.

15. Before he wrote, Bert made an outline of images. That outline required him to identify his images in active rather than passive form. In an active image, the subject performs the action. In a passive one, the subject is acted upon. Hence, Bert wrote a three-word sentence for each of his images, and in verbs or pictures he identified all the actions that expressed each image as well as the relationships between each image. The idea for this type of writing instruction comes from an absolute gem of a book: Jon Franklin, *Writing for Story* (New York: New American Library, 1986).

16. Again, Bert made an atypical outline, which he arrived at through questioning. First, Bert questioned himself and others. The questioning generated his thinking so that he could arrive at a point of view. He captured that point of view in a thesis statement, and that is the place where he actually began writing an outline. Bert captured the essence of his point of view in a single thesis statement that followed certain criteria: it stated an opinion rather than a fact; all

terms within the opinion were clarified; the opinion was not only arguable but worth the arguing; and for certain types of papers, his thesis statement had to call for a specific action. Once he wrote his thesis statement down, Bert sketched out a visual map of the paper, and the map captured in picture or in question form the function of each of its sections. Then he was ready to write argument.

17. A personalized list of rules are those actions writers must take to help them think clearly and to convey that thinking to their audience. Writers are very different from one another. We do not need the same set of actions. Some need more. Others less. The task of a teacher who is fortunate enough to instruct students in writing is not to tell them what to say or even how to say it but rather to help them identify the actions they need to take to express their thinking.

5 / Lucille, How Do You Do?

1. Lucille's difficulty was broader than organizing words into a sentence. Her difficulty was with grammar — "the sets of rules that relate ordered sound sequences to meaning . . . to communicate underlying propositions compactly and efficiently." She appeared to lack the knowledge about language needed to convey her ideas. See Dan Isaac Slobin, *Psycholinguistics* (Glenview, Ill.: Scott, Foresman and Company, 1979), 11.

2. Ibid., 171.

3. Lucille did not ask others to read for her for the same reason that Frank did not. She could not acknowledge the shame.

4. Articulation refers to the phonology of speech or the sounds that comprise it. Semantics refers to word meanings, and syntax refers to ordering conventions.

5. In his book *Grammatical Man*, Jeremy Campbell defines language as the fulfillment of our biology, an idea first proposed by Noam Chomsky. Campbell says, "The unique information system known as language comes to humans almost whether they want it or not. It is as natural as the appearance of arms and legs, an accomplishment on which nobody is likely to congratulate us, since, in developing as they do, arms and legs merely fulfill the plan of biology. It is true that a child needs to immerse himself in language and practice speaking it. But for that matter, he also needs nourishment and the experience of walking and running if his body is to develop strongly and well" (Jeremy Campbell, *Grammatical Man* [New York: Simon & Schuster, 1982], 173). We are not so surprised, then, when individuals develop language. Instead, we are amazed when they do not.

6. "The notion of a 'critical age' for acquiring language was introduced by Lenneberg: the hypothesis that if language were not acquired by puberty it would never be acquired thereafter, at least not with real, native-like proficiency. . . . Questions of critical age hardly arise with the hearing population, for virtually all the hearing (even the retarded) acquire competent speech in the first five years of life. It is a major problem for the deaf, who may be unable to hear, or at least make any sense out of, their parents' voices, and who may also be denied any exposure to Sign. There is evidence, indeed, that those who learn Sign late (that is, after the age of five) never acquire the effortless fluency and flawless grammar of those who learn it from the start (especially those who acquire it earliest, from their deaf parents). See Oliver Sacks, *Seeing Voices: A Journey into the World of the Deaf* (Berkeley: University of California Press, 1989), 83.

7. "You can only communicate with another person if both of you have the same underlying knowledge of the language" (Slobin, *Psycholinguistics*, 8).

8. Passive grammar means that we can interpret the meaning of a structure even though we might not be able to produce it ourselves. That explains, then, why very young children understand what adults tell them, or why, for that matter, we can understand a foreign language even though we are not yet able to speak it. See ibid., 76–78.

9. "Knowing a language means being able to produce new sentences never spoken before and to understand sentences never heard before. The linguist Noam Chomsky refers to this ability as part of the 'creative aspect' of language use." See Victoria Fromkin and Robert Rodman, *An Introduction to Language* (New York: Holt, Rinehart and Winston, 1983), 7.

10. The shapes have since been made out of plastic, three-dimensional pieces, and they have been used successfully with many other learners, including a deaf student who could not produce nor understand anything other than very simple structures. Both the color and the form of the shape help to capture the function of the grammatical category that it represents.

11. See the chapter "Taming a Bully" for the reason to label letters as well as a method to learn to link the labels to their correct letters.

12. Again, the goal here was not for Lucille to name parts of speech but rather to discover how words functioned in relation to one another.

13. See the chapter "The Giant with a Boy Tucked inside His Pocket" for a description of the visual note method for learning words.

14. Asking a question is a more difficult syntactic feat than answering one, but it is a vitally important one. The inability to formulate the correct form of a question undermines understanding as well as performance, as Sacks illustrates in *Seeing Voices*, 57.

6 / I Bit Him 'Cause I Bit Him

1. The idea that one of the functions of language is to guide one's actions and to orient oneself was proposed by Russian psychologist Lev Vygotsky. See Lev Vygotsky, *Thought and Language*, trans. and ed. Alex Kozulin (Cambridge, Mass.: MIT Press, 1987).

2. "Why is this sort of schematization in memory necessary?" asks psycholinguist Dan Isaac Slobin. "A moment's thought will make the answer obvious. If you want to recall what happened yesterday, for example, and if your memory were not of this sort, you would have to relive the entire day in memory, at the same rate at which you originally lived it. Obviously, you could make no progress this way. It would take you a whole day just to remember the previous day! So it is clear that we *must* reduce our memories to the point where we can deal with a summary of some sort. Exactly how this sort of recoding is done is still pretty much of a mystery," he concludes (Dan Isaac Slobin, *Psycholinguistics* [Glenview, Ill.: Scott, Foresman and Company, 1979], 156).

3. Some years ago a research team began the quest of teaching an invented language to chimpanzees. Two members of the team, David and Ann Premack, identified several questions of the study: "Can the chimpanzee manage abstract reasoning, for instance, analogies, such as, 'chimpanzee is to human as house is

to castle'? Could it be trained to read maps? To do simple arithmetic? Learn to lie? To deceive others who are intent on deception?" Several conclusions were drawn from the study, one of which is that with the exception of Walnut, the chimpanzees that received language training could interpret actions, but that the chimpanzees that did not receive the training could not. They "failed every aspect of the action questions, while the language-trained animals — Sarah, Peony, and Elizabeth — not only passed the tests, they replied correctly from the very first test." See David Premack and Ann James Premack, *The Mind of an Ape* (New York: W. W. Norton, 1983), 4 and 73.

If language training results in a chimpanzee able to interpret actions, can we expect that language would do anything less for a child?

4. Slobin defines the difference between speech and language: "To begin with, we must be careful to remember the distinction between language and speech.... Speech is a tangible, physical process resulting in the production of speech sounds, while language is an intangible system of meanings and linguistic structures" (Slobin, *Psycholinguistics*, 145).

5. Jerrold G. Bernstein, *Handbook of Drug Therapy in Psychiatry* (Boston: John Wright PSG, 1983).

7 / Patch for a Missing Chromosome

1. H. H. Turner, "A Syndrome of Infantilism, Congenital Webbed Neck and Cubitus Valgus," *Endocrinology* 23 (1938): 566–74.

2. Anne De Paepe and Maria Matton, "Turner's Syndrome: Updating Diagnosis and Therapy," *Endocrine Genetics and Genetics of Growth* (1985): 283. The incidence of Turner's syndrome at birth is + or −1/2500 live-born girls, but the frequency at conception is much higher since more than 95 percent of all monosomy X embryos are lost through first-trimester spontaneous abortion.

3. Bruce F. Pennington and others, "The Neuropsychological Phenotype in Turner Syndrome," *Cortex* (1985): 21, 391–404. "This syndrome was first described by Turner (1938). Subsequently, it was discovered that TS is a genetic disorder which is caused by the failure of sex chromosome segregation during early development, resulting in individuals with only one X chromosome in either all or some of their cell lines (either the 'pure' or mosaic karyotype). The principal features of the physical phenotype are (1) short stature; (2) gonadal dysgenesis, with failure of both primary and secondary sexual development; and (3) one or more characteristic congenital malformations, which include webbing of the neck, shield chest, horseshoe kidney and coarctation of the aorta, among others" (391).

4. Barbara Lahood, Ph.D., and George E. Bacon, M.D., "Cognitive Abilities of Adolescent Turner's Syndrome Patients," *Journal of Adolescent Health Care* (1985–86): 358. A specific spatial deficit may not be present in TSPs who have average and above average intelligence. Instead these individuals demonstrate an impairment in visual memory.

At the time Liffy was diagnosed, the typical prediction was severely impaired spatial function.

5. This concept is frequently put forth informally because it explains most of the major characteristics. Published research has not been located either to sustain or to deny this assertion.

6. Hermann Schone, *Spatial Orientation: The Spatial Control of Behavior in Animals and Man* (Princeton, N.J.: Princeton University Press, 1984), 93. "For the perception of the spatial orientation of objects it is necessary to know and integrate (1) the orientation of the object relative to the body and (2) the orientation of the body in space. Why do we perceive a telephone pole to be vertical? The visual information about the pole's alignment to the body is related to information about the body's position with respect to the vertical. This furnishes information about the orientation of the pole relative to the vertical. The information on body position depends itself on two sensory inputs: gravity and the visual input on the structure of the environment."

7. Ibid. "Sensory deprivation experiments identify the role of sensory input in the perception of space. . . . Man's perception of space is based on an image of the external world as registered by his senses and is continuously checked and stabilized by sensory feedback from his own activity" (148).

8. Mark G. McGee "Spatial Abilities: The Influence of Genetic Factors," *Spatial Abilities Development and Physiological Foundations*, Michael Potegal, ed. (New York: Academic Press, 1982). "Factor analytic studies conducted during the past five decades demonstrate the existence of at least two spatial factors, Visualization and Orientation. Spatial visualization is an ability to manipulate or rotate two- and three-dimensional pictorially presented stimulus objects whereas spatial orientation is an ability to remain unconfused by the changing orientation in which a spatial configuration may be presented. Visualization ability enters into abstract reasoning required in solving mathematical problems. Orientation ability enters into tasks requiring geographical sense of direction such as map reading and piloting an airplane through three dimensional space" (199).

McGee goes on to tell of the persistent sex differences that exist for tasks that rely on these abilities. He also details studies of how hormone levels have an impact on functioning. His conclusion is: "In sum, although available evidence suggests that hormone levels have an effect on sex-related differences in cognitive functioning, the precise nature of the relationship between spatial abilities and hormone balance remains an open question" (213).

Thus the hormone differences between males and females do not yet provide insight into the spatial problems of TS.

9. Beate Hermelin and Neil O'Connor, "Spatial Modality Coding in Children with and without Impairments," in *Spatial Abilities Development and Physiological Foundations*, Michael Potegal, ed. (New York: Academic Press, 1982), 35. The visual system is very important for coding input. The "availability of vision contributed to the structuring and stabilization of the spatial framework within which the stimuli were perceived. However, neither auditory nor kinesthetic information tended to be processed primarily in spatial terms. Since the cognitive requirements of the tasks were the same for all modalities, this must indicate a particularly close connection between space and vision" (50).

10. Herbert L. Pick, Jr., and John J. Rieser, "Children's Cognitive Mapping," in *Spatial Abilities Development and Physiological Foundations*, in ibid. Pick and Rieser conclude that at times a self-reference system can be very sophisticated as it is used to update position. Further, a self-reference system can be immature or mature. A mature system implies the creation of a reference system using more

than a single landmark. They go on to suggest that cognitive mapping should be viewed as a dynamic *process:* "We tended to use the term *cognitive map* to refer to the *set* of spatial relations that people knew, and we were particularly interested in the spatial relations people knew by virtue of making spatial inferences. As our work progressed, we have become more and more uncomfortable with this reification of such mental representations.... Rather we feel the focus should be on the *process* of maintaining spatial orientation. It does seem that some level of sophistication includes not only *making* spatial inferences about relations between locations but *updating* the relation between one's own position and all the other locations in a space. Although this shift may appear small, we feel it is important since it changes the emphasis from the thing to the process" (127).

Liffy learned a process for maintaining control of position through creating a base for her location and amending her image as she moved.

11. Geometry demanded that Liffy understand forms and be able to rotate or transpose them while retaining control. She constructed several hypotheses in toothpicks and "talked the process" until she was comfortable. Soon she could use language to "see" the movement. "Mental rotation is in any event both temporal and spatial, and the relative demands of either aspect may call upon the respective resources of left or right hemisphere. It may therefore be misleading to locate mental rotation exclusively or even predominantly in either hemisphere" (Michael C. Corballis, "Anatomy of a Paradigm," in *Spatial Abilities Development and Physiological Foundations*, 189).

8 / Coach's Choice

1. The etymological meaning of the word "dysgraphia" is "can't write," just as the etymological meaning of the word "dyslexia" is "can't read." Most individuals who are dysgraphic learn to write, just as most individuals who are dyslexic learn to read, but not without great effort and often atypical instruction.

The dysgraphic student usually finds that cursive writing is easier than printing. Learning to make the strokes through the large motor system first, rather than the small motor system, is easier for them. For the severely dysgraphic student, moreover, language often must accompany the instruction. In other words, in order to learn how to make a letter, the severely dysgraphic student often needs to devise a script that captures or describes in language the motion of the stroke. One student's script for the letter "w," for example, was "sweep, valley, valley, flag." Saying the script aloud as he made the letter helped him to code the motion. He said the script as he made the letter until the motion became easy and automatic.

2. For Steve, traditional instruction in handwriting and more and more practice at the skill never made it any easier. That is the case for the dysgraphic. The motor act of handwriting never becomes easier, only manageable.

3. The child with large motor planning difficulties usually benefits from sensory motor integration therapy, but the key is diagnosing the difficulty at a young age. Once the child is past a certain age, motor planning is resistive to change. Too often, however, motor planning problems are dismissed or misinterpreted, as they were with Steve.

4. Written demands increase as the grades advance. In the early grades, teachers often use handwriting as a method of imposing order, quiet, and calm.

As the grades advance, however, teachers use the written response as a way of measuring a student's knowledge. They give math and comprehension tests and assign writing tasks as a way of finding out what the student knows. The dysgraphic student is at a disadvantage, however, because the response required relies upon the motor channel. Steve's fourth-grade teacher recognized the unfairness of measuring his performance through the motor channel. She allowed him to demonstrate his abundant knowledge in ways other than writing.

5. For dysgraphics, handwriting is never automatic or easy. Dysgraphics must remain vigilant. They must literally think their way through the series of motions as they write. Such vigilance is tiring. As their visual control momentarily lapses, dysgraphics misspell, as Steve did.

6. Understandably, dysgraphic students do not take on typing skills with the ease or the speed of their nondysgraphic colleagues. They can learn to type, but learning the keyboard is only part of the challenge. For typing to be effective, dysgraphic students must learn how to use the keyboard in the same way that others use the pen or pencil. In short, dysgraphic students must learn how to use the keyboard as a communicative device.

7. Definition is a tactic, a communicative tool that individuals use upon others or upon themselves. It is a tool that carries a high price, however. "A person who allows himself to be defined by another," say Cornelis and Marianne Bakker, "gives up some of his freedom; a man who applies a definition voluntarily to himself does the same." For a discussion of definition and other communicative weapons see Cornelis B. Bakker and Marianne K. Bakker-Rabdau, *No Trespassing: Explorations in Human Territoriality* (San Francisco: Chandler and Sharp Publishers, 1973), 176–77.

9 / The Sun Sinks in the West

1. A. R. Luria in his book *The Mind of a Mnemonist* (Cambridge, Mass.: Harvard University Press, 1987) describes a man whose memory was so vast and accurate that he had to mentally burn unwanted information to be free of it.

2. *Thinking Visually* and *Seeing with the Mind's Eye* are two wonderful references full of imagery techniques. See Mike Samuels, M.D. and Nancy Samuels, *Seeing with the Mind's Eye: The History, Techniques and Uses of Visualization* (New York: Random House, 1975); Robert H. McKim *Thinking Visually: A Strategy Manual for Problem Solving* (Belmont, Calif.: Lifetime Learning Publications, 1980).

3. Our images are a base. We refer to them and wrap our language around them. An image that is anchored takes on power.

4. The rationale for this instruction was to teach Rollo to attend to the meaning of the language message as well as to remember that message. Too often students try to remember the *exact* language that they hear or read. They do not sift through the language to get at the heart of its meaning, the image it attempts to convey. Hence, when they try to retrieve what they heard in a lecture or read in a book, they cannot remember. Small wonder. They did not get below the surface level of the language. They did not get to its meaning.

5. Taking visual notes (or picture notes) to incoming language does not rely upon the drawing ability of the student. Scratches, squiggles, and stick figures will do. A picture note is effective if, later, the student can recall the content from

the drawing alone. The reason this method works is that it forces the student to mentally examine the meaning of the language.

6. To be effective, picture notes should be able to answer the type of questions that the teacher would ask us on a test.

7. See McKim, *Thinking Visually: A Strategy Manual for Problem Solving.*

8. In his book *Extraordinary People*, Darold A. Treffert, M.D., uses the term "islands of intellect" to describe the unusual abilities of the "idiot savants." At the clinic, we prefer to think of intellect as a series of pools where the waters of one can be joined to the waters of the other and thereby strengthen both.

10 / I'm Talking as Loud as I Can!

1. Like blindness in some children, spatial difficulties that have an impact on more than one sensory modality can also have pronounced effects on the organization of personality. Selma Fraiberg, *Insights from the Blind: Comparative Studies of Blind and Sighted Infants* (New York: New American Library, 1977).

2. For a narrative account of pronounced visual-spatial confusion, see the title story of Oliver Sacks, *The Man Who Mistook His Wife for a Hat and Other Clinical Tales* (New York: Harper & Row, 1987), 8–22.

3. Spatial thinking, or the lack of it, affects an individual's performance in many ways. It has an impact on the ability to make estimations, for example, manage or even tell time, compute, solve the simplest of story problems, and understand relational language. For a discussion of spatial processing as well as measures to test it, see Alexander Luria, *The Working Brain: An Introduction to Neuropsychology*, trans. Basil Haigh (New York: Basic Books, 1973), 169–86.

4. Evidence suggests that children learn much about the world through the active exploration of it and that "enactive representation" or muscular imagery is an early means for mentally representing objects. See Dan Isaac Slobin, *Psycholinguistics*, 2d ed. (Glenview, Ill.: Scott, Foresman and Company, 1979), 148–50.

5. For many years, psychologists and educational philosophers, discredited the very existence of imagery as a form of thinking, dismissing it instead to the realm of the artist or the mystic. Unless it could somehow be measured, quantified, and analyzed, the psychologists argued, imagery did not exist. With the brain mapping studies as well as the split-brain studies, imagery came to be accepted as an actual phenomenon. For a discussion of imagery see Stephen Michael Kosslyn, *Ghosts in the Mind's Machine* (New York: W. W. Norton, 1983), and *Image and Mind* by the same author (Cambridge: Harvard University Press, 1980).

6. Like many other individuals who demonstrate spatial confusion, Janine invaded the territories of others. She did not do so intentionally, of course, because for her territories did not exist. Just as she did not recognize the physical boundaries within her environment, Janine did not perceive social boundaries. She ignored or invaded the psychological space of others, for example, and she invaded the physical space of others as well. She did not give others the amount of attention they needed or wanted, not even her parents. She behaved as though others did not exist. She did not give others the amount of physical space they needed to feel comfort. Instead, she came uncomfortably close and talked at an uncomfortably loud level, unaware that by doing so she invaded the listener's physical space. For a discussion of these and other territories observed in social

exchanges, see Cornelis B. Bakker and Marianne K. Bakker-Rabdau, *No Trespassing! Explorations in Human Territoriality* (Novato, Calif.: Chandler & Sharp Publishers, 1973).

7. Constancy of form is one of the precursors to reading. For a discussion see Frank Smith, *Understanding Reading: A Psycholinguistic Analysis of Reading and Learning to Read*, 3d ed. (New York: Holt, Rinehart and Winston, 1982), 107–8.

8. The "melody" of speech appears to be a spatial concern. See Luria, *The Working Brain: An Introduction to Neuropsychology.*

9. Janine's continual dialogue resembled the egocentric speech of very young children. Egocentric speech is characterized by its vocal quality, outward as opposed to inward. Its function is self-guidance, a vehicle designed to free the individual from dependence upon the immediate events in the environment so that mental planning and voluntary behavior can occur. Hence, egocentric speech is the stage at which the child begins to anticipate, program, and regulate behavior.

Young children cannot direct their actions verbally in covert fashion the way that adults do, and as a result their dialogue remains outside. As the child develops, egocentric speech "goes underground" to become inner speech. Janine's speech never did so. See the following sources: Philip S. Dale, *Language Development: Structure and Function*, 2d ed. (New York: Holt, Rinehart and Winston, 1976), and Alexander Luria, *The Making of Mind: A Personal Account of Soviet Psychology*, ed. Michael and Sheila Cole (Cambridge: Harvard University Press, 1979).

10. Scripting is different from inner speech. Whereas inner speech can be, as it was all the previous years for Janine, a commentary on the world, scripting became a strategic way for her to impose her language *on* the world and *on* her behavior. Scripting allowed Janine to guide herself with intent, to program and plan her behavior.

11 / Everything's Related to Everything Else

1. By feeling the letter, John had to refer to his memory match for it. The task was hard. When he felt a letter, he could not easily identify it because the memories he had stored for letters and words were diffuse.

2. Individuals, like John, who have an inaccurate memory match for words should never be tested this way in spelling. They should never be forced to sort through a number of misspellings to the one word that is correct. Tested this way, they will not know which word is correctly spelled because their memory match is tenuous. Instead, they should be tested by simply spelling the word.

3. A reader who does not have an accurate memory match for printed words must rely even more than usual upon the sense of the sentence to figure out the word in question. When a reader constantly refers to an inaccurate memory match for words, fatigue is the result.

4. Many individuals who have difficulty learning to spell (as well as read) simply do not recognize the distinguishing features symbols. In other words, they do not attend to the unique characteristics of a word. For a discussion of this concept, see note 5 of the chapter "Taming a Bully."

5. A desensitization scale is a technique borrowed from counselors who use it to teach clients to manage their fears. A desensitization scale slices the fear into manageable tasks. The client rehearses the easiest, least fearful task until the client feels under control and ready to go on to the next task on the scale. A person who is terrorized by the thought of going to the dentist, for example, might begin by looking up the list of dentists in the phone book. Once the fear leaves, the person is ready to proceed to the next task on the scale. John continued writing lists until he felt ready to move on to the next task on his scale: writing notes to himself. He had nearly twenty different tasks on his scale. Writing a letter to his father was at the top, the scariest task of all.

6. Over the years John had tried to remember the spelling of words by writing them over and over again. Motor rehearsal did not improve his spelling performance. He tried looking at them over and over again, hoping that somehow he would remember how they were spelled. That didn't work either. More and more traditional practice does not work with the genuinely poor speller, however. The function of John's clinic program was to help him code more accurate memories for symbols, not merely rehearse what he already knew about them.

7. What's the difference between those who spell accurately and those who don't? Good spellers know what a word "looks like" in their heads. They don't even need to close their eyes to "see" the word's spelling. The image pops before them, and they know with certainty what symbols (or letters) to attach to the word and the sounds within it. Poor spellers don't, in varying degrees. Feeling letters, identifying their tactual and visual features, and linking the sound to an image help the really poor speller like John become an accurate one.

Another Door to Learning in Tacoma, Washington, has been a crucible for the research and development of innovative methods and materials for over a decade.

Our mission is to help all individuals achieve their potential. In this spirit, we offer educational resources and learning tools for teachers, parents, and communities nationwide. These include the following:

- On-site workshops
- Clinic internships
- Teaching materials
- Videos
- Audio tapes

For more information, please call or write:

Another Door to Learning
3519 S. 30th St.
Tacoma, WA 98409
(206) 627-0139

BIBLIOGRAPHY

Arnhein, Rudolf. *Visual Thinking*. Berkeley: University of California Press, 1969.

Bakker, Cornelis, and Marianne K. Bakker-Rabdau. *No Trespassing: Explorations in Human Territoriality*. Novato, Calif.: Chandler & Sharp Publishers, 1973.

Bernstein, Jerrold G. *Handbook of Drug Therapy in Psychiatry*. Boston: John Wright PSG, 1983.

Bronowski, Jacob. *The Origins of Knowledge and Imagination*. New Haven: Yale University Press, 1978.

Bruner, Jerome. *Child's Talk: Learning to Use Language*. New York: W. W. Norton, 1983.

Campbell, Jeremy. *Grammatical Man: Information, Entropy, Language, and Life*. New York: Simon & Schuster, 1982.

————. *The Improbable Machine: What New Discoveries in Artificial Intelligence Reveal about the Mind*. New York: Simon & Schuster, 1989.

Carrol, Patrick L., S.J., and Katherine Marie Dyckman, S.N.J.M. *Chaos or Creation: Spirituality in Mid-Life*. New York: Paulist Press, 1986.

Cavey, Diane Walton. *Dysgraphia: Why Johnny Can't Write*. Danville, Ill.: Interstate Publishers, 1987.

Chomsky, Noam. *Syntactic Structures*. Paris: Mouton Publishers, 1957.

Corballis, Michael C. "Anatomy of a Paradigm." In *Spatial Abilities Development and Physiological Foundations*, ed. Michael Potegal. New York: Academic Press, 1982.

Dale, Philip S. *Language Development: Structure and Function*, 2d ed. New York: Holt, Rinehart and Winston, 1976.

De Paepe, Anne, and Maria Matton. "Turner's Syndrome: Updating Diagnosis and Therapy." In *Endocrine Genetics and Genetics of Growth* (1985): 283.

Eccles, John C. *The Understanding of the Brain*, 2d ed. New York: McGraw-Hill, 1977.

Fraiberg, Selma. *Insights from the Blind: Comparative Studies of Blind and Sighted Infants*. New York: New American Library, 1977.

Franklin, Jon. *Writing for Story: Craft Secrets of Dramatic Nonfiction by a Two-Time Pulitzer Prize Winner*. New York: New American Library, 1986.

Fromkin, Victoria, and Robert Rodman. *An Introduction to Language*, 3d ed. New York: Holt, Rinehart and Winston, 1983.

Gardner, Howard. *The Shattered Mind: The Person after Brain Damage*. New York: Vintage Books, 1976.

———. *The Mind's New Science: A History of the Cognitive Revolution*. New York: Basic Books, 1985.

Gazzaniga, Michael S., and Joseph E. LeDoux. *The Integrated Mind*. New York: Plenum Press, 1979.

Hart, Charles. *Without Reason: A Family Copes with Two Generations of Autism*. New York: Harper & Row, 1989.

Hermelin, Beate, and Neil O'Connor. "Spatial Modality Coding in Children with and without Impairments." In *Spatial Abilities Development and Physiological Foundations*, ed. Michael Potegal. New York: Academic Press, 1982.

James, P. D. *Innocent Blood*. New York: Warner Books, 1980.

Johnson, Pauline. *Creating with Paper*. Seattle: University of Washington Press, 1975.

Kail, Robert. *The Development of Memory in Children*. San Francisco: W. H. Freeman, 1979.

Kosslyn, Stephen Michael. *Image and Mind*. Cambridge, Mass.: Harvard University Press, 1980.

———. *Ghosts in the Mind's Machine: Creating and Using Images in the Brain*. New York: W. W. Norton, 1983.

Kozol, Jonathan. *Illiterate America*. New York: New American Library, 1985.

Lahood, Barbara, Ph.D., and George E. Bacon, M.D. "Cognitive Abilities of Adolescent Turner's Syndrome Patients." In *Journal of Adolescent Health Care* (1985–86): 358.

Levine, Melvin D., M.D. *Developmental Variation and Learning Disorders*. Cambridge, Mass.: Educators Publishing Service, 1987.

Livingston, Robert B., M.D. *Sensory Processing, Perception, and Behavior*. New York: Raven Press, 1978.

Loftus, Geoffrey R., and Elizabeth F. Loftus. *Human Memory: The Processing of Information*. Hillsdale, N.J.: Lawrence Erlbaum, 1976.

Luria, A. R. *The Working Brain: An Introduction to Neuropsychology*. New York: Basic Books, 1973.

———. *The Making of Mind: A Personal Account of Soviet Psychology*, ed. Michael Cole and Sheila Cole. Cambridge, Mass.: Harvard University Press, 1979.

———. *The Mind of a Mnemonist*. Cambridge, Mass.: Harvard University Press, 1987.

McGee, Mark G. "Spatial Abilities: The Influence of Genetic Factors." In *Spatial Abilities Development and Physiological Foundations*, ed. Michael Potegal. New York: Academic Press, 1982.

McKim, Robert H. *Thinking Visually: A Strategy Manual for Problem Solving*. Belmont, Calif.: Lifetime Learning Publications, 1980.

Miller, Jonathan. *States of Mind*. New York: Pantheon Books, 1983.

Nicolaides, Kimon. *The Natural Way to Draw*. Boston, Mass.: Houghton Mifflin, 1969.

Payne, Lucille Vaughan. *The Lively Art of Writing*. Chicago: Follett Publishing Company, 1965.

Pennington, Bruce F., et al. "The Neuropsychological Phenotype in Turner's Syndrome." In *Cortex* 21 (1985): 391–404.

Piaget, Jean. *Structuralism*. New York: Harper & Row, 1968.

Pick, Anne D., ed. *Perception and Its Development*. Hillsdale, N.J.: Lawrence Erlbaum, 1979.

Premack, David, and Ann James Premack. *The Mind of an Ape*. New York: W. W. Norton, 1983.

Readings from Scientific American: The Mind's Eye, with Jeremy M. Wolfe. New York: W. H. Freeman, 1986.

Sacks, Oliver, M.D. *The Man Who Mistook His Wife for a Hat and Other Clinical Tales*. New York: Harper & Row, 1987.

————. *Seeing Voices: A Journey into the World of the Deaf*. Berkeley: University of California Press, 1989.

Samples, Bob. *The Metaphoric Mind: A Celebration of Creative Consciousness*. Reading, Mass.: Addison-Wesley, 1976.

Samuels, Mike, M.D., and Nancy Samuels. *Seeing with the Mind's Eye: The History, Techniques and Uses of Visualization*. New York: Random House, 1975.

Schone, Hermann. *Spatial Orientation: The Spatial Control of Behavior in Animals and Man*. Princeton, N.J.: Princeton University Press, 1984.

Slobin, Dan Isaac. *Psycholinguistics*, 2d ed. Glenview, Ill.: Scott, Foresman, 1979.

Smith, Frank. "The Learner and His Language." In *Psycholinguistics and Reading*, ed. Frank Smith. New York: Holt, Rinehart and Winston, 1973.

————. *Understanding Reading: A Psycholinguistic Analysis of Reading and Learning to Read*, 3d ed. New York: Holt, Rinehart and Winston, 1982.

————. *Reading without Nonsense*, 2d ed. New York: Teachers College Press, 1985.

Snyder, Solomon H. *Drugs and the Brain*. New York: Scientific American Books, 1986.

Treffert, Darold A., M.D. *Extraordinary People: Understanding "Idiot Savants."* New York: Harper & Row, 1989.

Vygotsky, Lev. *Thought and Language*, ed. Alex Kozulin. Cambridge, Mass.: MIT Press, 1987.

THE CROSSROAD
COUNSELING LIBRARY
Books of Related Interest

James Archer, Jr.
COUNSELING COLLEGE STUDENTS
A Practical Guide for Teachers, Parents, and Counselors
"Must reading for everyone on campus—professors, administrators, dorm personnel, chaplains, and friends—as well as parents and other counselors to whom college students turn for support."—*Dr. William Van Ornum*
$17.95

Denyse Beaudet
ENCOUNTERING THE MONSTER
Pathways in Children's Dreams
Based on original empirical research, and with recourse to the works of Jung, Neumann, Eliade, Marie-Louise Franz, and others, this book offers proven methods of approaching and understanding the dream life of children. $17.95

Robert W. Buckingham
CARE OF THE DYING CHILD
A Practical Guide for Those Who Help Others
"Buckingham's book delivers a powerful, poignant message deserving a wide readership."—*Library Journal* $17.95

Alastair V. Campbell, ed.
A DICTIONARY OF PASTORAL CARE
Provides information on the essentials of counseling and the kinds of problems encountered in pastoral practice. The approach is interdenominational and interdisciplinary. Contains over 300 entries by 185 authors in the fields of theology, philosophy, psychology, and sociology as well as from the theoretical background of psychotherapy and counseling. $24.50

David A. Crenshaw
BEREAVEMENT
Counseling the Grieving throughout the Life Cycle
Grief is examined from a life cycle perspective, infancy to old age. Special
losses and practical strategies for frontline caregivers highlight this
comprehensive guidebook. $17.95 hardcover $10.95 paperback

Paul J. Curtin
HIDDEN RICHES
Stories of ACOAs on the Journey of Recovery
A book of hope and healing for every ACOA or for anyone who knows
and loves someone who grew up in a dysfunctional family.
$8.95 paperback

Paul J. Curtin
TUMBLEWEEDS
A Therapist's Guide to Treatment of ACOAs
A book for those who are ACOAs and for those who wish to help ACOAs
in their search to experience and share themselves honestly.
$7.95 paperback

Paul J. Curtin
RESISTANCE AND RECOVERY
For Adult Children of Alcoholics
The ideal companion to *Tumbleweeds, Resistance and Recovery* shows how
resistance is vital and necessary to recovery when obstacles are turned into
growth opportunities.
$7.95 paperback

Reuben Fine
THE HISTORY OF PSYCHOANALYSIS
New Expanded Edition
"Objective, comprehensive, and readable. A rare work. Highly
recommended, whether as an introduction to the field or as a fresh
overview to those already familiar with it."—*Contemporary Psychology*
$24.95 paperback

Reuben Fine
LOVE AND WORK
The Value System of Psychoanalysis
"A very perceptive approach to psychoanalytic thinking and one that will
gain momentum as time goes on. ... Fresh, insightful, and daring."
—*Choice* $24.95

Raymond B. Flannery, Jr.
BECOMING STRESS-RESISTANT
Through the Project SMART Program
"An eminently practical book with the goals of helping men and women
of the 1990s make changes in their lives."—*Charles V. Ford, Academy of
Psychosomatic Medicine* $17.95

Marylou Hughes
THE NURSING HOME EXPERIENCE
A Family Guide to Making It Better
A book of encouragement and answers to help the relatives of the forty-three percent of Americans over 65 who will live in nursing homes before they die, before, during and after the difficult experience. $17.95

Marylou Hughes
MARRIAGE COUNSELING
An Essential Handbook
Concise, practical, and up-to-date—an effective guide to counseling individuals, couples, and groups. $17.95

E. Clay Jorgensen
CHILD ABUSE
A Practical Guide for Those Who Help Others
Essential information and practical advice for caregivers called upon to help both child and parent in child abuse. $16.95

Eugene Kennedy
CRISIS COUNSELING
The Essential Guide for Nonprofessional Counselors
"An outstanding author of books on personal growth selects types of personal crises that our present life-style has made commonplace and suggests effective ways to deal with them."—*Best Sellers* $10.95

Eugene Kennedy and Sara Charles, M. D.
ON BECOMING A COUNSELOR
A Basic Guide for
Nonprofessional Counselors
New expanded edition of an indispensable resource. A field guide to understanding and responding to troubled people.
$27.95 hardcover
$15.95 paperback

Eugene Kennedy
SEXUAL COUNSELING
A Practical Guide for Those Who Help Others
Newly revised and up-to-date edition, with a new chapter on the counselor and AIDS, of an essential book on counseling people with sexual problems. $17.95

Judith M. Knowlton
HIGHER POWERED
A Ninety Day Guide to
Serenity and Self-Esteem
"A treasure! Not only those in recovery, but everyone seeking peace and self-assurance will benefit from the ideas and inspiration in this excellent book."—*Thomas W. Perrin*
$9.95 paperback

Bonnie Lester
WOMEN AND AIDS
A Practical Guide for Those Who Help Others
Provides positive ways for women to deal with their fears, and to help
others who react with fear to people who have AIDS. $15.95

Robert J. Lovinger
RELIGION AND COUNSELING
The Psychological Impact of Religious Belief
How counselors and clergy can best understand the important emotional
significance of religious thoughts and feelings. $17.95

Sophie L. Lovinger,
Mary Ellen Brandell, and
Linda Seestedt-Stanford
LANGUAGE LEARNING DISABILITIES
A New and Practical Approach for
Those Who Work with Children and Their Families
Here is new information, together with practical suggestions, on how
teachers, therapists, and families can work together to give learning
disabled children new strengths. $22.95

Helen B. McDonald and Audrey I. Steinhorn
HOMOSEXUALITY
A Practical Guide to Counseling Lesbians, Gay Men, and Their Families
A sensitive guide to better understanding and counseling gay men,
lesbians, and their parents, at every stage of their lives. $17.95

James McGuirk and Mary Elizabeth McGuirk
FOR WANT OF A CHILD
A Psychologist and His Wife Explore the Emotional
Effects and Challenges of Infertility
A new understanding of infertility that comes from one couple's lived
experience, as well as sound professional advice for couples and
counselors. $17.95

Janice N. McLean and Sheila A. Knights
PHOBICS AND OTHER PANIC VICTIMS
A Practical Guide for Those Who Help Them
"A must for the phobic, spouse and family, and for the physician and
support people who help them." —*Arthur B. Hardy, M. D., Founder,*
TERRAP Phobia Program $17.95

John B. Mordock and William Van Ornum
CRISIS COUNSELING WITH CHILDREN AND ADOLESCENTS
A Guide for Nonprofessional Counselors
New Expanded Edition
"Every parent should keep this book on the shelf right next to the
nutrition, medical, and Dr. Spock books."—*Marriage & Family Living*
$12.95

John B. Mordock
COUNSELING CHILDREN
Basic Principles for Helping the Troubled and Defiant Child
Helps counselors consider the best route for a particular child, and offers
proven principles and methods to counsel troubled children in a variety
of situations. $17.95

Cherry Boone O'Neill
DEAR CHERRY
Questions and Answers on Eating Disorders
Practical and inspiring advice on eating disorders from the best- selling
author of *Starving for Attention*.
$8.95 paperback

Thomas W. Perrin
I AM AN ADULT WHO GREW UP
IN AN ALCOHOLIC FAMILY
At once moving and practical, this long-awaited book by a leader in the
addiction field provides new hope to other adult children of alcoholics and
those who love them.
$8.95 paperback

Dianne Doyle Pita
ADDICTIONS COUNSELING
A Practical Guide to Counseling People with
Chemical and Other Addictions
"A fresh and greatly needed approach to helping the whole person—it fills
a great gap in the existing literature."—*Thomas W. Perrin* $17.95

Paul G. Quinnett
ON BECOMING A HEALTH
AND HUMAN SERVICES MANAGER
A Practical Guide for Clinicians and Counselors
A new and essential guide to management for everyone in the helping
professions—from mental health to nursing, from social work to teaching.
$19.95

Paul G. Quinnett
SUICIDE: THE FOREVER DECISION
For Those Thinking About Suicide,
and For Those Who Know, Love, or Counsel Them
New Expanded Edition
"A treasure— this book can help save lives."—*William Van Ornum,*
psychotherapist and author $9.95 paperback

Paul G. Quinnett
WHEN SELF-HELP FAILS
A Guide to Counseling Services
 "Without a doubt one of the most honest, reassuring, nonpaternalistic,
and useful self-help books ever to appear."—*Booklist* $11.95

Judah L. Ronch
ALZHEIMER'S DISEASE
A Practical Guide for Families and Other Caregivers
Must reading for everyone who must deal with this tragic disease on a
daily basis. Filled with examples and facts, this book provides insights
into dealing with one's feelings as well as such practical advice as how to
choose long-term care.
$11.95 paperback

Theodore Isaac Rubin, M. D.
ANTI-SEMITISM: A Disease of the Mind
"A most poignant and lucid psychological examination of a severe
emotional disease. Dr. Rubin offers hope and understanding to the victim
and to the bigot. A splendid job!"—*Dr. Herbert S. Strean*
$14.95

Theodore Isaac Rubin, M.D.
CHILD POTENTIAL
Fulfilling Your Child's Intellectual,
Emotional, and Creative Promise
Information, guidance, and wisdom—a treasury of fresh ideas for parents
to help their children become their best selves.
$18.95 hardcover
$11.95 paperback

John R. Shack
COUPLES COUNSELING
A Practical Guide for Those Who Help Others
An essential guide to dealing with the 20 percent of all counseling
situations that involve the relationship of two people. $17.95

Milton F. Shore, Patrick J. Brice, and Barbara G. Love
WHEN YOUR CHILD NEEDS TESTING
What Parents, Teachers, and Other Helpers
Need To Know About Psychological Testing
A clear and helpful map of the world of psychological testing that will
ease fears and encourage better decision-making among parents and
others who care for children and adolescents. $18.95

Herbert S. Strean as told to Lucy Freeman
BEHIND THE COUCH
Revelations of a Psychoanalyst
"An entertaining account of an analyst's thoughts and feelings during the
course of therapy."—*Psychology Today*
$11.95 paperback

Stuart Sutherland
THE INTERNATIONAL DICTIONARY OF PSYCHOLOGY
This new dictionary of psychology also covers a wide range of related
disciplines, from anthropology to sociology. $49.95